WILLIAM LEVI DAWSON

American Made Music Series

ADVISORY BOARD

David Evans, General Editor
Barry Jean Ancelet
Edward A. Berlin
Joyce J. Bolden
Rob Bowman
Susan C. Cook
Curtis Ellison
William Ferris
John Edward Hasse
Kip Lornell
Bill Malone
Eddie S. Meadows
Manuel H. Peña
Wayne D. Shirley
Robert Walser

WILLIAM LEVI DAWSON

American Music Educator

Mark Hugh Malone

with content design and pre-editing by Meagan Elizabeth Malone,
University of Alabama at Birmingham

UNIVERSITY PRESS OF MISSISSIPPI / JACKSON

The University Press of Mississippi is the scholarly publishing agency of
the Mississippi Institutions of Higher Learning: Alcorn State University,
Delta State University, Jackson State University, Mississippi State University,
Mississippi University for Women, Mississippi Valley State University,
University of Mississippi, and University of Southern Mississippi.

www.upress.state.ms.us

The University Press of Mississippi is a member of
the Association of University Presses.

Copyright © 2023 by University Press of Mississippi
All rights reserved

First printing 2023

∞

Library of Congress Cataloging-in-Publication Data

Names: Malone, Mark Hugh, 1952– author. | Malone, Meagan Elizabeth, contributor.
Title: William Levi Dawson : American music educator / Mark Hugh Malone ; with
content design and pre-editing by Meagan Elizabeth Malone.
Other titles: American made music series.
Description: Jackson : University Press of Mississippi, 2023. | Series: American made
music series | Includes bibliographical references and index.
Identifiers: LCCN 2022049654 (print) | LCCN 2022049655 (ebook) | ISBN
9781496844798 (hardback) | ISBN 9781496844804 (trade paperback) | ISBN
9781496844811 (epub) | ISBN 9781496844842 (epub) | ISBN 9781496844828 (pdf) |
ISBN 9781496844835 (pdf)
Subjects: LCSH: Dawson, William L. (William Levi), 1899–1990. | Composers—Alabama—Biography. | African American composers—Biography. | Choral conductors—Alabama—Biography. | African American choral conductors—Biography. |
Musicologists—Biography. | Music teachers—Biography. | LCGFT: Biographies.
Classification: LCC ML410.D276 M35 2023 (print) | LCC ML410.D276 (ebook) |
DDC 780.92—dc23/eng/20221209
LC record available at https://lccn.loc.gov/2022049654
LC ebook record available at https://lccn.loc.gov/2022049655

British Library Cataloging-in-Publication Data available

CONTENTS

Acknowledgments VII

Introduction 3

Chapter 1: Dawson's Early Years and Education: 1899–1930 8

Chapter 2: The Development of the Music School at
    Tuskegee Institute: 1930–55 37

Chapter 3: The Rise of the Tuskegee Choir to National
    Prominence: 1931–55 52

Chapter 4: Dawson the Composer: 1921–90 74

Chapter 5: Dawson the Pedagogue: 1921–90 116

Appendix A: Choral and Orchestral Compositions
    and Arrangements 133

Appendix B: Awards and Honors Received
    by William Levi Dawson 140

Appendix C: Significant Letters, Speeches, and Interviews
    Regarding the Life of William Levi Dawson 143

Notes 163

Bibliography 189

Index 198

ACKNOWLEDGMENTS

Though this journey began over forty years ago, the image and aura of William Levi Dawson is vibrant, has been refreshed, and further enhanced through continued study and research over years that amount to nearly a half century.

Gratitude still resides within me for my major professor, Colleen Jean Kirk, for her guidance and wisdom toward completion of my dissertation.

Appreciation also exists for former Tuskegee University Archivist Daniel Williams, who continued to provide me with updated information concerning William Dawson nearly a decade following the attainment of my PhD.

In the quest to learn even more about Mr. Dawson, after a successful teaching career that spanned more than forty-five years, I encountered kind, thoughtful, efficient faculty/staff in the Stuart A. Rose Manuscript, Archives, and Rare Book Library at Emory University in Atlanta, Georgia, which houses the William Levi Dawson Collection. Courtney Chartier, Head of Research Services, and Kathy Shoemaker worked diligently to provide materials during in-person visits. However, once the world was impacted by the COVID-19 pandemic in March of 2020, these two women spearheaded efforts to provide papers and compositions, as well as audio/video recordings in a virtual manner, going above and beyond normal measures to provide library services in the midst of worldwide health protocols. Heartfelt thanks are genuinely extended to these women.

Likewise, Jennifer Randolph, grandniece of William Dawson, who serves as Donor Executor of the gift of his papers to Emory University, was instrumental in granting special permission for virtual use of copyrighted music and materials. I am most grateful for her efforts to facilitate easy access of these vital research documents and her genuine interest in the research concerning her uncle.

Kind thanks go as well to Dana Chandler, Archivist at Tuskegee University. Despite current global health challenges, Mr. Chandler was extremely gracious in opening the university archives for on-site access to the repository of materials housed on the campus founded by Booker T. Washington, where William L. Dawson spent most of his professional life teaching and composing. Archival Assistant, Cheryl Ferguson, was invaluable in establishing contact for personal interviews and procuring resources.

Published novelist Claire Matturo kindly read the manuscript to offer wise counsel in placement of historical information to enhance the biographical storyline, encouragement to consider chapter reorganization, and careful overall editing. How grateful I am for her expertise and willingness to assist in the preparation of the manuscript.

Finally, in any human endeavor, the love and support of family is crucial to reaching a personal life goal. My brother Patrick R. Malone, PhD, EdD, MA, served as an editor in the early shaping and formatting of the manuscript for submission to the publisher and was adept at acquiring references, citations, and other quotations during revisions. His insight into crafting clear ideas, as well as the brotherly love we share, is highly valued. My wife, Patty Sharpe Malone, DM, was of immeasurable support by listening lovingly to my latest research findings with avid interest and encouraging my work. Our love has continued for over forty years. My daughter, Meagan Elizabeth Malone, PhD, eagerly leant her expertise by providing steps for submission of materials for publication, giving advice as to how to proceed with peer revisions, keys to successfully becoming published, as well as by editing the final document. Through Meagan's vision the manuscript was molded into a more cogent narrative with clear direction and purpose throughout. How thrilling to collaborate with a daughter of whom I am most proud and love dearly.

WILLIAM LEVI DAWSON

INTRODUCTION

In the spring of 1979, I knocked on William Levi Dawson's door for the first of five visits. We had corresponded by mail for several weeks before he was able to find time in his busy schedule to host me for an all-day interview session. At the time, I was working on a dissertation prospectus as part of the requirements for a master's and then a PhD in music education at Florida State University. Having completed my undergraduate studies in music and social studies, I was keen on conducting primary research on a prominent figure in American music and pedagogy. At the time, Dawson was a familiar and beloved composer. I had always admired his choral arrangements, performed them as a high school and college choir member, and then conducted them in my first job as a high school choir director.

The selection of William Dawson as a worthy topic of study was fortuitous, as there was a paucity of in-depth writing about his life, teaching, and compositions. William Dawson's life and work exemplified a thirst for knowledge, a desire for professional competence in numerous areas, an ability to organize and capably administer a school of music at the college level during a nationwide financial depression, a willingness to mold young minds through educational endeavors, and to celebrate folk music of his race through composition and arrangement.

When a friend and fellow graduate student mentioned in passing that his father was an optometrist in Montgomery, Alabama, and that William Dawson was one of his patients, I jumped at the opportunity to track down his address and request a meeting.

In his reply Dawson agreed to be interviewed as a part of a prospectus and doctoral dissertation project but, revealing his humility and self-deprecation, wrote, "I don't know what you're going to write about." At that time there was a dearth of available information and a lack of extant research about Dawson. His life story, told in his own words, would provide an overwhelming wealth of material about which to write.

On each of the five visits, I made the three-hour drive to Tuskegee, Alabama, from Tallahassee, Florida; Dawson welcomed me into his home and spent the entire day narrating the events of his life. Despite the availability of recording devices, Dawson asked that he not be recorded, making it necessary to take copious notes during the extended sessions. We would always pause for lunch, and I easily forgot my aversion to raw vegetables when Dawson's wife, Cecile, prepared homemade chicken salad served in quartered tomatoes.

At the conclusion of each interview session, I made my way to the Tuskegee library and archives, where I sought out documents to corroborate and further detail Dawson's stories. Dawson himself provided me access to his own personal archives, an impressive collection of papers including carbon copies of most letters he had sent. During and well beyond the interview period, the Tuskegee archivist, Dan Williams, continued to mail me newspaper clippings and other documents, and provided me with supplemental information for my project.

Over the next few years, I knitted together a narrative of Dawson's life, based largely on his own words, and supplemented his story with additional available documents. While he read and approved my final manuscript, he also requested that an esteemed colleague, Bess Bolden Walcott, have access to the manuscript in order to verify and complement it. Walcott, born in 1886, was hired in 1908 at Tuskegee Institute by its founder, Booker T. Washington, where she served as science and English teacher, librarian, museum curator, and publishing editor until her retirement in 1962. Walcott was employed at the school while Dawson was both student and faculty and therefore was able to provide invaluable insight into Dawson's story.

My dissertation received committee approval in 1981. By that time other students and scholars had finally begun serious research projects focused on Dawson's work. Prior to the 1980s, one could find only sentence-, paragraph-, or page-length mentions of Dawson in sources that focused on broader topics. Since then, a variety of work on Dawson has proliferated, and much of that scholarship references my 1981 dissertation. Vernon Huff, who completed his dissertation on Dawson in 2013, asserts that "by far the most comprehensive examination of the life of Dawson [is] Mark Malone's PhD dissertation at Florida State University, 'William Levi Dawson: American Music Educator.'"[1] While appreciative of that source, Huff nevertheless notes "that the most substantial sources" on Dawson's life are unpublished works written over thirty years ago."[2]

Shortly after my graduation, I intended to pursue publication opportunities for this biography; yet my career, much like Dawson's, led me to teaching institutions where I worked primarily as a choral director and then administrator. While unable to pursue writing projects over the last decades, I nevertheless remained abreast of Dawson's career and have been grateful to maintain connections with those who know and research his impressive accomplishments. In 2017, musicologist Gwynne Kuhner Brown wrote to alert me that Dawson's papers had found a home at the Rose Archives at Emory University in Atlanta, Georgia. After I retired from full time teaching in 2018, my first priority was to conduct archival research with the aim of updating, expanding, and finally publishing a biography of Dawson. Such a volume not only fills a large gap in scholarship on important 20th century American musicians; it also represents a tribute to a man whose love for music pushed him to subvert and transcend seemingly insurmountable boundaries created by white America to oppress and subjugate Black Americans.

The following work reveals William Levi Dawson's quest to become a musician, school administrator, choral director, composer, and pedagogue. As the interviewer, archival historian, and author, my vision and voice inevitably influenced what appears here; nevertheless, my aim was not to construct an ironclad, linear narrative of Dawson's life, nor to present some larger argument about his legacy. Instead, through my archival research efforts to update and extend my original dissertation, I endeavored to uncover, collate, and present additional information on Dawson that could be used by a variety of scholars such as historians, musicologists, critical theorists, and others.

My research and writing approach aligns with what archivist and composition scholar Kelly Ritter calls "archival ethnography" in which the researcher "[views] archival spaces as sites of communal representation with historical scholars at the helm, poised to report from the location and embed themselves in the multivocality of the past."[3] Whereas archival historians often aim to assemble historical traces found in archives into a *tidy* story that reflects a particular argument, Ritter's approach asks researchers to avoid taking on the role of storyteller, instead seeing themselves as "curator" and *reporter* of these traces. In keeping with the archival ethnographic approach, like a foreign correspondent, I embedded myself within the archives at Emory University, Tuskegee University, The University of Missouri-Kansas City, and the Missouri Valley Collection of the Kansas City Public Library. The result of my time in the archives did not necessarily result in some clear, neat narrative about Dawson. Rather, I uncovered and reported an abundance of historical traces that I present here, traces that have the potential to unfold subsequently into more detailed sites of inquiry and discovery.

In the following chapters, you will find lengthy reproductions of newspaper articles, excerpts from correspondences, and quotes from Dawson and his colleagues. I hope that in my heavy use of untreated primary sources, it is clear that this work does not attempt to represent *the* life and career of Dawson as an objective, "naturally appearing phenomenon";[4] rather, my approach creates opportunities for "more discovery and presentation rather than validation and proof" and exposes the constructed nature of this or any historical account.[5]

Chapter 1 presents the early events of Dawson's life based on his own words. It spans a thirty-year period during which Dawson came of age, received an education at the Tuskegee Institute, took his first job in Topeka, Kansas, and pursued additional training in music. Parallel and integral to Dawson's story is that of the Tuskegee Institute.

Chapter 2 chronicles not only his years as the head of the School of Music at Tuskegee but also the history of music education at the institute. Using a variety of documents such as the school's catalogue, or bulletin, this chapter follows the School of Music's initial growth, its changes during years of economic depression and war, and its attempt to serve the needs of students.

The nationally renowned Tuskegee Institute Choir, under Dawson's direction, is the focus of chapter 3 which traces the choir's multiple tours and appearances on radio and television broadcasts. The chapter also includes the voices of many newspaper and media critics who responded to the choir's performances at the time. This allows present day readers to form a sense of the way Dawson and his group were received by mainstream—and largely white—America.

In chapter 4, I sketch a timeline of Dawson's life as a composer, using his publishing record, his personal correspondences, and critical reception of his work. Furthermore, the chapter situates Dawson's musical output within the larger context of American music, delving into his approach to authentically conceiving of, composing, and performing African American folk music. Here, readers encounter Dawson's rationale for his personal preference for and against certain nomenclature; he embraced the term "Negro" to describe that which is African American and rejected the word "spiritual" to describe songs written by the enslaved.

The work ends in chapter 5. Therein Dawson's pedagogical legacy is examined, reflecting on the role he played in the lives of his students and chronicling his robust career as a guest conductor and clinician.

When I began this project in 1979, at a time when information on Dawson was scant, I could not imagine the overwhelming volume and high quality of research that would be available about him four decades later. As I combed through box after box of Dawson's papers at the Rose Archives, discovering photographs and letters and pocket calendars, I was most taken with the recordings from a March 3–5, 2005 conference on Dawson at Emory University entitled, "In Celebration of William L. Dawson: An Exploration of African-American Music and Identity at the Dawn of the 21st Century." I sat transfixed in the archival reading room in Emory's Woodruff Library while listening, jotting notes, and feeling the unique thrill of making new and unexpected scholarly connections. It is my most sincere hope that this revised and updated biographical text will contribute to and encourage further excellent research on a man who has been an inspiration to me and so many others.

Chapter 1

DAWSON'S EARLY YEARS AND EDUCATION

1899–1930

THE DAWSONS

The birth of a male child to George W. and Eliza Starkey Dawson on September 26, 1899, was a joyous occasion. The infant was the first of seven children born to the Dawsons who lived in Anniston, Alabama. In honor of Eliza's father, William Starkey, and George's brother, Levi Dawson, they named their son William Levi Dawson.[1]

Eliza Starkey Dawson was an educated woman from a family with extensive property holdings. Just two decades after the close of the Civil War, the hardworking and successful Starkey family was able to purchase land in Calhoun County near the Brewtonville community. They were firm believers in the value of an education and succeeded in providing educational opportunities for their children. Eliza's parents extended complete support for her brother's decision to attend Talladega College in Talladega, Alabama, just over twenty-five miles from Brewtonville. Eliza, who received a primary and secondary school education, was a devoutly religious woman who would often sing the songs she knew from camp meetings, revivals, and other religious services. She also sang folk songs she heard her formerly enslaved grandparents sing.

George W. Dawson, a native of Albany, Georgia, migrated to Anniston, Alabama. According to William Dawson, George was probably born into slavery. He did not have the opportunity to acquire an education but was able to find a job with an ice company in Anniston. Later he unloaded coal to earn a living. Because he had no formal schooling, George Dawson saw little value in an education and thought the pursuit of formal schooling was a complete waste of time, believing hard work was much more profitable.

Following their marriage, Eliza urged her husband to purchase a house, because her family's prosperous investment in land had taught her the value of owning property. George and Eliza had little money, so Eliza's family provided the twenty-five dollars necessary for the down payment on the house. At the closing of negotiations for the purchase of the home, George signed his name with an "X," making it obvious he could not read or write.

As William grew he was curious about everything he came across. Watching every man busy at an occupation in and around Anniston was fascinating to him. He aspired to every profession he saw: a brakeman on a train, a carpenter, a brick mason. He discounted no occupation from his hopes of "being something" in his future.

There were few formal music concerts in Anniston, but there was a great deal of informal singing. William heard the singing in his community and eagerly joined the music-making. His precocious perception of music manifested itself in many ways. Frequently hearing music, he picked out rhythms and experimented with them, sometimes using the rhythmic patterns he heard to make up dances based on current events he heard. Once he tried to fashion a stringed instrument out of a cigar box to investigate the vibrations created by a variety of pitches. He delighted to use his homemade instrument to accompany his own singing.[2]

On Wednesdays and Sundays, William would walk to a small church near his home and stand outside partly to listen to the prayer meetings and services but mostly just to hear the singing. He had never heard such beautiful sounds and was always fascinated with the lovely tones emanating from the worship inside. Upon hearing a concert in Anniston featuring the Fisk University Jubilee Singers, he exclaimed, "Oh Mama, I know those songs." From this pivotal moment, his interest in music grew exponentially as he continued to experience pitches, rhythms, and timbres in many forms. Almost a half century later, William Dawson would be invited to conduct the choirs at Fisk University.

William was impressed by the African American men in town who played instruments, especially those in a fifteen-piece band. This small ensemble was directed by S. W. Gresham, who previously had been bandmaster at Tuskegee Normal and Industrial Institute in Tuskegee, Alabama. Gresham was an excellent trumpet player and a fine musician. William was enamored with all the musical instruments he saw and eager to play a horn. He would have played any horn but had his heart set on the trombone.

Dawson's father, on the other hand, was not interested in William studying music and had other ideas for his eldest child. Being the first child in a family always comes with great responsibility, but George Dawson added an extra burden, making it very clear that William was to help "take care of the family." Thus, at an early age, William was apprenticed to E. L. Langston, a shoemaker. In Langston's shop shoes were made entirely by hand. William's first job was to make and tend the fire for burnishing soles and heels on the shoes. He would watch other workers sew the soles and soon took up the practice, having learned the procedure through keen observation. Despite the work in the shoe business, William's interest in music did not wane. Young Dawson desperately wanted to play an instrument.

Understanding his father's dislike of educational endeavors and refusal to allow the study of music, William knew he could not bring a trombone into the house, even if he could procure one. Realizing Dawson's extreme desire to play an instrument, the trombonist in the "Anniston Negro Band," a Mr. Fleming, counseled William that his father might concede if the choice were a mellophone, a brass instrument similar to a French horn. Sure enough, George Dawson acquiesced, and William began to work at this new challenge.

Band director S. W. Gresham loaned him his own mellophone, and young Dawson avidly experimented with the horn. Following a heuristic approach, Gresham allowed him to discover the horn and seek assistance from the other men in his band. He made rapid musical progress through his own diligent study, but the more musically experienced men enhanced his development. Realizing the young musician's potential combined with his seriousness about learning the instrument, Gresham began to give William private music lessons. Almost as soon as these individual lessons began, however, they ended. Sadly, S. W. Gresham died after only a month of providing personal coaching for young Dawson.

From time to time, graduates of Tuskegee Institute would pass through Anniston, and some even decided to settle in Calhoun County. Recognizing that these young men and women were different from Anniston inhabitants, William was impressed and emulated them. He had heard about the Tuskegee Institute Band from Gresham, the newly settled residents from Tuskegee, and others. The prestigious aura of Tuskegee Institute emanated throughout the South, and it seemed each mention of the school and the band painted glowing, yet accurate pictures for Dawson of both the institution and ensemble. Desiring to pursue an education, gain further experiences in music, explore instruments, and be a part of the Tuskegee Band, William Dawson resolved to somehow attend the school. Yet, even getting a head start with an early education in his community was a challenge, as public primary and secondary schools were not yet established for African American children in Anniston during the first part of the twentieth century.

BOOKER T. WASHINGTON AND THE TUSKEGEE INSTITUTE

In 1881 Booker Taliaferro Washington began working to provide educational opportunities for African Americans in Tuskegee, Alabama. The citizens of Tuskegee summoned Washington from his alma mater, Hampton Institute in Virginia, to begin the secondary school that was to be called Tuskegee Institute. On July 4, 1881, classes at Tuskegee Institute began in a small shanty near the Butler Chapel African Methodist Episcopal (AME) Zion Church. Despite the many hardships of those early days, the school soon prospered. Notwithstanding problems such as a leaking roof—at which time the pupils would hold an umbrella over Washington's head so that he could continue to teach—and the lack of materials and equipment, the enrollment grew from the original thirty students to over four hundred within seven years.

His convictions about the best way to achieve racial equality affected the way he founded and fostered Tuskegee Institute. Washington was both author and proponent of what came to be known as the Atlanta Compromise: one strategy for working toward a world in which Black and white people experienced the same privileges and opportunities. Outlined in his speech to a largely white audience at Cotton States and International Exposition in Atlanta on September 18, 1895, the Atlanta Compromise called for white and Black Americans to work together peacefully to create a mutually prosperous society. Segregation, in this view, was not inherently bad; instead, it provided a framework from which members of both races could fulfill responsibilities to one another. Black people, he suggested, ought to seek out practical education and training while white people should work to make America accommodating to all races.

Acknowledging the desire of African Americans for social equality, Washington promoted the idea of "interlacing [Black] industrial, commercial, civil, and religious life with [that of white people] in a way that shall make the interests of both races one."[3] Rather than challenging the segregated society of the Jim Crow era, he suggested, "In all things that are purely social we can be as separate as the fingers, yet one as the hand in all things essential to mutual progress."[4] Critics such as W. E. B. Du Bois, Locke, and others rejected this approach as one that merely pandered to a white America that was, despite its show of support for the Atlanta Compromise, doggedly unwilling to share power, resources, and influence with fellow Black citizens. Washington nevertheless based his own actions, including his efforts toward developing the Tuskegee Institute, on these principles, emphasizing the need for Black students to achieve racial equality through hard, practical work.

Believing that young people needed to learn to use their hands as well as their heads, he endorsed the beliefs of Frederick Douglass, cited in a letter to Harriet Beecher Stowe, regarding the education of African American youths. Washington agreed with Douglass that:

> We must become mechanics; we must build as well as live in houses; we must make as well as use furniture; we must construct bridges as well as pass over them; before we can properly live or be respected by our fellow men. We need mechanics as well as ministers. We need workers in iron, clay, and leather. We have orators, authors, and professional men, but these reach only a certain class, and get respect for us in certain select circles. To live here as we ought we must fasten ourselves to our countrymen through their everyday cardinal wants. We must not only be able to black boots, but to make them.[5]

For Washington, then, industrial education was just as important as an academic education. From the earliest days, the institute emphasized the importance of agriculture, believing that it would facilitate self-sufficiency of both the individual and the school. Yet beyond agriculture and academics, the school's offerings expanded to include training in mechanics, the domestic sciences, nursing, music, and theology. Regardless of the robust curricular offerings, many students were unable to attend the school due to lack of finances.

Two years after the opening of Tuskegee Institute, a night program was established so that students could work during the day and attend classes at night. Once a student earned sufficient funds to cover expenses, enrollment in the day school was possible. Even after enlisting in the regular day program, each student continued to work at a particular trade two days a week. No one was permitted to enroll in academic instruction only, because manual labor was viewed as a necessary component of a worthwhile education. As a result of the night program, Washington noted that "industrial work is now as popular as the academic branches" and that "some of the most successful men and women who have graduated from the institution obtained their start in the night school."[6]

Washington also expanded Tuskegee Institute by developing a portable school in which a teacher would take materials and travel by wagon to outlying towns and communities to teach people who could not come to Tuskegee. As a result of the mobile school, those who might never have had any education opportunity learned current agricultural methods, modern home economics techniques, and simple mechanical skills. Washington's remarkable vision and commitment to teaching made education possible for even those living a distance from the school, through the creation of night classes and the use of a roving, satellite campus.

Despite the dual emphasis on industrial and academic training, music was considered an important part of education at Tuskegee. Writing about the school in the early days of the twentieth century, Washington indicated that music had always been encouraged at the school and proudly described the musical offerings there in 1893. As early as 1891 plans for a complete course of music study were established that included vocal and instrumental ensembles as well as piano instruction. By 1893 a four-year course in piano instruction had been designed, and the school provided eight pianos, two cabinet organs, and a suitable music library to support the program.

As Principal Washington was extremely fond of what he called "the plantation melodies," the school placed great emphasis on singing "these old, sweet slave songs" which provided a "source of pride and pleasure to the students."[7] Not only did the entire school sing the spirituals, but the choirs also sang harmonized arrangements of the tunes in much the same fashion that African American colleges at the time had made famous through concert tours across the nation and abroad. Dr. Washington[8] boasted that the extensive choral ensembles contained impressive enrollments in "The Choir of 75 voices, The Choral Society of 150 voices, Men's Glee Club of 40 voices, Women's Glee Club of 20 voices," and "Male Quartette, that traveled throughout the northern United States performing to raise support money for the school."[9]

Despite the smaller numbers enrolled in instrumental music-making, Washington was proud of "The Brass Band of 30 Pieces" and "The Orchestra of 14 Pieces."[10] While the choral directors were not mentioned specifically in the description of music offerings, President Washington indicated that the director of the band also conducted the orchestra and was hired by the school. Auditions were required for membership in instrumental ensembles, but knowledge of the instruments was not considered essential for joining the organizations, as the director was charged with providing music instruction to build a strong instrumental program. The band, patterned after a military instrumental ensemble, played each morning before school during inspection and drill. The orchestra played every school evening during devotions.[11]

Washington's genuine compassion for people from all walks of life was made manifest in his work at Tuskegee Institute. He built a school that provided young people with both knowledge and skills to enhance their lives, and his influence throughout the nation spurred the development of educational opportunities for all Black people. Using his gift of oratory, Washington shared the great work occurring in Alabama, making Tuskegee a sought-out destination for Black Americans. Not only were students from the United States drawn to the school, but young people also seeking an education from as far away as Africa and as near as Puerto Rico came to study at the great institution.

DAWSON AT TUSKEGEE

While apprenticed to shoemaker Langston, William began to shine shoes on Sundays. His work with Langston provided invaluable experience for shining shoes through later periods of Dawson's life. Not only did his childhood work experience provide Dawson with a strong work ethic, he also continued to polish and buff his own shoes in adulthood and was overtly boastful of his shoe-shining skills. Young Dawson worked hard at his trade and shortly thereafter undertook the work full-time. He prided himself on being the best shoe-shiner in the business, and soon, people were waiting in line for his spectacular shine. Rather quickly, Dawson's shoe-shining reputation spread through the town, and he was working permanently in the local barber shop.

When not busy shining shoes, Dawson would listen unobtrusively to the "white folks" talk. Frequently, they talked of former days of slavery and the inhuman treatment to which the enslaved were subjected. Dawson gave the money he earned shining shoes to his father to help with family support. George Dawson, believing in hard work as the key to success, continued to regard education as a fruitless endeavor. It was evident that even if Dawson's father could afford to send him to school, George would not do so because it conflicted with his anti-education principles. After making further inquiries regarding Tuskegee Institute, he learned that the school had been founded by a great man, Booker T. Washington, who wanted to help African Americans get an education. Dawson was told that no one would be turned away because of lack of funding to attend school. He believed that if he could only get to Tuskegee, everything would work out. Nevertheless, he still needed funds to travel to the school.

It became increasingly clear that the only way he was going to get to Tuskegee was by saving some of his shoe-shine money rather than giving it all to his father. Dawson shared: "I was shining shoes and if I made $3, I would take 50 cents and keep it for myself. We call that 'knocking down.' I would give my father $2.50 and maybe he would give me 10–15 cents."[12]

Dawson found a snuffbox and designated it his bank for school money. He placed the box in a hole in the ground that he dug close to one of the pillars of the house next door. The regular deposits were noticed by Dawson's "friends," who then stole the money. The discouraged young man thought his dream of going to Tuskegee was a hopeless endeavor.

Dawson postponed his intended journey and attempted to secure tutoring in basic subjects: reading, writing, and arithmetic. There were two men in Anniston who taught African American children. Professor Moses taught school on the west side of town, and Professor N.W. Carmichael had a school in south Anniston, where Dawson lived, yet these were not public schools. The men leading these "schools" had to charge fees in order to earn a living. Since William was unable to attend school during the day because of his job, Professor Carmichael agreed to work with him for a fee of fifty cents a month. The eager boy would go secretly to the teacher in the early evening and return before dark so that his father would not discover his mission. This individual study represented a forward movement toward his educational goal and stood in stark contrast to what he felt he had been doing previously: "simply marking time." He thought that whatever skills he could acquire at this point would benefit him once he arrived in Tuskegee.

Dawson soon renewed his efforts to get to Tuskegee and secured a job as errand boy with Mr. Black, the owner of the dry-goods store in Anniston. He made deliveries with a used bicycle he was able to purchase. Black trusted young Dawson and allowed him to stock as well as inventory exclusive items. Dawson worked hard at his new job and with the money he saved was able to buy a trunk for his planned trip. Diligently he began once again to save his money. Throughout this time of preparation, Eliza Dawson was a source of great encouragement to her son. Having been reared in a family that highly prized an education, she successfully concealed her son's plans from her husband and urged William to go on to school at Tuskegee.

In September of 1913, the time had finally come for young William to leave home. The sale of his bicycle yielded the six dollars necessary for the train fare from Anniston to Tuskegee. On Sunday afternoon George Dawson went to church, which enabled William to put his plan into action. The Beavers Family, Dawson's neighbors, collaborated with him and took his trunk for safekeeping. The following morning the Beavers' own son George planned to check the trunk as his own on his ticket to Tuskegee. Upon returning from church, George Dawson quickly noticed that William's trunk was missing and immediately began searching for his son. William had already walked to another railroad depot several miles distant, so the elder Dawson did not find his son at the Anniston station.

Once aboard the 2 a.m. Southern Railroad train bound for Birmingham, William locked himself in the men's room and emerged only after the train had departed. After he arrived in Birmingham, he boarded the Louisville and Nashville train that took him to Tuskegee. When the train pulled right onto the Tuskegee Institute campus, Dawson was in awe of the buildings that composed the school he had sought so long to attend. With only $1.50 in his pocket, he stepped off the train to begin a new challenge.

At Tuskegee all entering students were given diagnostic tests for proper placement. William Dawson's test results placed him in the most basic division, the "C" Preparatory Class. His name first appeared in the 1914–15 school-year bulletin under the classification of "special agriculture student." During the day he would work at the Institute to meet his educational expenses, and he attended classes at night.[13] Mr. L. J. Watkins oversaw vocational guidance and, aware of the need for extra farm hands, offered Dawson an agricultural job. Having been counseled by his friend George Beavers, Dawson was reluctant to accept a position on the farm. Yet the wise Watkins euphemistically presented the more cumbersome tasks by giving them great appeal with special titles. A "civil engineering" job was Dawson's first assignment. Recalling an earlier desire to work with the railroad, the thought of "engineering" excited the adolescent.

For several days after joining the crew that was building a road on the institute farm, Dawson still had hopes of getting on the train. He finally asked one of his peers about the train and, to his dismay, learned the true meaning of "civil engineering." His work for nearly five years at Tuskegee was farm related. Following the first few years of daily work and nightly schooling, he was promoted to the "A" Preparatory Class. He then attended school during the day three days a week and did manual labor only two days, spending all summers working on the school farm.

It was on the school farm that Dawson met a young man who had come from Africa, though he does not mention which region or country, to study at Tuskegee Institute.[14] As the two became friends, Dawson found a marked difference between himself and this friend. Despite their similar skin color, Dawson concluded that he himself was not African and could never identify in this way. Because of differences in their environments, "the Negro man" in America, according to Dawson, was entirely distinct from "the African man," the product of both African and American influences. Dawson explains that his encounter with this man sparked a desire to visit Africa:

> When I was at Tuskegee Institute I was working on the farm, picking peas in the summer to try to stay in school. And, alongside of me was

a boy from Africa. He had just been brought there by a missionary. And I asked him if they had any music in Africa and he said yes, and he sang something for me. Now prior to that time I just knew Africa and just the word Africa, but I didn't realize how important it was, and how large it was, and how many countries were involved in Africa—the West Coast of Africa. And so, I got interested and I always wanted to go there.[15]

CHORAL MUSIC AT TUSKEGEE

Booker T. Washington realized the value of music and wanted everyone to be able to enjoy it; in particular he wanted his to be a student body capable of singing. When the school celebrated its twentieth anniversary in 1901, philanthropist Andrew Carnegie was invited to speak at the festivities. Washington had hoped that the generous man would give the institute money to buy a pipe organ. After hearing the student body sing at the celebration, Carnegie remarked that the students' choral abilities were better than any musical value an organ could provide, so he donated money for a library instead, in keeping with his history of providing funding for the construction of a library on many other school campuses. Despite having no organ, the students were always singing. Singing was a part of every chapel service, every Sunday evening vesper service, and any special school assembly. Tuskegee students also sang grace before each meal. Dawson especially remembered the morning blessing, "Awake My Soul," sung by all the pupils before breakfast began. It was thrilling to hear hundreds of voices lifting praise and thanks to commence each day's activities.

At the school, each pupil was given music instruction in sight-singing and ear-training. Everyone was taught music notation and learned how to sight-read hymns. Students listened, sang, played rhythm instruments, and responded to music much in the same way children in elementary classes learn today. William Dawson received piano instruction from a niece of Booker T. Washington, Alice Carter Simmons, and also studied harmony with her. As a member of the Institute Choir, Dawson was exposed to choral and vocal solo literature. Directed by Jennie Cheatham Lee, the choir developed into an excellent performing ensemble. Jennie Lee's extensive background in choral music was highlighted by her having known the original Fisk University Jubilee Singers. Her impeccable speech and careful personal example in rehearsal resulted in flawless, clear choral diction. Mrs. Lee was a very special person in William Dawson's life, for she encouraged him at every turn. She would allow him to sit in the back of her other classes when he could be excused from work. He loved and admired her, often calling her "Mother Lee."

Every Sunday evening, a vesper service was held in the chapel. Students were required to attend, and many townspeople frequently came as well. These worship experiences also served as opportunities for the choir and orchestra to perform. For each service, Booker T. Washington would enter and ascend the stairs to the platform. At this point everyone would rise while the orchestra played a prelude. The service opened with a congregational hymn followed by a responsive reading. The middle portion of the program consisted of special music, featuring the choir and orchestra, and a vocal solo. During the fifteen-minute message, Principal Washington would speak to his students. Many of these sermon-talks were compiled by Dr. Washington and published in 1900 under the title *Sowing and Reaping*. Following the discourse, participants would sing a closing hymn. The orchestral recessional was always a lively march to which all would file out of the chapel. The girls would exit first, followed by the boys, marching 120 steps per minute. Clearly, then, the musical ensembles were a central element of this important Tuskegee tradition.

Principal Washington also knew of the extramusical importance of a band. The Tuskegee Institute Band drew attention to the school and was an effective public-relations extension of the institute; it was the reputation of the band that had greatly influenced Dawson's decision to come to Tuskegee. When he first arrived on campus, Capt. Frank L. Drye was director of the instrumental program. Although Dawson could play the mellophone, he wanted to play the trombone. He was given a trombone and a chance to audition for the band. Realizing he would have to sight-read, he obtained a copy of *Music Self Taught*, published by J. W. Pepper of Cincinnati, to study the rudiments of music. At night he went straight to his room without supper and studied diligently. He put together the scales and melodies he had experienced with the theory he was reading. His brief self-help study course was successful, because he was able to pass the audition and become a member of the band. Acceptance into the band was one of Dawson's most ardent dreams and stood out to him as an early milestone in his career.

Dawson's acceptance into the band was just one of his many ambitions; he was also eager to learn the sound of all the instruments and carefully explore each one. Although he did not have a strong background in theory, his director, Captain Drye, encouraged all bandsmen to write scales and, later, write melodies. Dawson seemed to be an insatiable music student. The young man's bubbling, energetic spirit led his geometry teacher, Professor Perkins to state, "Dawson, your head is just a musical prison!" Encouraged by "Cap," as Captain Drye was affectionately called, Dawson student-conducted the band and the orchestra. Cap knew that experience was a good teacher, so he emphasized learning through doing. William soon began to realize that everything the man did was for the purpose of learning. Cap also encouraged the eager musician to help others learn their instruments. By working with other students in groups and individually, Dawson learned about musical concepts, musical instruments, people, and, especially, himself.

The band was not the only organization that was successful in bringing recognition to Tuskegee Institute. The Male Quartette was equally effective, as ensembles made up of Black men, especially quartets, were particularly popular. The Quartette, first mentioned by Washington in the description of the work at Tuskegee in 1893, was later expanded to an octet around the turn of the century. By 1918, though, the group consisted of one first tenor, two second tenors, a baritone, and a bass. William Dawson auditioned in 1918 and was chosen to sing second tenor with the ensemble, then called the Quintette. Friends of Tuskegee and the trustees of the school would schedule singing engagements for the group throughout the northern United States.

When Dawson first joined the Quintette, Charles Winter Woods was spokesman and manager. The performances began with a few numbers by the ensemble, followed by Mr. Woods's telling of the school's work, with emphasis on its current needs; the men would sing again to close the performance. Dawson's first trip with the Quintette began in April 1918, when they rode the train to New York, sang during the entire summer throughout the northern United States, and returned to Tuskegee in time for the fall term.

Dawson's best friend in the Quintette was Alonzo Small. Small was a highly talented pianist from Charleston, South Carolina, and was as enthusiastic about music as Dawson. The two musicians called each other "Ludwig," in their great admiration of Ludwig van Beethoven (1770–1827). As the young men studied the history of music, they found that many composers worked under the domination of some authority, being responsible to monarchs and patrons. Yet they observed that Beethoven was a "free" composer, not tied to a patron for support, and therefore wrote as his soul dictated.

Indeed, public concerts slowly began to appear in the late Baroque and early Classical periods of music history that seemed to challenge the exclusive performances in palaces for the elite. Along with the revolutions of 1776 and 1789, public concerts in Paris (1725), Dublin (1741), Leipzig (1763), which continued in 1781, Vienna (1771), and Berlin (1790) signaled the beginning of the demise of the patronage system. The status and livelihood of composers had heretofore been tied to a patron. Beethoven's creativity and output, however, was not hindered by a king or an aristocrat.[16] The freedom to compose was important to the young men. This conviction, along with the many experiences they shared and their thirst for music, kept William and Alonzo close friends throughout their lives.

After several summers of traveling on its own, the Tuskegee Quintette was asked to join the Redpath Chautauqua Circuit. The Chautauqua Movement, which began in 1874 and continued throughout the 1920s, featured summertime educational experiences for adults in Chautauqua, New York. Originally of a religious nature, the offerings soon included general education and arts entertainment. The success of the New York Chautauqua program led to an expansion of the movement into traveling shows into many parts of the United States and Canada. The shows traveled on circuits, each circuit traversing a different path by train throughout North America. Each circuit featured a unique group of performing ensembles that were accompanied by college students who put up and took down the huge tents where the events were held.

The traveling Chautauqua programs offered communities situated on or near the railroad system quality entertainment but also provided all necessary equipment and an on-site team to manage the production. The only requirement for the local community was to guarantee sale of a certain number of tickets. The Tuskegee Quintette, on the circuit managed by the Redpath Lyceum Bureau, toured the northeastern United States and included several stops in Canada. Other independent Chautauqua circuits were underwritten by philanthropists and businessmen. In all, the Chautauqua circuits provided "popular education" for audiences. The tone of the circuit was educational for the audience and performers alike. Hugh A. Orchard in his book *Fifty Years of Chautauqua* said that ideas and music migrated from the older centers of culture and population to villages, towns, and farms by means of the Chautauqua circuit. In a time when radio was not yet developed nationally, the Chautauqua circuit was a way to enrich the cultural lives of many people.[17]

Dawson remembered that a traveling Chautauqua program had passed through Anniston when he was a child, but he was not able to attend, because African Americans were not allowed entry. His first exposure to the programs came as a member of one of the performing groups. In addition to exposure for Tuskegee Institute, a further benefit of joining the circuit was the sum of money the Redpath Lyceum paid the school for its participation. The speakers and other attractions were all outstanding. Some of the speakers who made an impression on Dawson were William Jennings Bryan, the three-time presidential nominee; a governor of Pennsylvania; a poet laureate of Kentucky; and a British production of Gilbert and Sullivan's *Pirates of Penzance*.

Captain Alvin J. Neely was the leader of the Quintette when they joined the Chautauqua circuit.[18] Following his graduation from Tuskegee, Neely was appointed by Booker T. Washington to direct and manage the ensemble, as well as to sing. He would speak about the philosophies of Dr. Washington, the school he had built, and the educational opportunities for African Americans.[19] The Quintette would sing and occasionally present soloists. William Dawson was featured as trombone soloist many times and was accompanied on the piano by his companion Alonzo Small.

The Burlington, Vermont, newspaper related the impact of the Tuskegee Male Quintette in an August 17, 1921, article.

> The dark-skinned vocalists from the Tuskegee Normal and Industrial Institute, Tuskegee, Alabama furnished the musical part of yesterday's program to the entire satisfaction of everyone concerned. These singers, who are well-known the country over through their Victor records, gave a short prelude to the afternoon lecture and presented the entire program in the evening. Their numbers consisted of the old-time negro melodies, including many sacred numbers. The blending of their voices was well-nigh perfect and the result was beautiful harmony.
>
> William L. Dawson, second tenor, was also a trombone artist of note. His three trombone solos during the day were among the features of the program and the patrons would gladly have heard more had there been time for it.
>
> Alvin J. Neely, leader and manager, took a few minutes in the evening to tell something about the Tuskegee Institute, its 2,200 students, 100 teachers, and more than 100 buildings, which was founded by Booker T. Washington about 40 years ago. A pleasing and convincing speaker, Mr. Neely gave many interesting facts about the negro race and its growth out of slavery into American citizenship. He emphasized the service which the white race in this country has done for the negro and spoke especially of the part which General Howard, whose home was in this city, had in helping along this good work in the South. He praised the better class of white people in the South who have stood by the negro and helped in his upward progress, and closed with an appeal for an extension of the educational opportunities to both whites and blacks in the South.[20]

The Burlington newspaper's reference to General Howard describes Oliver O. Howard, head of the Freedmen's Bureau after emancipation of the enslaved at the end of the Civil War, who lived his final years in Burlington, Vermont.

The general was a founder and eventually served as president of Howard University, now known as a Historically Black College and University (HBCU) in Washington, DC, which was later named in his honor.

It is important to note that Negro, a common twentieth-century term for African Americans that Dawson preferred, was not capitalized. Du Bois led a letter-writing movement beginning in 1926 to encourage publishers and newspaper editors to capitalize this reference to African Americans.[21] The *New York Times* initially refused, though Du Bois indicated that to use a lowercase letter to refer to African Americans worldwide was insulting. Four years later the paper agreed, saying that the decision was "not merely a typographical change" but "an act in recognition of racial self-respect."[22] In the 1920s Du Bois also had the opportunity to write an article on "The Negro in the United States" for *Encyclopedia Britannica*. In his initial draft, Du Bois wrote: "The legislation of the South at the time showed a determination to re-establish Negro slavery in everything but name." Then-editor Franklin H. Hooper, however, removed this from the final published version.[23]

Despite Du Bois's victory in convincing the paper to capitalize Negro, nearly a century passed before the *New York Times* made the move to capitalize "Black" in reference to African Americans. In July of 2020, the paper's executive editor, associate managing editor for standards, and national editor issued a statement:

> We believe this style best conveys elements of shared history and identity, and reflects our goal to be respectful of all the people and communities we cover.... It seems like such a minor change, black versus Black, but for many people the capitalization of that one letter is the difference between color and a culture.[24]

The paper's 2020 decision to change its capitalization conventions came on the heels of Black Lives Matter protests that erupted globally following the deaths of George Floyd and Breonna Taylor at the hands of police. Both in 1930 and in 2020, the *New York Times* appeared to respond to strong challenges from vocal Black activists.

Members of the Quintette and their leader Captain Neely would often encounter difficulties because of their skin color. The men were initially refused hotel accommodations at stops in Massachusetts despite the fact that the Redpath Lyceum Bureau had made the reservations. The group was also harassed when boarding the train in the same state. Dawson recalled the irony that some of the speakers on the circuit in the Northeast focused on the inhuman treatment of Negroes in the South when the same discrimination occurred openly in the North.

Dawson recognized the complete disregard for the 14th Amendment that granted full citizenship to the formerly enslaved and promised equal protection under the law. While the states that fought for the Union during the Civil War did not join those former Confederate states in overtly contesting the amendment, for Dawson, it appeared that much of the northern sentiment toward African Americans matched that of the South. The members of the Tuskegee Quintette were continually subjected to prejudicial and unequal treatment while traveling and performing in the northern United States, making a mockery of the amendment, the letter of which promotes equal protection under the law.

Dawson's experience on the Chautauqua Circuit had a deep impact on his understanding of himself as a Black man operating in a white-dominated world. Dawson saw more clearly than ever that the people of his race had to exist within the confines of laws designed by whites to maintain white supremacy through segregation. Despite the blatant inequalities he faced on the circuit, he chose to peacefully persist within the given racial hierarchy, believing it necessary for eventual social change leading to racial equality. Yet, even after the hardships endured by those African Americans who chose a more active and, at times, combative role in the fight for racial justice—from the Civil Rights Movement in the 1960s to the Black Lives Matter Movement nearly a half century later—it seems not much had changed. Following an insurrection in the form of a storming of the Capitol Building in Washington, DC, on January 6, 2021, African American sports star LeBron James, echoing Du Bois, lamented, "We live in two Americas."[25]

Upon completion of all the requirements for graduation, William Dawson graduated from Tuskegee Institute in May of 1921. Graduation at Tuskegee was not assured for members of the senior class until two to three weeks prior to the commencement ceremonies. Each potential graduate was discussed before the entire faculty. The most important question asked about each candidate was whether that student would represent the school in an honorable fashion. The faculty wanted to be certain that the ideals and philosophies of their founder, Washington, would be infused into the character of each graduate so that the "Tuskegee Spirit" would live on.

Dawson would become not only one of the greatest ambassadors of that spirit but a dear friend of Washington's, as well as an advocate of his strategy for achieving racial equality. Many have said that Washington was a strong father-figure for Dawson. Marva Carter asserted the existence of an inseparable triumvirate that included Dawson, Tuskegee Institute, and Booker T. Washington, writing that "at Tuskegee [Dawson] found a home and a mission. Both were tied to his love for music, which coincided with the Institute's founder." Carter indicated in an interview with Lucius Wyatt of Prairie View College that Dawson made manifest his feelings about his mentor, exclaiming, that "Booker T. Washington was the greatest! He was a giant." Their relationship was so strong that Dawson was amongst the musicians "in the Tuskegee band in his funeral procession behind his coffin."[26]

To commemorate Washington, Dawson recalls that he "saved a flower from his funeral. After the funeral, they placed all of the flowers received in the form of a pyramid, and I have kept this flower in my scrapbook all of those years."[27] Furthermore, Washington's nephew gave Dawson a stone from the cabin in which Washington was born, which was treasured on the fireplace in Dawson's Tuskegee home. Following his death in May of 1990 William Dawson was buried near Booker T. Washington's gravesite in the on-campus cemetery behind the chapel.

Throughout his life and career, Dawson would largely emulate Washington's approach to living as a Black man in a racist, segregated society. Just as Washington promoted peaceful persistence in the face of white supremacy and discrimination—what detractors of Washington's approach at times called acquiescence to white violence—Dawson maintained what some might consider a conservative approach to the life of an African American man years after the death of his mentor. He worked to compose and educate in ways that would lead white society to accept and embrace African American art and, eventually, Black people. Yet, in his own way, William Dawson quietly refused to accept the limits forced on his life by white society, rejecting the view that Black people should adhere to their "proper place."[28]

Whatever he faced in life, including discrimination on the Chautauqua circuit, a blocked door to college entrance, having to use back doors to gain access to buildings, segregation at college commencement, and other issues, Dawson was not dissuaded from pursuing his goals. Dawson's nephew, Milton Randolph Jr., lauded Dawson's persistence and praised his tenacity in getting to school and launching a career. Dawson encountered incredible obstacles just to get to Tuskegee to complete his education. But further struggles ensued, both in getting along in what was an "exclusive" white society and working to further his career within the rigidity of operating space for African Americans. Randolph stressed, however, that his uncle approached these difficulties as challenges rather than obstacles. Dawson viewed such roadblocks as minor setbacks "to either go around, to go over, to go under, to go through."[29] None of the struggles dampened William Dawson's determination to succeed.

Unfortunately, Dawson's parents could not attend the graduation exercises. Disappointed but not dejected, Dawson did catch a little of the excitement the festive occasion brought to the Tuskegee campus. He felt a real sense of accomplishment, yet he could not share the extreme revelry of the other graduates. Deep down, he knew there was something more to commencement, so he looked up the word in the dictionary. Its definition—a formal beginning, a new start—made perfect sense to him. He had not arrived; rather, he had merely begun.

DAWSON'S EARLY CAREER AND FURTHER EDUCATION

Tuskegee Institute's reputation as an educational institution for Negroes had grown tremendously under the leadership of Washington. After Washington's death in 1915, the school saw continued growth under the careful guidance of successor Robert Russa Moton of Hampton, Virginia. Tuskegee's musical influence was known throughout the nation, which afforded many Tuskegee graduates the opportunity to serve as bandmasters in schools in many parts of the United States.

The former head of the agriculture department at Tuskegee Institute had accepted an administrative position at Kansas Vocational College in Topeka, Kansas, in 1920. Although the main purpose of the school was industrial training, the school considered music to be an important aspect of education. As a result of his association with Tuskegee, Dawson was called to be the first bandmaster and to form the first band at the college, but the school lacked sufficient money to purchase instruments for an entire band. The head of the college sent a telegram to Dawson while he was touring with the Tuskegee Quintette in Canada and asked him to bring all the instruments he could find when he reported to begin teaching. Dawson assumed duties as band director at Kansas Vocational College in the fall of 1921. Not only was he conductor of the band, but he also taught applied music lessons on all the band and orchestral instruments. With the instruments he could find, borrow, or purchase, he was able to put together a twenty-piece ensemble.

The need for self-improvement, the desire for continuing education, and his insatiable interest in learning drove William Dawson to seek further instruction in music. While teaching at Kansas Vocational College, Dawson sought to enroll at Washburn College, established in 1865 by the Congregational Church in Topeka (now Washburn University and municipally supported). When asked by the registrar if he had any previous college credit, he sadly admitted he had none. It was also obvious that because he was

Black, the officials were reluctant to admit him. The Dean of the School of Music, Henry V. Stearns, however, was not without compassion and gave the young man a special examination. Although he was lacking actual college credit, Dawson had acquired a rich background of musical experiences that provided him with the practical knowledge enabling him to pass the exam. He was then given permission to take composition classes at the school.

Dean Stearns taught classes in composition and orchestration, courses which William was eager to take, desiring to build on his previous musical experiences. The Washburn College orchestra was significantly larger than Tuskegee's had been, and through his participation in that group, Dawson was able to expand his understanding of orchestral sound while studying the theoretical aspects of orchestration. It was also here that he sought to further his knowledge of instruments by experimenting with strings. He worked especially hard to become competent on the double bass. Stearns took a personal interest in Dawson and offered comments and suggestions for the improvement of his compositions. The Dean recognized the potential in the young man and urged him to seek further compositional study with Adolph Weidig in Chicago. William Dawson, however, had other ambitions.

Having heard great things about an outstanding trombone player, Pat Conway, Dawson became interested in studying with him at the Ithaca Conservatory of Music in Ithaca, New York. Dawson resigned his post as bandmaster at Kansas Vocational College after only one year of teaching and moved to Kansas City, Missouri. In order to raise money for his impending trip to Ithaca for further studies, he sought to publish his first composition, "Forever Thine," which is a vocal solo with piano accompaniment. To pay for publishing his song, Dawson was able to borrow money from Captain Alvin J. Neely at Tuskegee. As the summer months began, armed with freshly printed copies of his song, he set out on a door-to-door campaign to sell the copies for twenty-five cents each. William greeted each customer cordially, introduced himself and his song, then promptly demonstrated the music by singing. He not only canvassed the streets of Kansas City, Missouri, but also crossed the Missouri River and the state line to solicit sales in Kansas City, Kansas. His efforts netted him a small sum of money that he set aside for school.

In order to maintain his instrumental technique, Dawson sought to play his trombone in Blackburn's Negro Concert Band. Professor Dan Blackburn was one of several conductors paid by the Parks Department of the city of Kansas City to provide concert band music in all the public parks in Kansas City, Missouri. Blackburn's was the only ensemble composed of African American performers.[30] The concerts consisted of symphonic band literature, marches, and transcriptions of orchestral classics for band. The performances also featured soloists from time to time. Dawson approached the conductor about joining the group but was rebuffed. Blackburn told him he could not hire nonunion members. On a return trip to Topeka, Dawson promptly joined the American Federation of Musicians in order to be eligible for membership in Blackburn's band. Blackburn, however, continued to be hesitant, saying Dawson had not been a union member long enough.

Inquisitive Dawson, always seeking to improve himself through any learning experience, went to the rehearsals anyway. He quickly noticed that the band already had seven or eight good trombone players, which made it almost impossible to get into that section; however, after listening to the group rehearse several selections, he discerned that the euphonium player was rather weak. Dawson had brought his horn and sat in that section as they began to play a Sousa march. Then the conductor switched to some Barnum and Bailey circus favorites. Reading ahead, Dawson scanned the trio, and on the repeat of that section made his instrument sing out. The whole band was immediately impressed, and Blackburn then asked him to join the group. Dawson played with Blackburn's band all during the summer of 1922 and was even featured as vocal soloist, singing popular ballads.

At the time that William Dawson resigned from Kansas Vocational College, N. Clark Smith (formerly the band director at Tuskegee Institute) also resigned as band director at Lincoln High School in Kansas City, Missouri. Smith had been offered a position in Chicago working with the Pullman Railroad Car Porters. His assignment was to teach them to sing and play instruments for public performance. Smith had done excellent work at the Lincoln High School, and the principal, H. O. Cook, was looking for an appropriate replacement. Cook received a strong recommendation from Tacitus Gaillard and his wife, Lilla Washington Gaillard, niece of Booker T. Washington, to hire William Dawson. Gaillard taught masonry at Lincoln High School. Cook was already familiar with Dawson's work, having heard the Kansas Vocational College Band under Dawson's direction the previous year. The Gaillards praised Dawson's musical skills and vocal experience in the Tuskegee Quintette. Based on their recommendation and his teaching experience, Cook offered Dawson the position as band director. Remembering his desire to go to Ithaca for study with trombonist Pat Conway, William was reluctant to accept the job despite strong encouragement from the Gaillards. He nevertheless acquiesced and began work at the school in the fall of 1922.

The duties at Lincoln High School were many and varied. Not only was he conductor of the band and small orchestra, but Dawson also directed the huge chorus at the school. The choir had as many as 150 singers and performed a variety of music. They soon specialized in Negro folk songs which William Dawson had begun to arrange for mixed voices (both genders). Under his careful direction the choir gained local fame and was asked to sing on many occasions. After the choir sang Dawson's arrangements of "King Jesus Is A-Listening" and "My Lord, What a Mourning" at an immense music convention in Kansas City, music publishers swarmed him, eager to publish his arrangements. One of them, William Arms Fisher, editor and publishing manager of the well-known Oliver Ditson Company, even went so far as to invite Dawson to his hotel for a chat later that evening. Fisher, a student of Antonin Dvořák, had set many African American folk tunes himself and was interested in Dawson's work.

Dawson walked up to the Muehlebach Hotel and asked for the number of Fisher's room. The reaction he received was not one of warm greeting and courteous smiles but one of incredulous surprise that a Black man would be so impudent as to enter an establishment meant for white people only. He was immediately informed that even though he had an appointment with Mr. Fisher, he would have to use the kitchen elevator at the rear of the hotel. Remaining calm, Dawson quietly refused to be insulted by such action and merely waited silently, patiently. Following a period of much turmoil, the hotel administration had the elevator cleared and appointed someone to take Dawson up alone. Despite the difficulties in getting to see Fisher, the meeting was not profitable. Another publisher, H. T. FitzSimons of Chicago, also showed interest in Dawson's work and succeeded in publishing one of Dawson's arrangements by late 1925.

It was at Lincoln High School that Dawson would meet visual artist Aaron Douglas, where the two forged a friendship that would last a lifetime. While Dawson directed the musical arts organizations, Douglas was the visual art instructor and sponsor of the art club. Douglas was already an avid reader of the NAACP publication, *The Crisis*, and it seems very likely that the two arts instructors discussed the current social, economic, and artistic endeavors of their race and were influenced by the writings of Alain Locke.

At the close of the 1924–25 school year, Aaron Douglas left Missouri for New York and eventually became a leader in the Harlem Renaissance movement. Later, Dawson would move to Chicago for further education. While both men left Missouri to pursue other interests, the bond formed between Dawson and Douglas at Lincoln High School continued. Biographer Helen Kirschke related the importance Aaron Douglas placed on his newfound friendship with Dawson and the impetus for Douglas to leave Missouri for New York.

For Douglas, it was like an "embryo or first step" of a renaissance or revival. Finding a friend of the same racial and cultural background who lived and worked "in the same milieu" raised Douglas from the isolation he later called "the cross the Black artist had to bear, who was often isolated physically, as well as in time, interest, and out-look." His decision to go to Harlem would be precipitated by this desire to overcome isolation.[31]

The job of directing music at Lincoln High was very demanding, yet Dawson was an industrious worker, continuously improving band and choral music instruction, as well as adding courses in theory and harmony. His job description was expanded to include responsibility for developing and maintaining instrumental programs in eleven elementary schools in the city. Remarkably, he was able to establish small orchestras or bands in all the schools in which he taught.

Dawson was not too busy, however, when a church needed a choir director. The Reverend Peck of the Ebenezer African Methodist Episcopal (A.M.E.) Church contacted him to fill a music vacancy. Dawson agreed to work with the group and indicated he would serve without remuneration. Peck, though, urged him to accept a small salary. This extra income enabled him to further aid his family in Alabama. The Ebenezer A.M.E. Church choir grew and prospered musically under Dawson's tutelage. The choir was asked to present several programs on a local radio station in Kansas City, and Dawson was also featured as trombone soloist. Yet, despite many enriching musical experiences, an excellent teaching record, and exceptional personal achievements, he still felt a pressing need to further his education. To this end, he sought to enroll at the Horner Institute of Fine Arts in Kansas City.

In the 1920s, the segregation of African Americans from white society was de facto in many parts of the United States, regardless of law. African Americans were not allowed to enter most public buildings, businesses, or restaurants, at least by the front door. They were second-class citizens despite the abolition of slavery and constitutional amendments that guaranteed equality to members of all races. Dawson had already encountered many difficulties because of his skin color, and he knew he would face additional discrimination. The registrar at Horner Institute refused to enroll Dawson in the school, just as officials at Washburn College in Topeka had done a year earlier. He was told that they had a policy that did not allow "Negroes" to attend classes. Dawson astutely replied that he wanted to "study," not attend classes. Dawson's response probably caught the admission committee off guard, but he was told to come back in two weeks, possibly with the hope that he would give up the idea of matriculation.

Historian John Horner surmises that the founder of the conservatory, Charles Horner, was present at the initial meeting. With the founder's extensive interest in and connection with the Chautauqua Movement, John Horner asserted that the head of the conservatory may have recognized Dawson and sought to provide a means for him to enroll.[32] Subsequently, trying to avoid controversy, institute officials went to music theory teacher Regina Hall, to inquire if there was a possibility of teaching a young African American man privately. Hall was a woman from New England with varied musical experience, and she welcomed the eager student, demonstrating her disapproval of the school's segregationist policies.

Hall saw to it that Dawson had as many opportunities as other students to receive the education he desired. Still, he was hampered by prevailing attitudes and opinions and, because of this, officials arranged for him to come to the school after the institute had closed for the day. While he first began studying theory with Hall, he later received instruction in piano, trombone, and composition from other professors. Dr. Carl Busch presented lessons to Dawson in composition, emphasizing eighteenth-century counterpoint. Busch was influential in creating an interest in symphonic music in Kansas City. Not only did he teach composition at Horner Institute, but he also conducted the community oratorio society and generated excitement for orchestral music in the city.

Dawson continued his studies at Horner for three years, earning high grades. Very few people even knew he was a student there until the local newspaper printed a list of would-be graduates in the spring of 1925. He was to receive the bachelor of arts degree with highest honors. He got word from school officials, however, that he would not be allowed to sit with his class on the stage at the graduation exercises. Afraid of a possible confrontation, the administration decided the best decision was to maintain segregation. When Regina Hall learned of the school's decision to segregate Dawson from the other graduates, she wept. William was allowed to attend the commencement ceremony only if he sat in the balcony. His *Trio in A* for violin, cello, and piano, was selected for presentation at the graduation festivities and members of the Kansas City Symphony Orchestra were asked to perform the work. Despite the apparent enthusiastic appreciation by the audience, Dawson was not permitted to stand and acknowledge the thunderous applause. Years later, when questioned about his commencement experience at Horner, Dawson said:

You don't let that disturb you—you have a goal.... So, if you want to learn something, you're willing to pay the price. And we had to pay the price. And I was willing to pay the price. Of course, I realized my shortcomings, and [education] was there for me to get. And there were people there to teach it. And I took advantage of that. And when I graduated, they opened it up to others. Somebody has to go in, and you've got to do it. No, I don't let that make me hate anybody.[33]

Roy Wilkins, editor of the *Kansas City Call* and a friend of Dawson, reported the commencement incident along with the negative reactions that were generated by the administrative decision at Horner. Nine years later, following an impressive national achievement by William Dawson, Wilkins recalled the Kansas City commencement in his column "Talking It over with Roy Wilkins."

> Nine years ago, I was sitting in a little cramped balcony there exclusively "for Mr. Dawson's colored friends." Bill was being graduated from Horner Institute, but he was right there among us in the tiny balcony, not up on the stage with the white graduates. The little orchestra there was playing Bill's melody, a composition judged to be good enough to have a star place on the graduation program. It was a sweet thing, wispy, haunting music for violin, cello, and piano. It brought applause and many in that audience, even though they were from Kansas City, looked around for William L. Dawson, not thinking for a moment that his brown face had sent him into the background where he could not even acknowledge the applause his brain-child called forth. He could not even march up from where he was and get his diploma.... It was "thought best" to deliver it to him the next day in the office. Might start a riot or something to pass it to him along with white graduates.
> .... Maybe Kansas City deserves some credit [for Dawson's success]. Maybe it made Bill's pathway so hard, made the insults so stinging that he HAD to go on. Maybe we ought to give thanks this year and this season for Kansas City's scorn, ignorance and cheap insults. Maybe, but then ...
> I can't be bitter against the town. I got deep satisfaction out of last night for Bill's sake. No matter what happens now—even if Bill should go back to Kansas City to live—I will know I was right in 1925. Dawson has proved it. He has proved that Kansas City had no right to treat him as it did. I felt then that he was too big for them to see. Now I am sure of it. I think they felt it too. Maybe Kansas City has grown in nine

years. Nearly every other place has. Maybe they can't be as little and mean again as they were in 1925. I hope so, but, as I say, after last night it doesn't matter. They can't stay mean, but they can't hurt me again as they did then.... Because now I KNOW.[34]

Soon after the initial reporting of the commencement incident at Horner, Wilkins assumed the role of assistant secretary of the National Association for the Advancement of Colored People (NAACP) in 1931 and followed W. E. B. Du Bois as editor of *The Crisis* in 1934. In 1964 Wilkins ascended to become executive director of the NAACP and would later serve a leadership role in the civil rights movement in the 1960s.[35]

DAWSON'S MOVE TO CHICAGO

A year prior to his graduation from Horner, Dawson's father passed away in Anniston. But, with William's financial support, the family was doing well. With the family's stability assured for a while, Dawson began to consider further compositional study. Remembering the encouragement of Dean Henry Stearns at Washburn College, as well as advice from others, William contemplated studying with composer Adolph Weidig in Chicago. In order to go to Chicago, Dawson first had to resign as music director at Lincoln High School. The resignation meant leaving his position as band and choral director as well as music supervisor for the eleven grammar schools. It also meant bidding a farewell to Principal Cook. Cook had recognized Dawson's outstanding musical talent and pledged that his support would be unlike any other administrator's. Indeed, Cook had proven to be a very easy man with whom to work. Realizing the value of music as a part of every child's education, Cook fully supported Dawson's programs in all of the schools, and Dawson did not want to disappoint the fine principal. It was a difficult decision, but Dawson decided to take a leave of absence to study with Weidig. Dawson did not know then, however, that he would not return to Lincoln High School.

German-born Adolph Weidig emigrated to the United States in 1892 and settled in Chicago. A composer, violinist, and teacher, Weidig played with the Chicago Symphony Orchestra from 1892 to 1896. He taught composition at the American Conservatory of Music in Chicago and became the assistant director there in 1898. His compositions include symphonic works, several choral pieces, chamber music, and a suite for piano. Weidig's music was performed in the United States and in his own native Germany.

In the fall of 1925, Dawson sought to enter the American Conservatory. He had a portfolio of his compositions and arrangements, which he presented along with his application for admission. Weidig was immediately impressed and awarded Dawson a scholarship for compositional study. He freed Dawson from strict counterpoint and helped Dawson see its usefulness as a compositional device without being bound to it as the only mechanism for thematic exposition and development. Diligent study resulted in Dawson's receiving a master's degree in composition from the conservatory in 1927.

Prior to graduation, William Dawson met and fell in love with Cornella Lampton, a pianist originally from Greenville, Mississippi. The Lampton family left the South and moved to Chicago. Eventually, Cornella matriculated at Howard University in Washington, DC, where in 1914 she became the first woman to earn a degree from the Conservatory of Music. Dawson met Cornella while she was continuing her piano study with Percy Grainger at the Chicago Musical College. The marriage took place in Chicago in May of 1927, but tragically, Cornella died just over a year later due to complications from an appendectomy.[36]

It was Weidig who encouraged Dawson to audition for the Chicago Civic Orchestra and subsequently recommended William as a fine trombonist. Established in 1920 by the Civic Music Association of Chicago and Frederick Stock, then conductor of the Chicago Symphony Orchestra, the Civic Orchestra provided young musicians with invaluable experience and training. All applicants were required to play in alto clef, and Dawson admitted, "I couldn't play it either . . . but Mr. Stock liked my attempt."[37] His successful audition netted him a first chair position, yet, of the 110 men in the orchestra, he was the only African American. Some of the orchestral instrumentalists were openly hostile toward him, while others ignored him. Most did not speak to him at all. The conductors, however, genuinely liked Dawson and were friendly toward him. Dawson would occasionally speak a little German to Stock and Eric DeLamarter, which pleased them.[38] To Dawson's great delight, the two men would share with him their experience and knowledge of Brahms and other German composers. William continued to hold first chair in the Civic Orchestra from 1926 to 1930.

Dawson took a position as editor and arranger for the Gamble Hinged Music Company soon after he arrived in Chicago. Known as Gamble Hinged Music upon opening its doors in 1906, the company gained fame for designing a process to extend the life of choral octavos and other sheet music by binding a cloth hinge to the spine, which they called "Gamble-izing."[39] Dawson also worked for the music publishers H. T. FitzSimons Company.

Both music companies published some of Dawson's choral works while he was in their employ.

While in Chicago, Dawson was approached by the Reverend Kingsley at Good Shepherd Congregational Church. The choir at the church consisted of twelve to fourteen members and needed a conductor to recruit additional singers and enhance their musicianship. Busy as he was already, Dawson accepted the position for $100 a month. He directed the choir in rehearsal and presented special music each Sunday morning. He worked to provide necessary sight-reading instruction and helped improve the choral sound of the group.

In addition to staying active in performance circles, William Dawson joined a dance band. Charles "Doc" Cook organized a fourteen-piece combo called the "Doctors of Syncopation." Cook, who had received his doctorate in music from the Chicago Musical College, was the head arranger for Remick Music Corporation for fifteen years.[40] Cook's ensemble played regularly in the White City Amusement Park's Casino Dance Hall, which was located at South Parkway and Sixty-Third. Between 1927 and 1928, at least six tracks were recorded by Doc Cook's jazz ensemble by Columbia Records. Dawson said he was the most versatile member of the group, playing euphonium, string bass, and trombone; he was even the featured soloist in some performances. The list of performers on the recordings, however, list him only as the trombonist.[41]

Much like writings about William Dawson over forty years ago, despite knowledge and respect paid to Doc Cook, little is written beyond a brief biography of several sentences or a mere mention in passing in several books about jazz history.[42] Yet, when one listens to the six pieces recorded by Doc Cook's band, the sophisticated musicianship demonstrated is hard to miss. Some say the performance style may be referred to as "flapper style," while others think it may be termed as a nascent, emerging swing style. The quality of the recording is amazing, especially considering the tracks were laid down in the 1920s.[43] All of the recordings made by Columbia can be found in the Brian Rust Discographies, with the recordings of Cook's band contained in Volume 3.[44]

Even though he had received a master's degree in composition, Dawson was compelled to pursue further study. He was able to receive compositional direction from Danish composer and teacher Dr. Thorvald Otterstrom. Born in Copenhagen, the composer came to the United States in 1892 and chose Chicago as his new home. Otterstrom's compositions included chamber instrumental, vocal, piano, and orchestral works; one of his orchestral pieces is entitled *American Negro Suite*. Dawson had begun work on a symphony based on themes from what he called Negro folk songs. Otterstrom was anxious for Dawson's work to be completed because he believed it would help change the prevailing prejudicial opinions about African American composers as well as the entire race. Dr. Otterstrom believed that many white people viewed the African American as having childlike intellects, and he thought that the performance of a major symphonic work written by a Black man would force anti-Black sentiments to be reevaluated. Regardless of Otterstrom's wishes, Dawson was not able to complete the symphony while in Chicago.[45]

Chicago had been the site of the 1893 World Columbian Exposition, a commemoration of the four hundredth anniversary of Christopher Columbus's initial exploration on the North American continent. Forty years later, the city hosted the exhibition entitled Century of Progress. The 1933 Chicago fair marked the progress made in America since 1893. While the Columbian Exposition had emphasized the classical past, the Century of Progress pointed toward the future. Serious planning for the gigantic exhibition began in 1929 and eventually resulted in the creation of man-made islands and lagoons along the lakefront, upon which buildings with elaborately designed landscaping were erected. Although the United States was plunged deep in an economic depression by 1933, the fair was a huge success, attracting crowds of more than 100,000 each day.

An important consideration in plans for the 1933 World's Fair in Chicago was music. Well in advance of the fair, organizers prepared for the selection of a principal bandmaster for the festivities. In 1929 the *Chicago Daily News* devised a contest to choose a suitable conductor, which resulted in many musicians applying for the position. Doc Cook was approached about entering the contest, but he refused and suggested Dawson instead. Even union members in the American Federation of Musicians recommended Dawson for the contest. The rules of the contest included a required performance audition for each entrant. Contestants were asked to conduct their own group in a scheduled concert on the *Daily News* Plaza. Most of the contestants were conducting or playing in large bands and did not have difficulty securing the necessary forces. Dawson, on the other hand, started from scratch and put together a sixty-piece band for his audition. He even gathered twenty voices for a choir to perform vocal works on the concert.

> The white conductors used the same band. All the symphonic players in the Loop in Chicago (I was playing with some of them in the

orchestra). But I had to organize my band, the Negro band of 60 players. And, the union made it possible for me to call anybody I wanted out of the cabaret.[46]

The reaction was overwhelming acclaim for Dawson's conducting. A large picture of Dawson conducting his ensemble appeared on the front page of the September 18, 1929, edition of the *Chicago Bee*. The *Bee* was an African American publication established in 1926 to rival *Chicago Defender*, the largest Black newspaper in the nation at the time. As a result of that 1929 contest, Dawson was selected to lead the Negro division of the 1933 fair's musical aggregation. Yet, unbeknownst to Dawson, he would soon be summoned home to Tuskegee Institute. Thus, he would find it necessary to return to Chicago to assume his position of honor at the fair.

Chapter 2

THE DEVELOPMENT OF THE MUSIC SCHOOL AT TUSKEGEE INSTITUTE

1930–55

TRANSITION FROM SECONDARY TO HIGHER EDUCATION: 1925–30

On November 14, 1915, only two years into William Dawson's schooling at Tuskegee Institute, Booker Taliaferro Washington, the beloved founder of the school, died. It was Washington's reputation and aura that compelled Dawson to run away from home and get an education in the setting Washington had created in east central Alabama. Only sixteen at the time of Washington's death, Dawson joined thousands of mourners from across the nation who took part in memorializing the great man. In two short years at Tuskegee, Washington had taken Dawson under his wing, mentored the young man, and paved a path to enable him to realize his dreams of becoming a musician. The great leader had also shaped Dawson's beliefs about how to succeed as a Black man in America, but the young musician had no idea that Washington's successor would eventually provide an opening that would impact Dawson's life for sixty years.[1]

In 1915 there was little doubt as to who would succeed Dr. Washington at Tuskegee Institute. The man he favored, Robert Russa Moton, had cultivated an outstanding reputation at Hampton Institute in Virginia where Washington had worked before moving to Macon County, Alabama, to begin the work at Tuskegee. The trustees agreed with Washington's assessment, and Moton assumed his position as head of the institute on May 24, 1916. Moton said of his first few years at the school that despite a few minor changes, he diligently continued Washington's vision and policies. In his biography, *Finding a Way Out*, Moton extolled the former president's unique leadership and persona, lauding the fact that few changes were necessary in the transition due to Washington's planning.[2]

The prosperity of the 1920s led to great change for most Americans, including African Americans. In a biographical sketch of Portia Pittman Washington, the daughter of the former Tuskegee president, historian Ruth Ann Stewart alluded to the Harlem Renaissance of the 1920s that witnessed the emergence of the "New Negro" and an outpouring of artistic and intellectual accomplishments of African Americans. Stewart concluded that the aesthetic awakening of Black scholars and the flowering of the arts in New York completely shifted the focus away from what was considered the appropriate industrial education for all Black students, rendering this old educational idea obsolete.[3]

The industrial-academic dual education model had been the foundation upon which Tuskegee Institute was built, and while there were additions to this basic educational concept in terms of new programs and courses, the industrial aspect remained the chief reason for Tuskegee's influence. In a chapel address at Tuskegee Institute, Dr. Will Alexander, director of the Commission on Inter-racial Cooperation from 1919 to 1930, stated that the incredible strides made in vocational education at both Tuskegee and Hampton not only indicated a new path for American education but also influenced educational offerings at other levels. Vocational education was included in secondary schools nationwide and resulted in rural schools receiving federal educational funding.[4] Yet earlier in his speech, Alexander referred to Dr. Moton's proposed expansion of the educational mission to include both vocational and liberal arts education.

In the 1920s officials and educators in Black colleges continued to question and debate the purpose of higher education. While many Black colleges began emphasizing a liberal arts approach, others focused exclusively on industrial education. Black institutions such as Texas Agricultural and Industrial College, and Mississippi Industrial College (later absorbed by Rust College), were founded with an industrial focus. Moton understood that African American students needed the same education as other Americans and worked diligently to provide instruction to ensure success for all pupils under his aegis. Moton's decision to combine vocational and liberal arts education was probably significantly influenced by his closest friend, John Hope, president of Morehouse College and later Atlanta University, historically Black liberal arts colleges (now known as Historically Black Colleges and Universities, or HBCUs) in Georgia's capital city.[5]

Tuskegee began its transition from secondary to collegiate status in the 1925–26 school year. The *Institute Bulletin* for that year explained the need for change, first giving honor and praise to Booker T. Washington for his vision and determination to establish a school for industrial education that reflected sound judgment in providing skills to ensure the success of his race and people. However, citing the variation in social and economic conditions at the close of World War I, the bulletin announced new college degree plans that would raise the level of academic achievement and coexist with the traditional vocational diploma courses. The new college degrees included the following programs within the Teachers College:

THE TEACHERS COLLEGE
1. The School of Agriculture—Offering a four-year course leading to the degree of B.S., and a two-year course leading to a diploma. The School of Education—Offering a four-year course leading to the degree of B.S., and a two-year course leading to a diploma.
2. The School of Home Economics—Offering a two-year course leading to a diploma.
3. The Trade-Technical School—Offering a two-year course leading to a diploma.
4. The Summer School for Teachers.[6]

Some questioned the addition of these degree plans, believing them inconsistent and incompatible with the original purpose of Tuskegee. Regardless of the controversy, Dr. Moton upheld his decision to expand the scope of the institute. In his annual report several years following the changes, he promised an adherence to industrial training but reminded his critics that education must keep pace with societal changes. Moton's role in expanding Tuskegee's course offerings led biographer Frederick Patterson to compare Moton's vision to Washington's; both presidents demonstrated a commitment to enhancing the social, economic, and intellectual standing of African Americans in the United States.[7]

THE ESTABLISHMENT OF THE SCHOOL OF MUSIC AT TUSKEGEE: 1930–37

One of the new programs launched as a result of Dr. Moton's expansion was a School of Music for Tuskegee Institute. This seemingly innovative phase was not without roots in the Washington philosophy, as the founder believed music to be an important part of each student's education. The addition of a course of study leading to a baccalaureate degree in music, then, was in keeping the with founder's principles of education. Plans for the School of Music began in 1926, five years prior to the Golden Anniversary of the founding of Tuskegee institute. The most important early decision to be made was the selection of a capable person to administer and oversee the music program.

William Dawson's name surfaced frequently in the discussions of those persons recommended or suggested for the music position. Moton remembered Dawson as a vibrant young student during his early tenure as an administrator at Tuskegee and was well aware of Dawson's instrumental skills and his extensive travels with the Tuskegee Male Quintette. Moton also knew of William's professional success achieved through teaching and playing in the Midwest. School officials approached Dawson several times to invite him to assume the role of administrator of the School of Music before he finally acquiesced and accepted the invitation in the late fall of 1930. Dawson related the sequence of events:

> For two or three years or more [before 1931] Moton said he wanted a School of Music, I was in Chicago at the time playing first trombone in the Chicago Civic Orchestra, Moton sent [his assistant] G. Lake Imes to see me. I told Imes, "I'm getting what I want here and I think I will stay. I'm sorry."[8]

Given the vibrant music scene of Chicago at the time, it is easier to understand why Dawson was initially reticent to accept an opportunity to return to Tuskegee, where he had blossomed and thrived as a young musician. Chicago provided opportunities to perform jazz, study with noted composers, play trombone professionally, and achieve accolades for amassing and conducting choirs and bands. The big city that was beginning to feel the effects of a Black Renaissance certainly had its allure for the young man. Moton, undeterred by the refusal, tenaciously continued to seek the person he thought would be the best fit. Dawson continued:

> Finally, Moton himself came to Chicago to see me. He wanted a School of Music at Tuskegee. I told Moton, "I don't know: I'm playing in an orchestra and everything is going my way." Then Moton said, "Bill, what do you have against a homecoming?" I accepted that and told him I would come to Tuskegee around Thanksgiving just to talk. Moton was a great lover of music, and he told me over and over how much he wanted a School of Music. The night I arrived on campus Moton showed me the chapel and introduced me to the soloists. The

next day he convinced me of his seriousness in creating a School of Music at Tuskegee. He said, "You can get rid of anybody you want to. Do whatever you want to the program."[9]

Little did Moton realize then that his initial trip to Chicago to convince Dawson to come back to Tuskegee would not be his last. Several times during his tenure as president of the institute he would have to travel to Chicago to find the temperamental Dawson, who had left the campus in a huff, and bring him back to Tuskegee.[10]

Dawson finally agreed to return to his alma mater to establish the School of Music and serve as its first Director in time for the Jubilee celebration of the founding of Tuskegee, which would occur in the spring of 1931. However, Dawson warned Moton that he would not be on campus in time for the fall term in 1930, as he was working on a special project. Later, it was revealed that the piece he was composing would become the *Negro Folk Symphony*, a work that was eventually completed in 1932. The magnitude of Dawson's acceptance of the leadership of the new School of Music was made evident in a trumpeting of the news to faculty and students during the first evening chapel service immediately following Dawson's assent to return to Tuskegee. An exclamation point was added to the announcement with the revelation that the salary for the Director of the School of Music would be second to the principal, Dr. Moton![11]

When September and October had passed and the fall term was well into November, Dawson had still not arrived. Mistrusting the previous announcement in chapel, the campus grapevine spread the word that he was not coming. It was not until December of 1930 that Dawson returned to his alma mater to organize and facilitate the opening of Tuskegee's School of Music. While his pay began, his duties did not officially start until the new year, affording him time to reacquaint himself with his surroundings, assess the status of the music program, and make plans for the fiftieth anniversary celebration.[12]

When Dawson arrived at Tuskegee as an administrator, he inherited a department whose work in developing music education began in the nineteenth century. Since he completed his own course of study at the elementary and secondary levels, he realized that the parameters of Tuskegee's music program went far beyond the typical high school curriculum in place in the early 1900s. During his student days at Tuskegee, the music faculty had been predominantly made up of women. Jennie C. Lee was in charge of vocal music and was assisted by Emily C. Moore. Allice Carter Simmons, with the help of Adelaide Towson, was the head of instrumental music. Men usually held positions as band and orchestra directors. Dawson's former trombone instructor in Anniston, S. W. Gresham, had previously been director of bands and was followed by N. Clark Smith. It was Captain Frank L. Drye, however, who was band director during William's student days at Tuskegee. In the elementary classes, students were first introduced to the fundamentals of music theory in the key of C, and they quickly began work with the staff, clef signs, and all note values. They learned pitches by solfege syllables and interval numbers. After undertaking work in the key of C, students then worked with G, D, A, and E major scales. The Music Department also offered piano instruction for all levels and provided ensemble experience in band, chorus, and orchestra.[13]

Music instruction at Tuskegee was of a practical nature, considered essential for every student, and was meant to combine religious, historical, social, and aesthetic aspects of art. Each Monday through Thursday evening was reserved for chapel Services, and every faculty member and student was required to attend. The entire assemblage was expected to sing the melodies created during the time of enslavement known as Negro folk songs, thus honoring the artistic and cultural contributions of enslaved Africans. The Tuskegee community viewed music as an expression of the challenges, hardships, mistreatment, and horrors experienced by Africans who were forcefully brought to the New World; therefore, the school expected the choir and student body to approach singing with gravity and sincerity.[14]

The purpose of the Male Glee Club was similar to that of nightly chapel singing. Every member of the band and orchestra was required to participate in a male chorus. The school taught choral arranging as a part of choral skills and encouraged students to create harmonic renditions to be sight-read and performed. The choral education program also provided experiences in ethnomusicology, giving opportunities for students to visit rural areas, notate songs sung by the villagers, and harmonically arrange the music for the Male Glee Club to perform. Yet the importance of industrial education remained alongside the exciting musical offerings. The Tuskegee bulletin, or catalog, made a point of aligning the importance of music study with learning a trade or vocational skills, underscoring Washington's educational approach. In all, the years 1915–30 saw very few changes in the music program at Tuskegee.[15]

When Dawson first arrived at the school for the 1930–31 school year, the *Institute Bulletin* listed him as head of the Music Department. But by the following year, the catalog designated him in the Institute's Executive Council as director of the School of Music. Within that year, he and officials developed and published a well-defined purpose statement for the School of Music, which was published in the 1931–32 *Institute Bulletin*. The purpose statement declared that due to the current demand for qualified music teachers in schools, churches, and private studios, the School of Music was recently created at Tuskegee to produce choir, orchestra, and band directors, as well as organists and concert performers.[16] Remembering that Washington had searched for and located the finest Black educators for his faculty at Tuskegee, Dawson sought to do the same. He wanted each person's credentials to be in good order, and as such he insisted that each faculty member hold at least a baccalaureate degree from an institution of good standing and that the musical talents of the faculty be demonstrated in the classroom and in performance.[17]

While he insisted that faculty members hold degrees, Dawson did not believe that such titles were a true mark of someone's musical abilities. When it came to his own experience, he admitted feeling a sense of accomplishment upon the attainment of a diploma, degree, or distinction, but the degree was not evidence of mastery; instead, it indicated readiness for further learning opportunities via professional experience or continued formal schooling. For Dawson, degrees were not as important as talent. Competency and experience far outweighed total academic credentials. Yet he valued education for the mental stimulation it provided, the direction it gave to learning, and the rugged persistence and determination it required of an individual pursuing a particular course of study. As director of the School of Music at Tuskegee, he wanted to hire professors who, like himself, had extensive practical experience in the professional music world but who had also achieved academic honor. Dawson believed it would be difficult for students engaged in baccalaureate degree programs to respect and emulate faculty members who had not attained such distinction.[18]

Portia Washington Pittman, the only daughter of Booker T. Washington, was one faculty member whose credentials were not complete. She had been given a position as choral director and teacher of piano at Tuskegee by her father's successor, Dr. Moton, and was already on the faculty when Dawson arrived in 1930. While she had engaged in collegiate work at Bradford College (Massachusetts), studied piano abroad in Germany, and taken summer courses in vocal music at Columbia University in New York City, her records did not show completion of any one program. Pittman admired Dawson but went into a panic at his appointment as the new director of the School of Music. She knew he adamantly upheld his stringent expectations for completion of degrees. She frantically wrote her contacts at Bradford College, a two-year liberal arts college for women, and learned that her former teacher Miss Pond had collaborated with the Bradford registrar to provide documentation of her music courses. Together the women assembled verification that Mrs. Pittman had completed coursework at the college level during her final two years at the institution. Once the differences were resolved, Pittman was allowed to maintain her music faculty status.[19]

Dawson's first faculty, like the Music Department two decades earlier, was predominantly female. There were twelve instructors in all: eight women and four men. Hazel Harrison was head of the Piano Department. In 1904, at twenty-one years of age, Harrison was featured as piano soloist with the Berlin Philharmonic Orchestra. In so doing she was the first person who had never studied outside of the United States to perform a solo with a European orchestra.[20] Under Harrison's aegis were O. Lexine Howse and Catherine Moton, who taught both piano and theory, as well as Pittman, who taught only piano.[21]

Abbie Mitchell was head of the Vocal Department, and in charge of voice culture and repertoire. Mitchell was a soprano renowned for her operatic and musical performances in New York. At age fourteen, she was cast in *Clorindy, or the Origin of the Cakewalk*, one of the earliest African American musicals. *Clorindy* was an 1898 collaboration between poet Paul Laurence Dunbar and composer Will Marion Cook, whom she later married. Following her tenure at Tuskegee, in 1935 Mitchell performed the role of Clara in George Gershwin's opera *Porgy and Bess* and was the first to record the hit song from the production "Summertime."[22]

As head of the Public School Music Department, Elizabeth Terry supervised music instruction on the elementary and secondary levels and taught voice and theory. Under the direction of Terry, Alberta Simms and Emily C. Neely served as public school music teachers.

The director of the orchestra was Andrew F. Rosemond, who served as head of the Stringed Instruments Department and taught violin and viola. Captain Frank L. Drye continued as director of the band and eventually became head of the newly formed Band Instruments Department. He also served as instructor for brass instruments. Ernest R. Bullock was the clarinet and saxophone instructor. Dawson not only directed the School of Music but also conducted the choirs and taught composition, instrumentation, and conducting.[23]

The organization of the School of Music consisted of a Children's Division for the elementary grades and a Preparatory Division for the secondary level. A conservatory approach was designed for the collegiate level. The first baccalaureate degrees offered were the bachelor of music (BM), and the bachelor of school music (BSM). The BM included majors in piano, voice, organ, euphonium, clarinet, saxophone, trumpet, trombone, and composition. The BSM. included majors in General Music Supervision and Instrumental Music Supervision. In July of 1932, a statement about the degree programs appeared in the school paper, the *Tuskegee Messenger*, to publicize the newly expanded music offerings. Training in music was offered to those who desired music study only as an elective as well as those pursuing professional positions as teachers or concert performers. Dawson emphasized that liberal arts courses, specifically literary classes, would be studied alongside music courses to provide "sound academic training." Completion of all required courses would lead to a bachelor of music degree.[24]

The *Institute Bulletin* was unique in that it listed not only courses required for each degree but also the competencies expected for each level of classification. For example, freshman piano majors were required to play all major and minor scales at a metronome marking of M.M. 80 with attention to dynamics. The sophomore trombone major would be working daily on embouchure studies, exercises in clef shifting, and duet, trio, and quartet playing, among other techniques. The senior Instrumental Supervision major was expected to organize and rehearse an ensemble of beginners in the elementary division. The student was also responsible for an appearance as conductor of the institute band or orchestra in concert, having selected the music and rehearsed the group prior to performance. Student conductors were encouraged to choose works by Black composers such as Samuel Coleridge-Taylor and Will Marion Cook, and melodies arranged by Harry T. Burleigh. The theory courses listed under requirements for the degree in composition included harmony, counterpoint, form and analysis, solfeggio, orchestration, military and concert band arranging, and modern dance orchestra arranging.[25]

Other specific degree requirements and courses were noted in the bulletin. All instrumental majors were required to spend three hours weekly practicing on their major instruments and one hour on their minor (secondary) instruments. The programs of study included two years of foreign language and a course in public speaking. Composition and Instrumentation, emphasizing "Negro idioms," was a course required of every major except General Music Supervision.

All instrumental and vocal students were required to take the solfeggio courses. The second level of solfeggio courses had students sight-singing melodies in the movable "C" clef as well as taking melodic and harmonic dictation. Music History and Appreciation was a junior-level course, universally required. Musical Acoustics was required of Instrumental Supervision majors only. Offered during the fall term each year, the acoustics course consisted of demonstration and lectures emphasizing the application of scientific knowledge to problems band and orchestra directors might encounter. Further, problems of tuning, fundamentals and overtones, beats, the vibrations of strings, and A-440 were topics to be covered.[26]

The curriculum for students preparing to teach music in the schools included a group of core courses listed under the heading "School Music." Students began these courses in their freshman year and continued through the senior year. The first two years encompassed the fundamentals of theory and musical terminology as taught in the elementary school, as well as conducting. On the junior level, the coursework involved arranging music for various instrumental ensembles, and students were expected to be able to complete an arrangement for full orchestra or band by the end of the junior year. In the senior year, students began preparation for the student-teaching phase through exposure to the various methods and principles of teaching. The student-teaching component was a practicum of sorts that students undertook simultaneously with coursework during their entire senior year.[27]

The *Institute Bulletin* lists the probable expenses for a complete school year at approximately $400. This figure included the following fees, all on a yearly basis:

> $50 college tuition, an estimated $20 for books, and $184 for room and board. The charge for room and board included laundry service and hospital fees but did not include the cost of a uniform. The men's uniform was $25, while the women's uniform was only $10.50. Music students were required to pay the usual athletic and entertainment fees, as well as special fees for using school instruments.[28]

Just as Dr. Moton tried to further the work of Washington, Dawson also maintained many of Washington's ideals. He wanted to continue the emphasis placed on "plantation melodies" that had been initiated by Tuskegee's founder. Dawson saw to it that African American folk idioms were stressed in all phases of the music program. It was a requirement of all voice majors that at least one Negro folk song be included in each recital program. Dawson also served as personal counselor to each of the music students. He wanted to help them plan the course of study that would prepare them for a successful career after commencement. He continuously steered them toward graduation so that they would use their school time most productively. Relying on his own experiences with composition in the Tuskegee band, and his extensive coursework during baccalaureate and graduate study, Dawson encouraged his students to gain practical experience in composition, understanding that students' knowledge of the elements of music (pitch, melody, harmony, rhythm, tempo, dynamics, timbre, form, medium, style, texture) would grow and develop as a result of this practice. Not only did he inspire students to compose, but he also urged them to perform these new works.[29]

Sara Stivers, the first graduate of the School of Music at Tuskegee, arranged a composition for band. Dawson defied the usual music conservatory practice of allowing the composer only one or two rehearsals with an ensemble and instead granted Stivers as much rehearsal time with the band as she thought she needed. This decision, born out of his personal philosophy, was to provide the students with experiences and skills that would equip them to think for themselves once they left the institution. In this way Dawson carried on an earlier practice at Tuskegee of encouraging diligent labor with one's hands, championing the cause of education for all, and instilling the love and importance of music to enhance life. His careful guidance and inspiration fostered the spirit of Tuskegee pride in the students under his direction, ensuring that following graduation they would represent the institute in an outstanding manner, just as the previous faculty had demanded of students decades earlier.[30] Indeed, Dawson was demanding, as related by former student Ralph Ellison in a ninetieth birthday letter extolling the greatness of the educator (see Appendix C). Despite his temperamental reactions to imperfection in rehearsal or less-than-perfect classwork, the students knew he had their best interests at heart.[31]

At the start of the 1932–33 school year, Dawson's second full year as director, a few changes occurred. Bullock, clarinet and saxophone instructor, had passed away and had been replaced by George Rankin. Van S. Whitted was added as professor of organ.[32] The 1936–37 school year, on the other hand, brought more significant changes as the Depression limited resources for the privately funded Tuskegee Institute. State-funded schools such as Alabama State University in Montgomery, just forty miles west of Tuskegee, experienced enrollment increases during this time, while student population at Tuskegee declined. Despite Tuskegee's fine reputation, funding inequities made it difficult for the private school to compete with a state-supported institution. As a result of financial difficulties, the 1936–37 School of Music faculty at Tuskegee had only eleven members as compared with the thirteen in previous years. Harrison was still head of the Piano Department, but only Moton, Patterson, and Pittman continued to serve with her.

Florence Cole-Talbert, who had replaced Mitchell as head of the Voice Department, was the sole voice instructor. Born in Detroit in 1890, and the daughter of a mother who had sung with the Fisk Jubilee Singers, Cole-Talbert would later record vocal solos for three different labels. In 1919 she recorded on the new Broome Special Phonograph label. In 1921 she recorded four titles for the Black Swan label. Three years later Cole-Talbert recorded two pieces under the Paramount label, followed by three years in Europe, where she sang the title role in Verdi's *Aida* in Italy. Before coming to Tuskegee, Cole-Talbert taught at Bishop College in Marshall, Texas. She subsequently completed her teaching career at Fisk University, her mother's alma mater.[33]

Dorothy Sulton had succeeded Terry as head of Public School Music, and only Alberta L. Simms taught under her supervision. Rosemond and Drye remained as director of the orchestra and band director, respectively. Rankin was the clarinet and saxophone instructor, while Orrin Suthern, who replaced Whitted as professor of organ, also taught theory.[34]

The Great Depression significantly impacted Dawson and the Tuskegee School of Music. While economic woes plagued the School of Music, it nevertheless continued to offer two baccalaureate music degrees in 1936–1937. Major areas for the bachelor of music degree, however, were reduced from eleven to eight, and the instrumental supervisor's program was placed under the bachelor of music degree. The viola, euphonium, and saxophone majors were dropped due to lack of students electing those majors. The bachelor of school music degree was offered only in General Music Supervision (teaching), also due to low enrollment.[35]

THE DEPARTMENT OF MUSIC: 1937–55

Further changes occurred the following year, not only in the number of faculty and new personnel but also in the status of the School of Music and degrees offered. The description of the music program during the previous year, 1936–37, was listed under the heading "School of Music," but by the fall of 1937, all listings were under the description "Department of Music." The focus of the music program had also changed and was reflected in the stated purpose of preparing music teachers who, with the completion of a four-year curriculum, would earn a bachelor of science in music education. Accommodating the need for flexibility as a music teacher, the coursework was broadened to enable graduates to conduct both instrumental and vocal music. In keeping with Dawson's insistence on a firm literary background, those who enrolled in the B.S. in Music Education were required to take English as a minor.[36]

As the Depression continued, the faculty was further reduced from eleven to ten members, resulting in changes in personnel assignments. Cole was named head of the Piano Department, and Collins assumed the position as head of the Vocal Department. The remainder of the faculty included continuing members: Drye, band; Pittman, piano; Rankin, clarinet and saxophone; Rosemond, orchestra; Simms, Public School Music Department;

Suthern, organ and theory.[37] The breadth of course offerings was trimmed considerably. Private instruction was offered only in organ, piano, violin, voice, and trumpet. Courses in School Music, Instrumental Techniques class, and Student-Teaching remained under the heading "Music Education." Conducting, Instrumentation, Music Appreciation, and Solfeggio rounded out the music curriculum.[38] By 1941 enrollment decreases led to further reductions in faculty, just two members in addition to Dawson: Drye and Simms.[39]

Earlier, in the fall of 1940, the War Department opened the door for African Americans to enter aviation service, paving the way for Black men "to train as pilots and vital support personnel."[40] By 1942 the Tuskegee Army Airfield, which was the largest of the training bases, opened just north of the campus, and the first cadets arrived to complete flight training. Known as the Tuskegee Airmen, the graduates of pilot training served the US Army in many important, dangerous missions in defense of the country during World War II (WWII). While Dawson lamented the declining student enrollment in music, he was nonetheless proud of the contribution of all African Americans in WWII efforts, most especially those from Tuskegee.

By 1943, however, the department created a new curriculum and hired two additional faculty members. The prescribed new curriculum led to a bachelor of science degree in a particular department or school and a diploma in music. The Department of Music no longer offered a baccalaureate degree but continued to exist via this new "Joint Curriculum." To justify the change, the *Institute Bulletin* for 1943-44 pointed to the need for teacher flexibility given the expectation that teachers of traditional academic subjects would also need to conduct both vocal and instrumental ensembles. Students in Elementary Education and Physical Education were encouraged to minor in music. The hours required for the music minor varied from 36 to 50, depending on individual skills. All students were invited to select music courses that would stimulate their interest and meet their needs.

To facilitate the new program, the department added two more members to the music faculty, for a total of five instructors.[41] Electing to take music courses in preparation for the extra duties of music teaching, a minimum of a fifth year and a summer were added to the traditional curricula. The bulletin, however, warned that the student would need a high degree of aptitude and ability in order to achieve the musical growth required to earn the music diploma. One wonders what contribution Dawson made concerning this warning.[42]

With both the Great Depression and WWII behind the United States and Tuskegee, a new era developed for Dawson's music department. During this time, much of the department's original prominence was restored. To reflect this new phase, Dawson issued a restatement of the department's goals and objectives. The following statements are listed in the 1944–45 school bulletin under "Purposes":

1. To supervise and direct that part of the Institute's program of general education which pertains to the field of music. To offer to all students in the Institute the opportunity of gaining a knowledge and understanding of the art of Music, in its relation to the history of civilization, and to their own life in our time. To provide students in the Upper and Lower Divisions of all schools with opportunities for participating in musical activities.
2. To supplement the program of the School of Education through offering courses in School Music.
3. To give instruction in the piano, voice, and band, and orchestral instruments.[43]

Among the changes and improvements in the post- depression era, Tuskegee boasted the possession of superior music materials for student use. Using the analogy of "a museum gallery is to the artist as the collection of records is to the musician," the 1944 *Institute Bulletin* indicated that the college ranked quite high amongst other music departments in providing state-of-the-art equipment for all students.[44] The collection was due in part to the generosity of a rich donor. As mentioned previously, a visit from philanthropist Andrew Carnegie to the Tuskegee campus during the tenure of President Booker T. Washington resulted in the gift of a college library. Years later, in 1943, a magnanimous grant from the Carnegie Foundation bestowed a music listening library upon the music school. The school bulletin contained a description that seemed to be a proud declaration of this gift: a phonograph, an extensive collection of records, and written scores to accompany each music recording housed within the listening room.[45]

Changes in the 1945 bulletin indicate that under Dawson's direction the music department's focus continued to evolve. In the 1945 *Institute Bulletin*, the statement of purpose changed yet again, indicating that the department's primary purpose was "to prepare students of Agriculture, Education, Home Economics and Physical Education to direct choruses, bands, orchestras and other musical activities in the elementary and high schools."[46] The new statement reflects Dawson's mission to provide prospective teachers with multiple skills for success and to afford their future students with musical opportunities. The department continued to offer the joint curriculum until they dropped it in 1951. Until 1955 the Department of Music existed as an adjunct to the general education program of the institute to provide band, choral, and other experiences for the students.[47]

Despite all the changes in the status of the music program, the institute choir, under Dawson's tutelage, remained an outstanding organization that was nationally traveled and respected. Though the national concert tours of 1932–33, 1946, and 1955 were the most significant, from 1931 to 1955, the singers performed throughout the South, over the radio, and on television, which brought national attention to the school and to Dawson. The choir's fine reputation and long list of credits were a source of great pride for Tuskegee Institute and its notable conductor.

Chapter 3

THE RISE OF THE TUSKEGEE CHOIR TO NATIONAL PROMINENCE

1931–55

BACKGROUND OF THE TUSKEGEE CHOIR AND DAWSON'S RETURN AS CONDUCTOR, 1893–1930

The Tuskegee Institute Choir is an organization almost as old as the school itself, but it wasn't until the choir was placed under the direction of William L. Dawson that it achieved its distinctive, national reputation reflected in positive reviews of performances at Carnegie Hall, Constitution Hall, and the White House, among other honors.[1] Choral singing at Tuskegee was held in high esteem by founder Booker T. Washington.

The prevailing opinion of the day was that a choir of one hundred or more voices was a notable distinction for a school. It is clear that in its early days, at least one of the performing ensembles at Tuskegee had one hundred members.[2] Early descriptions of the effort to establish a center for education in Central Alabama are found in Washington's biography and in institute bulletins. In both publications Washington mentions not only the choir but the singing student body as well. In 1893 Washington refers to the institute's large choir of seventy-five members, a 150-voice choral society, male and female glee clubs of forty and twenty singers, respectively, and the traveling male Quartette.[3]

When Dawson arrived in 1930 to organize the School of Music, he developed a written statement for the school bulletin that described the purpose and value of the choir. The 1931–32 catalog explained that the institute choir was a choral organization whose purpose was to promote the highest excellence in choral singing. Dawson sought to use the vocal strength of the one hundred singers to interpret, rehearse, and perform works from a category of traditional, religious African American music for which he had a specific name: Negro folk songs.[4] In order to best prepare to perform these and other types of songs, the choir rehearsed daily and kept to a rigorous performance schedule that included Sunday morning and evening concerts presented during the school year.

College choirs in the twenty-first century may rehearse three to four days a week with the maximum of two performances during each semester; however, the Tuskegee Choir's ratio of rehearsal to performance was elevated and exhausting. These expectations are not surprising given Dawson's high expectations and his asking for the best from every vocalist. Dawson worked with his choir to produce an exciting, well-developed choral sound, and he accomplished this goal with a group of singers who were largely unauditioned. He listened to each person sing in a diagnostic testing session but never turned anyone away. Dawson believed in education not only to prepare for a specific vocation but to enhance one's life. Given that music was an important part of formal education, he believed everyone should have the opportunity to experience it and learn about it in school. Dawson taught every choir member to sight-read music. Those who were already proficient sight-readers were utilized as aides and were placed strategically throughout the choir to support less confident singers.[5]

The Institute Choir was an integral part of the educational life at Tuskegee during Dawson's tenure, just as it had been during Booker T. Washington's day. Dawson seemed to strive to replicate his choral experience at Tuskegee for the students in 1930 and beyond, continuing the vision of his mentor at the institute.[6] Dawson believed the establishment of women's choral groups to be as essential to a strong music program as that of men's groups, and he therefore frequently set or arranged folk songs for male, female, and mixed-gender voices. Some songs, like "Jesus Walked This Lonesome Valley," were even set in three parts for female voices of Soprano I, Soprano II, and Alto (SSA), and four-part women's voices of Soprano I, Soprano II, Alto I, Alto II (SSAA). The 1931–32 school bulletin notes that the glee clubs were auditioned groups, and that their participation was higher than in previous decades. The Men's Glee Club had a membership of seventy, while the Girl's Glee Club had expanded from twenty to fifty voices.[7]

In keeping with the sentiments of former principal Washington, the greater portion of the Tuskegee Choir's repertoire consisted of African American folk songs. Dawson himself arranged some of these songs and had succeeded in getting several of them published prior to returning to his alma mater as director of the School of Music. So important were these songs to thousands of African Americans who had first sung them while enslaved, and to their posterity, that complete concerts of early African American music were frequently presented by the choir.

One such choir concert was entitled "An Evening of Negro Folk Music."[8] It was specifically a "special rendition complimentary to George Foster Peabody, patron of Negro and Indian folk music." Peabody, a native of Georgia, promoted education for African Americans by funding new buildings at Tuskegee, Hampton, and other institutions. The introduction to this concert program is especially sensitive to general feelings about these folk songs. It is quoted here in its entirety to demonstrate the association of organic Black American cultural music with African heritage:

> The Negro is known everywhere for his singing. All the way from Jungle to civilization, his progress has been marked by his song. He has sung in the bush, he has sung on the bloody trek to the coast and the waiting slave ship; and whether at work, at play, in love, or at worship, he is still singing his way into the hearts and recognition of all mankind. The world has always listened—sometimes with curiosity, sometimes with amusement, always with a steady response to the compelling rhythm and the haunting melody of his songs. We offer them tonight for their intrinsic beauty, their artistic worth, and for the story they tell of the triumphant progress of a gifted race from the low-grounds of sorrow to a place on the heights of creative art.[9]

The most significant concert of Dawson's initial year at Tuskegee occurred April 13, 1931, to celebrate the fiftieth anniversary, or Jubilee, of the founding of the Institute. The special program weas titled, "Up from Slavery: A Festival of Negro Music Giving An Illumination of the Mind and Mood of the Negro in His Journey through Slavery to Freedom out of Sorrow through Hope to Joy."[10] "Up From Slavery" in the concert title references Booker T. Washington's 1901 autobiography. The assistants named in the program were most of the music faculty members. Works performed were by African American composers, including Nathaniel Dett, Harry T. Burleigh, Samuel Coleridge-Taylor, and William Dawson. Dawson composed a special choral work for the anniversary celebration entitled, "Hallelujah," the setting of a text written by G. Lake Imes, who had been a member of the institute staff since 1910. Unfortunately, there is no record to indicate the song was ever published.[11]

The choir worked diligently during Dawson's first year as director, and by the fall of 1931, the singers began preparing for their first concert tour. Touring was integral to marketing the music program, recruiting students, bringing notoriety to the institute, and most importantly, raising money for the college. Lawrence Jackson explained how Fisk University had increased both the size of its campus and investments in the late 1800s through its "world-class choir traveling far and wide and spreading the good news of Black Americans."[12] Tuskegee sought similar public attention. It is hard to imagine how traveling with such a large choir could be profitable, as opposed to sending just a male quintette as the college did in Dawson's years at Tuskegee. Whatever the cost, the investment in a traveling choir brought untold recognition to the Tuskegee Choir and its conductor.

THE TUSKEGEE CHOIR'S EARLY TOURS

The Tuskegee Choir's first concert journey under Dawson's direction began May 13, 1932, when the choir traveled to nearby Montgomery, Alabama, to sing in the Cramton Bowl, a large football stadium in the city. On the following day, the group gave an afternoon performance at Alabama College for Women in Montevallo (now the University of Montevallo, a coeducational institution) and an evening concert on the campus of the University of Alabama in Tuscaloosa. Following a May 15 appearance at Birmingham's Municipal Auditorium, the choir traveled on to Atlanta, where they sang at the Wesley Memorial Church. Before returning to Tuskegee, the choir made stops in Macon and Columbus, Georgia, for one-night engagements.[13]

The fame of the Tuskegee Choir soon spread beyond the South and rapidly climbed to preeminence in the world of music. Historian John Lovell attributes this success to Dawson, calling him a "directional genius" who seemingly willed his choir into national recognition and acclaim.[14] Musicologists Eileen Southern and Hildred Roach also praise Dawson. Southern claims that the Tuskegee Choir, under Dawson's direction and tutelage, was recognized as one of the finest choirs in the nation, while Roach calls Dawson an effective conductor.[15] Similarly, when Maude Cuney-Hare makes references to the fine Tuskegee Choir, she notes its outstanding director, William Dawson.[16] This accomplished choral group and its skilled conductor were soon to be invited to New York.

The Tuskegee Choir received a tremendous boost from Samuel Lionel Rothafel, better known as Roxy, who built Radio City Music Hall, the famed performing arts center in New York City. Roxy erected this famous theater on the corner of Sixth Avenue and Fiftieth Street, covering nearly one acre. It had an enormous stage that held up to 750 people and a magnificent foyer that was almost a block long. A *New York Times* article written on Christmas Day, just two days prior to the grand opening, told of the intent of the builder to initiate a new form of expanded vaudeville show that merged the traditional comedians, singers, and dancers with modern dance, ballet, choirs, opera, and symphony music, all without any moving or talking pictures. The new performance hall was, indeed, the most up to date at that time, having been equipped to provide quick transitions with steam-motorized curtain capabilities, and special lighting. While the facility itself was ahead of its time in terms of size and capabilities, the acts at Radio City Music Hall were often aligned with the backward, racist ideology of the day. The same *Times* article mentions expositions that include "blackface," a kind of performance that degraded and mocked Black Americans and kept them from participating in full, equal citizenship with white Americans.[17]

Roxy spent several months scouting the nation for top acts to appear in his planned spectacular opening of Radio City Music Hall. When he heard the Tuskegee Choir sing, he knew immediately that he wanted them to perform at the grand opening of his new hall and extended an invitation. Jackson wrote:

> [W]hen Radio City Musical Hall opened in 1933, it was Dawson's choir invited up from Alabama to christen the shiniest, and some thought gaudy, symbol of American audacity . . . It was a triumph for the young music school director and bespoke the potential for Black participation in a new age.[18]

Dawson accepted the invitation, and the Tuskegee Choir traveled to New York in December by train, staying in a hotel in the city for the duration of their visit. Dawson recalled sight-seeing with the choir while in New York, especially visiting the Empire State Building, explaining that the former governor of New York "Al Smith had [them] as his guests at the Empire [State] Building." While visiting, Dawson said, "We were on the 85th floor outside singing, 'O, What a beautiful City.' Everybody thought we were talkin' about New York City; we were talkin' about the New Jerusalem!"[19]

Dawson also remembers the advertisements for the grand opening that appeared in the New York newspapers days before the event. The ads were quite large and featured attractive artwork. Dawson's group was billed in the *New York Times* as "The Famous Tuskegee Choir of 110."[20] At the time of the performance, the country was plunged deep in the Depression, but a new president of the United States, Franklin Delano Roosevelt, had been elected, and the Christmas celebrations for the year had just concluded. Dawson indicated the city was buzzing with excitement over Radio City Music Hall.[21]

While the new hall had a seating capacity of 6,200, John Lovell related that an overflow crowd came to see the grand opening attractions on December 27, 1932. According to Lovell, "seven thousand people" were present for the event. Along with Dawson's choir, "Titta Ruffo, Coe Glad, Ray Bolger, Weber and Fields, DeWolf Hopper, Martha Graham and group, Patricia Bowman, the Berry Brothers and a ballet corps of eighty dancers" also performed.[22] A *New York Times* review of the show the following day reported that opening night proceeded as promised without any movies, consisting entirely of stage performances. The author compared Radio City Music Hall to the Hippodrome Theatre, just a few blocks away, which had a seating capacity of 5,200 and a large stage estimated to be ten to twelve times the size of a normal Broadway stage at the time of its completion in 1905. With modern lighting, plush trappings, state-of-the-art sound capabilities, lighting and placement of performers, Radio City far exceeded the aura of the Hippodrome. One attendee was overheard to verbally marvel at the spectacle, indicating particularly that Roxy had combined the greatness of well-known performers Ziegfield, Urban, Carroll, and White to exceed all expectations for the event.[23] A second *Times* article reviewed the subsequent show on December 28 in which reporter Brooks Atkinson gushed about the lavish trappings of the enormous performance venue and the perfectly synchronous performance of two organs that seemed like one. The writer was amazed that the opening of the program was billed as a "Symphony of Curtains," which displayed an impressive, motorized lifting of the curtain, an innovation of the time. Nearly a century later, theatregoers are still mesmerized by the incredible technology employed in theatrical productions on Broadway.[24]

Not only did reviews praise the facility, but they were overwhelmingly impressed with the Tuskegee Choir's performance. In his review Atkinson emphasized the "size" of Roxy's new music hall, and in keeping with the theme of enormity, he wrote that "the Tuskegee Choir, which sings gloriously until the ingenuity of the stage direction drown[s] it in clouds of Wagnerian steam, is large enough to form a political club."[25] The *Wall Street Journal* also applauded the choir's performance in a review of the opening festivities, writing, "Mr. Dawson plays upon the voices of his mixed chorus as if he were playing an organ, and an organ is the only instrument to which the tones he evokes are comparable. It is grand music."[26]

The grand opening of Radio City Music Hall was a four-week-long extravaganza, yet New York was still talking about the Tuskegee Choir months later. An April 1933 *American Business Survey* article entitled "A Striking Contribution to Musical America" suggested that while New Yorkers were familiar with the work of Black choirs from the South, until Tuskegee's performance they had not yet heard "such fullness of tone, such deep-throated resonance and clarity of the upper voice, perfect intonation, and careful attention to the [demands] of the music." The writer gave full credit to Dawson for the choir's impressive impact, recognizing his work in building the choral tone, developing vocal technique, conducting rhythmic intricacies, and writing the music. The writer not only documents Dawson's contributions to the historical music of African Americans but claims that Dawson is unparalleled in his role as composer and arranger of "Negro spirituals." He ended his article by ranking the Tuskegee Choir as among the finest choral organizations internationally.[27]

In between concerts and the month-long engagement at Radio City, the Tuskegee Choir accepted a late-January 1933 invitation to sing for the president-elect, Franklin Delano Roosevelt. At the behest of Roosevelt's mother, Sarah Delano Roosevelt, on the evening of January 30, at his Hyde Park residence, the choir sang a concert in honor of the newly elected president's birthday. Dawson was excited about FDR's enthusiastic impression of him as well as the president-elect's effusive praise at hearing the Tuskegee Choir:

> Mrs. Roosevelt, the mother of the President-Elect invited us to sing for his birthday party. We went up to Hyde Park. There was a long table, and the President was down there, and we sang. He liked "Good News." And he said, "Let's have them sing it again, sing it again. I want to shake hands with everybody." And so, we lined-up, [even] the Associated Press (they followed us). All got in line and shook his hand. He said, "I want you to come to the White House when I get there. When I get there, I want you to come to the White House."[28]

While performing at Radio City, the choir secured an engagement to appear at famed Carnegie Hall in New York City. The concert was given the evening of February 8, 1933, and a *New York Times* review was printed the following morning that touted the choir's "technical drilling in the precision of its attacks, its tonal unity, its excellent balance and the beauty of one of its solo voices." The author commented on the unique timbre of singers' voices that provides a richness of tone quality to the choral sound.[29] The body of the *New York Times* article, however, was not nearly as complimentary as the review in the *American Business Survey*. The article harshly criticizes Dawson's arrangements of the folk songs of Black Americans, reproving him for "not escaping the seduction of Classicism" and for over-embellishing a simple melody by placing it in grandiose harmonic clothing as heard in the Romantic music of the mid- to late-1800s. The reviewer believed that Dawson "[set] a simple, poignant melody in pretentious harmonic garment abounding [in] chromatic modulations suitable to Meyerbeer" and that the effect was "falsely rich a la Cyril Scott."[30]

A review by Stirling Bowen, a theater columnist for the *Wall Street Journal*, best exemplified the way derogatory, racist commentary lodged itself in otherwise praiseworthy reviews of the Tuskegee Choir. In his review of the choir's Carnegie Hall debut entitled "The World's Finest," Bowen simultaneously praises and mocks Dawson. Bowen, analyzing Dawson's conducting, concludes that Dawson was "partly prophet, partly plain old-fashioned deacon. With the aid of his strong and expressive hands, he delivers a sermon in pantomime with every number." Accustomed, perhaps, to a more reserved style of conducting, Bowen notes that "in spite of the fastidiousness of Mr. Dawson's attitude toward his music, his directorial gestures are as paddle-footed as the gait of a middle-aged waiter." Yet he claims that this style is "all a part of the essential simplicity of his approach," seeming to equate simplicity with Blackness.[31]

In keeping with his racially insensitive analyses, Bowen lauds the Tuskegee singers both for their impressive sound and for the way in which they defy his own prejudiced notions of what Black performers ought to look like, praising the fine voices and faces in the choir by commenting on the wholesome look of the singers, without any of the effects of what he called the raucous Harlem nightlife.[32] This "wholesomeness," he claims, was in keeping with the impressions he formed about the institute from a family trip to Tuskegee in the early 1920s. At that time, he took note of the student uniforms and of a brick-laying exhibit in particular, both of which signified the importance of "institutionalization and regimentation" to the school. The Tuskegee Choir's performance called to his mind these same concepts, given their military-style dress and their technical precision.[33] Bowen concludes his review with the pronouncement that the "Tuskegee Choir is probably the finest vocal ensemble in the world today."[34]

Abbie Mitchell, Head of the Voice Department at Tuskegee during the first three years of Dawson's tenure as director, recalled the New York trip:

> When Mr. Rothaphel [sic], better known as "Roxy," came down in 1931 to engage the choir to appear on the first program of the great Radio City in 1932, everyone was thrilled. That is history. The students saw the great sights of New York, went to the Metropolitan Opera where they heard Lily Pons in "Lucia de Lammermoor" [sic], sang a concert at Carnegie Hall and at the Academy of Music in Philadelphia, and received commendations everywhere. Last but by no means least, a private concert at the Roosevelt home, on 65th Street near Fifth Avenue . . . Mrs. Eleanor Roosevelt took the gang (all 100 of them) in groups up to the President's private suite to see all the interesting

things; the children were delighted. . . . It was a memorable evening, lasting from 8:30 till 11:30. To Mr. Dawson goes the credit for the arrangements of most of the spirituals, and for his conscientious efforts in working untiringly.[35]

On the return trip to Alabama in 1933, the Tuskegee Choir had the opportunity to sing at the Philadelphia Forum and for the outgoing president of the United States, Herbert Hoover, in the White House. The special concert of the Philadelphia Forum on February 9 was arranged as a replacement for singer *Göta* Ljungberg, who had just completed an appearance as Brünnhilde in the Metropolitan Opera's production of Richard Wagner's *Götterdämmerung*. Dawson remembered: "We left New York and went on to Philadelphia, the Forum. The Philadelphia Forum asked us if we'd take a concert that an opera singer was to sing. She got sick, and we took that."[36]

Continuing southward, Dawson's singers stopped in Washington, DC, to present a concert in the White House. They received a special invitation from President Hoover to present a choral program for a gathering of guests and friends. The president and the First Lady entertained the Alabama choir on February 10 providing ample space in the White House for a performance by the large chorus of singers. Dawson marveled at the difference between FDR and Hoover:

> Then we went on to the White House; Hoover invited us to sing for him. We were to sing 15 minutes. And, Hoover sat a safe distance, and he was just the opposite of Roosevelt, very staid. And, we sang and I looked at my stop watch—fifteen minutes, and I stopped and turned around and bowed to him. "Sing some more," [he said]. And I turned around and we sang 15 minutes more. I turned around and bowed to him. "Sing some more," [he said]. Forty-five minutes! And, uh. Then he came up and spoke to us.[37]

Later, Dawson couldn't help but laugh at the response of one of the attendees at the White House concert:

> When we came out of the White House one of the Associated Press men said, "You guys certainly did sing Hoover out of the White House this morning!" I said, What do you mean? [He said,] "Steal Away, I ain't got long to stay here, Soon-ah Will be Done With the Troubles of the World." We did the Russian piece, Hospodi—Lord have mercy upon us . . . I said, God, don't say anymore![38]

THE TUSKEGEE CHOIR ON THE RADIO, 1937–45

The national concert tour, spanning late 1932 and early 1933, was the last major tour the choir made until 1946. Declining enrollment due to the Great Depression, the competition of state-supported Alabama State University, and the advent of World War II limited school funding, keeping the choir at home. While Dawson continued to work with the choir, his immediate attention after the group returned from New York was focused on completion of the symphony he had begun earlier in Chicago. He busied himself with tidying the score, copying individual instrumental parts, and securing a conductor for a national premiere of the extended symphonic work, as well as advertising and promotion.[39]

Dawson's attention to the choir and his symphony also competed with a romantic interest. In 1934, six years after the death of his first wife, Cornella Lampton, William Dawson began an earnest courtship of Cecile De Mae Nicholson, who had just taken a position as a professor in the Home Economics Department at Morris Brown College in Atlanta. Despite being occupied with the premiere of his *Negro Folk Symphony*, Dawson pursued the hand of a young woman he had met in Kansas City, Missouri, while teaching there in the early 1920s. Nicholson and Dawson remained good friends while she completed degrees at Howard University and Kansas State Teachers College at Pittsburg, but it wasn't until she arrived in Atlanta that the friendship blossomed into romance. The couple married September 21, 1935, in a private ceremony in the home of Mr. and Mrs. Hale Woodruff. Dawson's composition, "Forever Thine," was chosen for the processional and performed by Tuskegee faculty members Andrew Rosamond, violin, and Mrs. F. D. Patterson, piano. The traditional "Wedding March" of Mendelssohn was selected as the recessional, performed by Mrs. Patterson.[40]

Following Dawson's preoccupation with the long-distance courtship of and subsequent marriage to Miss Nicholson, the choir continued to perform and enjoy popularity and demand nationwide respect, eventually resulting in a series of special concerts broadcast by the National Broadcasting Company's (NBC) radio network. These weekly music programs originated from the Tuskegee Institute campus on Sunday afternoons and began in October of 1937, ending in March of the following year. The contract for these broadcasts included an extra Christmas Day concert, which aired from the institute chapel.[41] Dawson recalled with excitement the beginning of the radio broadcasts.

[Radio listeners] heard the Tuskegee Choir on the air for about six months in this country, ['37], giving a half-hour broadcast every Sunday, a cappella. And I had to have the program in New York time 14 days ahead of each program. I had to teach these kids—they all read [music]. I taught them to read, and every week was a different program. And what happened, we were to sing one concert for NBC, now we had [an] open radio setting. The first night we held up the show for 10 or 12 minutes, then they stayed there six [months]. And, on this particular concert that Sunday, it was the [closing] day of the World Series and everybody had his radio turned on the red network. That was all in the East, the blue network went West. And we came on a half-hour before that game started. And they said that every hotel, every taxi driver after that had his radio on that day, and the churches in New England would bring radio sets and put in the church so the folks were going back to hear. And you should see those fan letters. The governor of Connecticut, those were the people who wrote fan mail! And we were on there those weeks. All a cappella.[42]

The response from the nation was overwhelming. The broadcasts were received with favor, as evidenced by the many letters extolling Dawson and the choir that quickly poured in. Several letters were particularly noteworthy. One example came from George Weida Spohn, professor of English at St. Olaf College in Northfield, Minnesota. At the time, and still to this day, St. Olaf was renowned for its choirs, first under the leadership of F. Melius Christiansen. Dr. Spohn wrote to Dawson explaining that while he normally avoided writing fan letters, he broke his personal rule after hearing the Tuskegee Choir via NBC radio.[43] Deeply touched by the meaningful choral singing, Dr. Spohn was inspired to write a poem entitled "Singing Hearts." Dawson treasured the poem and shared its words with many guests who visited his home.

SINGING HEARTS

Dedicated to the Tuskegee Choir
William L. Dawson, Conductor

In raptured zeal of ecstasy.
As though before the Master's face,
Unburdened hearts in song proclaim
The glory of a suffering race.

The mingled tones that thrill and throb
In joyful chorus and refrain
Beat down, but can not over bear
The aching undertones of pain.

Too long your frustrate hearts have borne
The weight of age-long woe and tears;
Now that your hearts are free you sing
The paean of the happy years.

The feet of those whose fathers sold
Your kin in mart, on auction-block
Exploited blood for use and gain,
As traders sell their market stock,

Are lighted by the torch you hold
Above the clouded doom of man,
Once more to walk on lighted paths
Since first the lust for gain began.

With burning zeal your voices rise
In raptured tones of ecstasy,
And lift the yearning hearts of men
Into the kingdom of the free.
(written October 18, 1937)[44]

Another exemplary letter of praise for the NBC broadcasts was from Nick Kenny, radio editor of the *New York Daily Mirror*, who wrote to "congratulate" Dawson "on the best job of directing a choral group [his] ears [had] ever heard." Kenny further indicated that Dawson's singers were without question "in a class by themselves" and promised to share this claim in future editions of the paper.[45] Columnist H. G. Tilghman, who at the time was serving as radio editor for the *Norfolk Virginian-Pilot*, a weekly paper in the Tidewater region of Virginia, also wrote Dawson with congratulations on the performances. Like Spohn, Tilghman admitted that the letter to Dawson was his first written message of commendation to any radio program. Calling the concert an enjoyable philosophy in song, Tilghman said he believed the broadcast to be a positive step toward improved race relations between Black and white people. Tilghman remarked that the Tuskegee Choir had quite a following in the Tidewater region of Virginia despite the fact that

Hampton Institute, another HBCU, was nearer to Norfolk. Hoping to prolong his enjoyment of Tuskegee's concert, the writer said he would gladly sacrifice his own on-air time and asked that the choir sing one full stanza or more of the closing number, "Deep River," prior to the sign-off by the announcer.[46]

The special broadcasts over the NBC radio network brought requests for the Tuskegee Choir to perform in many southern cities. The demanding rehearsal and performance schedule for chapel services and broadcasts left little time for an extended tour. As a result, the choir made small trips to various cities for one-night concerts, sometimes pairing cities in proximity for two successive performances.

In November of 1937, the choir traveled to Macon, Georgia, for a performance in the City Auditorium. Their first concert trip in 1938 was to nearby Alexander City, Alabama, in February. A month later the choir made an appearance in Montgomery's Municipal Auditorium. The energetic singers left Montgomery the next day and rode past Tuskegee to Columbus, Georgia, for a performance in a high school there. On April 14, less than a month after appearing in the Municipal Auditorium in Montgomery, the choir returned there and sang a concert to a large crowd. The last choir trip toward the end of April included programs presented in LaGrange and Atlanta, Georgia.[47]

Throughout this period, the Tuskegee Choir's repertoire continued to consist mostly of Negro folk songs, though not all of these spirituals were arranged by Dawson. As conductor, Dawson selected settings by several other well-known Black musicians, such as Robert Nathaniel Dett, Harry T. Burleigh, and John Wesley Work II. Dett was director of music at Hampton Institute in Virginia for nearly twenty years. Although most noted for his oratorio, "The Ordering of Moses," written for a chorus of Soprano, Alto, Tenor, Bass voices (SATB), soloists, chorus, and accompanied by orchestra, Dett also arranged the prime folk melodies of enslaved African Americans in the South. Dawson admired Dett and was often able to meet and talk with him. Dett encouraged Dawson to continue studying composition.

Burleigh was another of Dawson's favorite composers.[48] Music historian John Lovell "credited" Burleigh "with having done more than anyone else in preparing the spirituals for use by concert singers, both individuals and groups."[49] Dawson wrote in his personal pocket calendar-diary that he first met "Mr. Burleigh" in New York City on February 26, 1921, while traveling with the Tuskegee Quintette.[50] Burleigh's best-known arrangements of African American tunes are "Deep River" and "My Lord What a Morning." The Tuskegee Choir used Burleigh's "Deep River" to close its weekly radio broadcasts and included the work on many other concert performance programs.

John Wesley Work II, Frederick J. Work, and John Wesley Work III all continued the great spiritual tradition at Fisk University in Nashville from approximately 1898 to 1967. The three men scoured the South to collect and record African American music. Some of the Works' settings were sung by the Tuskegee Choir. Dawson's first choral director, Jennie Lee, had ties to Fisk, and Dawson would eventually direct the choirs there in the late 1950s.[51]

At their spring concert on April 1, 1938, the choir gave a complete performance of "The Death of Minnehaha," written by Samuel Coleridge-Taylor. A native of Great Britain, Coleridge-Taylor was influenced by African American folk songs and the literary works of Henry Wadsworth Longfellow. Coleridge-Taylor set these folk songs for symphony, voice, and piano.[52] President Washington displayed his great respect for Coleridge-Taylor by writing the introduction to *Twenty-Four Negro Melodies* Coleridge-Taylor composed in 1904, subsequently published in 1905.[53]

As the storm clouds gathered over Europe in 1938–39 that would eventually erupt into WWII, the Tuskegee Choir was soon able to add their voices to an international call for peace. The Foreign Mission Conference of North America organized the Christian Foreign Service Convocation radio broadcast for the benefit of world peace and missions, and the choir was invited to perform. On March 16, 1940, many religious leaders, lay-church workers, and interested Americans gathered in churches around the nation to listen to the broadcast. The NBC radio network originated the broadcast from the Waldorf-Astoria Hotel in New York City, and participants contributed to the program from various spots around the world, making the convocation a truly universal cry for peace. The president of the United States, Franklin D. Roosevelt, spoke from the White House in Washington, DC. Internationally renowned African American contralto, Marian Anderson, sang in a part of the program from Western Canada. Queen Wilhelmina of the Netherlands gave a speech from The Hague. The choir from Westminster Choir College in Princeton, New Jersey, traveled to New York City for their part on the program. The Tuskegee Choir performed from the campus in Tuskegee, Alabama.[54]

Following the world peace broadcast, Dawson conducted the Tuskegee Choir in a special concert in the Tuskegee Institute chapel on April 7, 1940. United States Postmaster General James A. Farley was the honored guest speaker for the celebration, which was organized for the release of the Booker T. Washington commemorative stamp. One of the choir's selections was Dawson's arrangement of the spiritual "Seeking for the City."[55] Like Dawson's composition of "Hallelujah," premiered in 1931, "Seeking for the City" was never published, and only "Hallelujah" is listed among Dawson's pieces found in the Emory University archives. Neither of the two works can be found at Tuskegee University.[56] Later that month the Tuskegee Choir appeared as the featured performing group at the Alabama Federation of Music Clubs' Twenty-fourth Annual Convention held in the sanctuary of the First Methodist Church in nearby Opelika.[57]

The Tuskegee Choir was first heard over the Columbia Broadcasting System (CBS) radio network in June of 1940. The choir was chosen to perform on a program entitled "Alabama—A Symphony of the New South." The "New South" referred not only to innovative music in the southern United States after the Civil War but also to changing social, economic, and political statuses for Black and white Americans. Given that the Tuskegee Airmen would soon begin training to become the first African American pilots to serve with the American armed forces in WWII, the Tuskegee Choir's appearance on this program was prescient. The overall response to the program was favorable, and the reaction to the choice of the choir for the program was especially complimentary. It was not until 1945 that CBS contracted Dawson's singers to present weekly concerts, resuming the practice begun in 1937 by NBC. For the entire month of May, the choir sang a series of four Sunday-morning programs over a nationwide hookup. These performances were equally successful as the earlier concerts aired over NBC radio. In February of the following year, the Tuskegee Choir was selected to perform another month-long series on CBS.[58]

THE TUSKEGEE CHOIR RESUMES TOURING AND SINGS ON TELEVISION, 1946–55

In 1946 William Dawson's Tuskegee Choir prepared for its most extensive tour since the 1932–33 opening of Radio City Music Hall. The choir, somewhat smaller than in the previous decade, was nonetheless vibrant and exciting. The singing entourage left Tuskegee for New York in late May and sang first on an all-star program in New York City over the American Broadcasting Company (ABC) radio network on May 22nd. On May 23, the choir was featured in a special ceremony honoring the founder of Tuskegee Institute, Booker T. Washington. This event united representatives from Washington's alma mater, Hampton Institute, and from the school he founded, Tuskegee Institute, through the performance of African American folk songs.[59] The *New York Times* reported that nine descendants of Washington and an audience of over 1,100 attended the festivities in New York University's Gould Memorial Library to unveil a bust of the famous educator. The sixty members of the Tuskegee Choir led a procession of teachers, friends, and colleagues of the late Tuskegee president that included his granddaughter, Gloria Davidson Washington, who unveiled the sculpture. The Creative Dance Group from Hampton Institute presented an enactment of the life of Washington in pantomime. Soprano Dorothy Maynor performed vocal solos and was a part of the choir, which sang spirituals.[60]

Soon after the Gould Library performance, the choir traveled to Newark, New Jersey, on May 26 to present a concert in the Mosque Theatre. The next day the singers went back to New York City for the Booker T. Washington Memorial Concert. A remarkable group of celebrities were a part of the Memorial Concert that included: Duke Ellington, Will Geer, Fannie Hurst, Sam Jaffe, Canada Lee, the Mills Brothers, Pearl Primus, and Bill Robinson. That the proceeds from the event went to the United Negro College Fund was a fitting tribute to the educational accomplishments of Booker T. Washington.[61]

Louis Biancolli, a reporter for the *New York World Telegram*, reviewed the choir's performance. In his May 28 article titled "Tuskegee Choir Shows Finesse in Memorial," Biancolli encouraged readers to include the Tuskegee Choir when compiling a list of the best choirs in the nation. Though the writer claimed that the Robert Shaw Collegiate Chorale, then based in New York, was the best choral ensemble in America, he pointed out specific areas in which the Tuskegee Choir excelled. He compared the choir's sustained, quiet dynamics to a whispered phrase or an imperceptible sigh and noted that the balance of sections was precisely controlled, at times giving the impression of "one unified sound."[62] It's not clear how to interpret Biancolli's observation that "it's possible to build a first-class ensemble out of second-class materials—it's possible, given a choirmaster who is also a genius." This seems to indicate his belief that talent recruited by Dawson was "second-rate," but he quickly pivots, suggesting that it was obvious the conductor had begun rehearsals with outstanding talent. Ultimately, he concludes that "Choirmaster William L. Dawson has trained the school unit to calm finesse and split-second timing. The balances last night never tilted faultily, and the group at times rang out like one voice."[63] The *New York Times* review was equally favorable and included a brief description of the program's offerings by Dett, Dawson, Burleigh, Work, and Palmgren, vocal soloists, and The Male Chorus. The review noted that in addition to the works listed in the program, the choir performed many encores in response to the enthusiastic applause of the audience.[64]

Continuing southward, the Tuskegee Choir stopped in Philadelphia to present a concert at the Academy of Music. Despite the sparse crowd, reviewers from two local newspapers were impressed by the singing of Dawson's group.[65] Samuel L. Singer of the *Philadelphia Inquirer* wrote a glowing report of the first appearance in Philadelphia of the Tuskegee Choir in over thirteen years, but noted those in attendance represented possibly the smallest number of patrons that season. Singer indicated the choir was impressively disciplined in vocal technique as well as military dress and praised the choir's exquisite quality of tone, contrasting dynamics, extensive vocal range, and nuances in phrasing.

> Both in performance and appearance the group is perfectly disciplined. The men were in R.O.T.C. uniforms, the women in white "gym suits." But more important than appearance was the way the group sounded.
>
> It seemed capable of anything a chorus can do. It rivals the famous Cossack choirs in sonority and range up and down the scale, and while the group achieved wispy pianissimos and full-bodied tone, and obeyed the conductor's slightest indication of nuance there were not sudden or gradual changes of volume solely for their own sake, but only to heighten the artistry of interpretation.[66]

He was particularly impressed with the soloists as well as the selection of pieces the choir performed:

> Outstanding was the sweet tenor of Otis D. Wright in "There is a Balm in Gilead," and the clear soprano of Ella W. Norwood in "Oh, Po' Little Jesus." The program consisted of spirituals and kindred works, so as to provide contrast. The final encore was the "Hallelujah" from "Messiah" by Handel.[67]

The *Evening Bulletin*'s reporter, Max de Schauensee, was moved even more by the concert than other writers, lamenting that only four hundred took advantage of the opportunity to hear the most outstanding choral singing of the entire performance season in Philadelphia. The writer groused over the prevailing choral norm for the women's voices to overpower the men's voices but noted that in the case of the Tuskegee Choir, the choral balance "was as delicate as a string quartet."[68] Above all, the reporter was impressed by the choir's technique, saying: "Of course the Tuskegee Choir sings everything a cappella. Its intonation is perfect; its rhythm, the rhythm of a people whose mainspring it is. Its leader, Mr. Dawson, is apparently a great artist."[69]

Leaving Philadelphia, the choir journeyed to the famous tourist spot of Atlantic City, New Jersey, for an appearance at Convention Hall and then to Baltimore, Maryland, for a concert in the National Guard Armory. From Baltimore, the group traveled to Washington, DC, for a June 3rd performance at Constitution Hall. Owned by the Daughters of the American Revolution (D.A.R.), a national organization, Constitution Hall and its restrictive segregated policies had long been the source of heated controversy. Noted African American singer Marian Anderson and other Black performers had not been allowed to perform there. Possibly to combat their racist image, the D.A.R. invited the Tuskegee Choir to sing in the hall. The gesture was met with some resistance from African Americans, however, as some suggested that it was hypocritical to allow a Black choir to perform while banning Black soloists.[70] A crowd of African Americans paraded in front of Constitution Hall and held picket signs decrying segregationist policies prior the concert. The *Washington Post* reported the incident the next day.

> A mass picket line chanting "Jim Crow Has Got to Go," marched before the entrance to Constitution Hall last night, but failed to keep more than five or six members of an estimated 3,400-person audience from going in to hear the all-Negro Tuskegee Choir.
>
> James Baker, head of the Committee for Racial Democracy in the Nation's Capital, said the line was thrown around the Hall because "the DAR has not changed its policy on the restriction of Negro artists. Marian Anderson still can't come here."
>
> The pickets formed about 7 p.m. and dispersed quietly at 9 p.m.
>
> Fred E. Hand, manager of Constitution Hall, said that all but 200 of the 3,844 seats in the hall were occupied. He estimated that about 75 per cent of the audience was Negro.
>
> Dr. Fred D. Patterson, president of Tuskegee, said, concerning the picket line, "I don't think it's done us any harm and I think it helped—a synthetic commotion about nothing."[71]

Indeed, Tuskegee's president, Dr. Patterson, who was also head of the United Negro College Fund (UNCF), had scheduled the concert as a fundraiser for the organization. Tensions flared within the organization, however, when the Tuskegee president refused to withdraw the choir from the venue despite the blatant discrimination. Though he was initially at odds with UNCF officers and members, the success of the event helped to defuse the controversy.[72]

In his report, Glenn Dillard Gunn, a columnist with the *Times Herald* in Washington, DC, noted the skirmish prior to the performance but chose to spend the majority of his piece describing the choir's program in considerable detail. Gunn contradicted the *Washington Post* reporter, suggesting that there was an equal mix of Black and white concertgoers. Considering a benefit for the UNCF, the writer mistakenly referred to the organization as the "Union of Negro Colleges."

> These 3,800 music lovers included may of the city's habitual concertgoers. In addition, there were Negroes prominent in education, such as the faculty members of Howard University. It was a responsive gathering, but its reaction was restrained. No soloist or ensemble making music in Constitution Hall this past season has stimulated quite the same quality of attention as these Tuskegee Singers provoked. They were heard in breathless silence. Applause persisted until the program had been lengthened by many encores.[73]

Gunn praised the beauty of the choir's sound, suggesting that the group had a distinctive "racial" quality to their voices. In keeping with the other reviewers, he gave credit to Dawson for developing the choral ensemble and for his diligent research work in the field of spirituals and choral composition. He recognized Dawson's use of compositional devices such as antiphonal singing and off-stage soloists and attested to being mesmerized by the beauty of tone, rhythmic impulse, and the pathos of the music that had also been heard in choirs from Russia. Despite praise for Dawson's impressive compositions of African American spirituals, Gunn admitted a preference for the works of Dett and Burleigh performed during the concert.[74]

Another newspaper in the nation's capital, the *Evening Star*, sent reporter Alice Eversman to cover the event. Like Gunn she was enthralled with the sound of the Tuskegee Choir and appreciative of its director, William Dawson, and stated that the concert was unforgettable. It was significant that Eversman referred to the demonstration prior to the concert as an obstacle for the choir to overcome and declared that the music brought peace to the event.

> The Tuskegee Choir came to this city last night as many another chorus has done, but it left a remembrance that will not be forgotten soon. Of the near capacity audience in Constitution Hall, where the group overcame obstacles to give its program, there were few who did not carry away a softened spirit and an unfamiliar peace of soul. The material success of the concert could be measured by the size of the audience and the enthusiastic applauding after each song.[75]

Credit was given to Dawson for creating an ethos between the conductor and choir that extended to the audience emotionally, binding together the audience and performers. The writer likened the choral dynamics and vocal range of the choir to the "tonal gamut of an orchestra."

> But in listening to the men and women in this ensemble the mechanics are something one's mind appreciates while the heart is moved by the sheer beauty of the performance. It is not a performance that called for the passive acquiescence on the part of the audience but one in which the singers and public were held together in a strong emotional bond.[76]

While Glenn Gunn of the *Times Herald* preferred the compositions of other African American composers, Eversman was partial to Dawson's songs and specifically listed "Behold the Star," "Ain'a That Good News," "Hail Mary," "There Is a Balm in Gilead," and "Soon-Ah Will Be Done" as fine selections. Praise for Dawson continued:

> The full tone of the group which sings a cappella is powerful yet its strength is seldom called upon as light flexible handling and chiaroscuro of color is Mr. Dawson's specialty. The precision with which the singers respond, their superior sense of rhythm and their elasticity in nuances achieves a flowing line that bends at the will of the conductor.... A giften [sic] composer and an expert leader, his power to obtain a spontaneous and heartfelt response from every member of his group puts a particular stamp on his choir.[77]

The next stop after leaving Washington, DC, was Richmond, Virginia where the choir gave a concert to a sparse crowd in the Mosque Theatre that also benefitted the UNCF. In her newspaper column of June 5, Helen deMotte chided the Richmond citizens for not attending the performance and was baffled that the Russian Cossack Choirs could fill the auditorium but a fine domestic choir could not. Selecting the word "fine" for an overall description of the concert, the reporter praised the simplicity and dignity of the performance, the high quality of literature on the program as well as that literature's deep historical roots in the American South, and the tremendous display of musicianship by both conductor and singers.[78] She wrote:

> [The Tuskegee Choir] has an unusual fine fullness and body of tone, and the warmth and ingratiating quality so characteristic of this race, its own emotional color its spontaneity and vitality. In its tonal unity it is almost like a great instrument, and there were times when it had an almost supernatural beauty.[79]

The long spring choir tour closed with a performance at North Carolina Agricultural and Technical College (now North Carolina Agricultural and Technical University), an HBCU in Greensboro, North Carolina, and a concert at the City stadium in nearby Winston-Salem.[80]

During the next three and a half years, Dawson busied himself with other musical projects. The next significant appearances of the Tuskegee Choir therefore did not take place until 1950. In February of that year, the choir sang on the *Edgar Bergen and Charlie McCarthy Show*. Sponsored by the Coca-Cola Company, the program was produced in the Tower Theatre in Atlanta. In April, Dawson secured the services of over forty players from the Atlanta Symphony Orchestra for a combined orchestra and choral performance of *Stabat Mater* by Antonin Dvořák. The concert was given in the chapel at Tuskegee Institute and was carried over the ABC radio network. Later that same year, the choir sang at the Cloister Hotel in Sea Island Beach, Georgia, at the request of the Business Advisory Council of the United States Department of Commerce. ABC radio contacted Dawson in December of 1950 in regard to a special Christmas program featuring the Tuskegee Choir. The program was set for Christmas Eve and broadcast from the Institute Chapel. ABC was pleased with the program and scheduled another such program for December 23 of the following year.[81]

The Tuskegee Choir made several short concert trips to Georgia and Alabama in the spring of 1952. The group sang at the Wheat Street Baptist Church in Atlanta; the City Auditorium in Albany, Georgia; Maxwell Air Force Base Theatre in Montgomery, Alabama; and at the Municipal Auditorium in Anniston, Alabama, Dawson's hometown. Each of these concerts took place during the month of March. On April 1 of the same year, the Tuskegee Choir sang for the Golden Anniversary of the Crawford Johnson Coca-Cola Company, the local soft-drink bottler in Birmingham, Alabama.[82]

Having sung on the radio many times, the Tuskegee Choir made its television debut on April 6, 1952. The singers were guests of Ed Sullivan on his show *Toast of the Town*, produced in New York City's Maxine Elliot Theatre. On April 7 the choir was featured on Kate Smith's television show, which originated from New York City's Hudson Theatre. While in the city, the Tuskegee Choir sang to open the 1952 campaign for the United Negro College Fund. The group also performed at Great Neck High School on Long Island. After these concerts the choir returned to Tuskegee for a special Easter concert.[83]

William Dawson took a sabbatical leave during the 1952–53 school year to fulfill a lifelong dream of visiting Africa but returned to Tuskegee in the fall of 1953. He then prepared the Tuskegee Choir for additional concerts and took them to New York once again for special appearances on Eddie

Fisher's television show, *Coke Time*. Sponsored by the Coca-Cola Company, the telecast was broadcast from NBC television studios in New York City. The choir sang a Christmas program and, a week later, presented a New Year's Eve program to usher in 1954.[84]

The Warm Springs Foundation asked the Tuskegee Choir to sing at the dedication of Franklin D. Roosevelt Hall in Warm Springs, Georgia, in mid-April 1954. Warm Springs was considered a haven for those afflicted with polio. President Roosevelt had been attracted to the area and had a home built there in 1932. Warm Springs served as the "Little White House" during Franklin Roosevelt's four terms as president of the United States. Along with the Tuskegee Choir, Helen Hayes, noted stage and screen star, was on the program.[85]

The final trip to New York made by the Tuskegee Choir under the direction of William Dawson occurred in March of 1955. This trip proved to be a significant journey with important milestones in Dawson's career at Tuskegee. In a single day, March 20, Dawson's group sang on the television show *Frontiers of Faith* over the NBC television network and also appeared in concert at the Metropolitan Opera House. The performance marked the closing of the United Negro College Fund's Convocation Week. The principal speaker for the last meeting was John Foster Dulles, then US secretary of state.[86]

The highlight of Mr. Dawson's last year as conductor of the Tuskegee Choir took place the following day in New York City—the recording of his singers by Westminster Records. So impressed by the choir was Westminster's musical director, Kurt List, that he later wrote to Dorothy Barker of the UNCF. List marveled that in his entire recording career, which was extensive, he had not encountered a more capable conductor than William Dawson. He bestowed upon Dawson the title of "finest choral conductor in the country" and related how pleasurable it was to observe the Tuskegee director's skill in evoking beautiful sounds from the singers.[87] Westminster Recording Company soon released the Tuskegee Choir album. Even twenty-five years later, the album was still in demand. Dawson's wife, Cecile, sold copies of the album in her Tuskegee gift shop, The Petite Bazaar, until it closed in the 1980s. Selections from the recording can be heard on YouTube.[88]

Despite having led the Tuskegee Choir to a national reputation, spearheaded accomplishments in the School and Department of Music at Tuskegee, and coached the many fine musicians, William Dawson resigned as director of Tuskegee's music program on September 1, 1955. Wishing to devote time to composing and to the ever-increasing requests for leading clinics and workshops, Dawson left the position he had held for twenty-five years.[89]

Chapter 4

DAWSON THE COMPOSER

1921–90

William Dawson experimented with composition from an early age. While formal concerts of choirs, bands, and orchestras were not a part of the social life in Dawson's hometown of Anniston, he nonetheless enjoyed the singing in his community, local church choirs, and the yearly concert of Gresham's Negro Band on Emancipation Day. Even as a small child, he was able to perceive the structure of music and, for the rest of his life, remained interested in the analytical elements of musical composition and dance, and expressed himself through these mediums. For example, to artistically present the local news of the day, Dawson would choreograph intricately patterned dance steps. Similarly, after hearing poetry, he would try to fit melodies to the phrases. Furthermore, in his haste to learn to play a musical instrument, Dawson tried to make his own stringed instrument by using materials at hand so that he could experiment with the many tunes he knew.[1] In other words, his creativity manifested in unique musical and dance expressions.

Reflecting on Dawson's career as a composer, Milton Randolph Jr. said that Dawson sought the sounds of Black America by venturing into the highways and byways of the Alabama countryside, visiting people, attending church with them, and toiling by their sides. This allowed him to gain understanding of their plight, dreams, and emotions to share with others through music.[2] Dawson strove to be the voice of his people, using the culturally rich tones and drawing on his own history of musical experiences in Anniston as a child.[3] Robert O'Meally noted, "Dawson was classically trained . . . in the often harder school of the jazz world, the hard knocks school there, of the church, and the blues, and wanted to present all those worlds . . . in his work." O'Meally further suggested that Dawson was trying to create musical forms that told the "panoramic history of African Americans."[4]

LOCATING THE AMERICANNESS OF MUSIC

Dawson came of age and began composing at a time when the nation was seeking to define what was distinctly "American" about American music. In 1892 Bohemian-born Antonin Dvořák was invited to the United States to become director of the newly created National Conservatory of Music in New York City. Dvořák's personal goal was to seek out the strains of a national music in America. He was chosen to direct the teaching and creative endeavors at the American conservatory largely because of his strong desire to compose music using the indigenous folk music of Bohemians who were under the aegis of the Austro-Hungarian Empire. Forced to speak German, rather than the native Czech, and experiencing music dominated and led by musicians from Germanic countries, Dvořák sought to promote the spontaneity and excitement of Czech folk music by weaving cultural motifs into standard musical forms of the day. Along with his contemporary Bedrich Smetana, Dvořák hoped to instill a strong sense of national pride in the people of Bohemia. Despite being from a small Czech village, Dvořák rose to become a recognized artist in Europe by creating music in the prevailing accepted musical style that featured folk idioms from his native country. Those making the selection for director of the new National School of Music in America believed Dvořák the perfect mentor to encourage young composers in the United States to seek sources of indigenous "American" sounds in lieu of overdependence on European sonorities.[5]

At first Dvořák felt unable to pinpoint a distinct American sound; however, upon working with his African American students, he identified "Negro songs" as the clear source of a national music. Believing these songs to be the fabric from which American music ought to develop, he explicitly encouraged African American musicians to seek musical education and to compose. It is highly likely that Dvořák had previously heard strains of African American melodies and rhythms in works by Louis Moreau Gottschalk, the Fisk Jubilee Singers, and others while he was still in Europe. Yet when his American students shared the music of those who had been enslaved, he was inspired. Among other courses, Dvořák taught two-hour composition lessons at the New York Conservatory. Though not one of Dvořák's composition students, Harry T. Burleigh, a young Black student, eventually rose to prominence in the early twentieth century for his arrangements of African American spirituals. Jay van Straaten wrote that Dvořák would, over and over, "ask H.T. Burleigh . . . to sing spirituals for him." Dvořák eventually claimed in a *New York Herald* article, "In the Negro songs I have found a secure basis for a new national music school.... America can save her own music, a fine music growing up from her own soil and bearing its own special character, the natural voice of a free and great nation."[6]

Dvořák caused agitation among many over the value of this African American song material. The prevailing musical opinions in America then had fostered an atmosphere that resulted in the outcry of disagreement with Dvořák. In the 1880s at Columbia University, Edward MacDowell, America's foremost musical luminary at the time, openly refuted Dvořák's contention that "Negro" music should be the basis for an American music sound, believing that "to classify music according to nationalities is to narrow its scope."[7] Despite his American origins, MacDowell spent twelve years, from age fifteen to twenty-seven, studying music in Europe, and his anger toward the proposed use of native plantation music in America seemed to be a result of his Old World education. MacDowell's attitude was echoed by his contemporaries Elson and Ritter, both American musicologists. MacDowell furthermore held the belief that music was not art. Rather, he believed that "the high mission of music ... is neither to be an agent for expressing material things; nor to utter pretty sounds to amuse the ear; nor a sensuous excitant to fire the blood, or a sedative to lull the senses." Instead, "it is a language, but a language of the intangible kind, a kind of soul-language."[8] Historian John Rublowsky says that closed-minded beliefs such as MacDowell's cut off otherwise serious and important music from the mainstream of everyday life, thereby creating an intellectual attitude that ignored significant American musical developments. Rublowsky also observed that, unlike perhaps Dvořák's few works by MacDowell and his peers have remained in public consciousness since their lifetimes.[9]

Gilbert Chase, who lauded African American melodies as a source of inspirational material for American music more broadly, indicated that MacDowell, who thought the Bohemian composer was offering a pattern for "an American national musical costume," misunderstood Dvořák's intent.[10] MacDowell's argument, in Chase's view, was likely against that of forcing American composers into a pigeonhole that required adherence to nationalistic norms.[11] However, Dvořák was not advocating the required use of folk songs in a literal sense. Unlike Glinka, who thought of himself as an arranger who enhanced folk tunes with instrumental coloring, Dvořák took elements of folk tunes and used them to craft a new sound, cultivating within the composition those folk characteristics that gave it a sense of place. Chase further clarified Dvořák's goal: to explore the use of ethnic melodies and rhythmic patterns when creating new music to reflect a given culture.[12] Still, America continued to debate Dvořák's controversial opinions.

Even the publicist for the National Conservatory, James Gibbons Huneker, did not agree with Dvořák's contention that the origins of the "unique voice" of the music of America were in the organic cultural music of African Americans and possibly Native Americans. Condescendingly referring to Black people as "darkies," Huneker was adamant that musical contributions from the enslaved during the antebellum period in American history would not constitute the basis for a national music. Instead, he had already decided that the music of Stephen C. Foster, a white man, was most original.[13]

Two decades following Dvořák's visit, the turn-of-the century raging controversy still centered around whether the songs of the previously enslaved should be considered the roots of American music. Henry E. Krehbiel, music editor of the *New York Tribune*, music critic and respected historian of the early twentieth century, noted the outrage from critics over Dvorak's selection of African American folk songs as the "true" source of an American musical sound. Krehbiel chided the responders for being short-sighted in not seeing the worth of this body of musical compositions that had been neglected by white society. In so many words, Krehbiel labeled their reaction as racist.[14] Krehbiel's 1914 book, entitled *Afro-American Folksongs*, was an attempt to settle the debate. He defined folk song as "the song of the folk; not only the song admired of the people but, in a strict sense, the song created by the people."[15] As the spontaneous expression of a particular group, such music is characterized by musical elements that are identified with a particular sect or national individuality that reflects hopes, feelings, beliefs of a people, as well as an insight into their history and pulse of life.

Historians often described the origination of the folk music of the African Americans in bondage on the plantations in America through the movement of field workers at the end of the day, dances, and baptisms, as well the many sounds of animals, work songs, and field hollers, that often culminated in music for worship, weddings, and funerals. In his book, Krehbiel attacked the ideas of Wallascheck, Jackson, and others who held that the folk songs from the plantations are mere copies of songs the enslaved Black people had heard from their captors, arguing that all folk songs contained similar characteristics due to universal patterns of human interaction over time. Krehbiel asked his detractors: if African American songs were merely copies of songs they heard in America, "why did white men blacken their faces and imitate these imitations?"[16] He ultimately asserted that African American folk songs are original American works that do embody some musical traditions of Africa but are made distinctly American as a result of their development out of shared experiences in the new land and their heartfelt expression of suffering under enslavement.

W. E. B. Du Bois corroborated Dvořák and Krehbiel's claims, arguing that "the Negro folk song—the rhythmic cry of the slave—stands today not simply as the sole American music, but as the most beautiful expression of human experience born this side of the seas."[17] To support Krehbiel's contention that Negro folk songs were not blatant copies of white folk songs they had heard, Du Bois outlined a four-stage development process by which these unique compositions came to be. The process was inspired by "African Music," that which comes from the homeland and gets complemented by "Afro American music," or the new expressions upon arrival in America. Then there was a "blending of Negro music with the music heard in the foster land." The resulting music, according to Du Bois, "is still distinctly Negro and the method of blending is original, but the elements are both Negro and Caucasian." At this point, "songs of white America," such as those by Stephen Foster, for example, begin to be "influenced by songs of the enslaved and Negro melody."[18] This dynamic process resulted in distinctively American music.

Subsequent works by musicologists laud the early work of Krehbiel and add support to his contention that African American folk songs should be recognized as the roots of original American music. For example, at the height of the Harlem Renaissance, the 1925 publication on American spirituals by African American scholar James Weldon Johnson asserted that these spirituals composed the *only* body of folk music in America, and her finest offering in art, at that.[19] In 1936 Alain Locke asserted, "Negro music is the closest approach America has to folk music, and so Negro music is almost as important for the musical culture of America as it is for the spiritual life of the Negro."[20] Locke believed that, since the latter part of the nineteenth century, African Americans had "been the main source of America's popular music, and promises, as we shall see, to become one of the main source of America's serious or Classical music, at least that part which strives to be natively American and not derivative of European types of music."[21] It was within the context of this cultural debate that Dawson launched his own composing career.

DAWSON'S EARLY COMPOSITIONS

Perhaps the first evidence of Dawson's interest in composition is in a letter from Harry T. Burleigh dated March 17, 1921, while Dawson was in his final year as a student at Tuskegee Institute.[22] Dawson's pocket calendar for that year indicated a meeting with Burleigh in New York on February 26 while on tour with the Tuskegee Quintette; it is likely that Dawson provided Burleigh with one of his early compositions during that meeting and asked for the composer's feedback.[23] Based on Burleigh's comments in the letter about the lyric "honey," the song Dawson offered was an arrangement of a piece from the 1898 musical *Clorindy, or The Origin of the Cakewalk*[24] with music by Will Marion Cook and lyrics by poet Paul Laurence Dunbar.[25] The text for the song was published by Dunbar as a poem under the title "A Negro Love Song" with words written in dialect.[26] Upon further investigation, however, Dawson's work was not an arrangement of Will Marion Cook's song from *Clorindy*. Instead, inspired by Dunbar's lyrics, Dawson composed a new melody and harmony for Dunbar's poem, the result being a delightful duet between a young Black couple. Dawson kept Dunbar's poetry in dialect exactly as written, adding a final repetition of "Jump back, Honey, jump back."[27]

Given that *Clorindy* was written, orchestrated, performed, and conducted entirely by African Americans, its initial performance represented an important milestone in the history of American music. Not only was it groundbreaking in its all-Black production, *Clorindy* also represented the first musical in which singing and dancing occurred simultaneously. Prior to this performance, singers and dancers performed their roles separately; yet the entire chorus of *Clorindy* sang and danced, performing the cakewalk to the syncopated rhythm of Cook's score.[28] Having heard selections from this historic African American musical performed at Tuskegee, Dawson was inspired to experiment with setting Dunbar's texts musically. In his letter to Dawson, Burleigh did not spare any words in pointing out flaws: "In looking over your song more carefully than I had time when you first showed it to me, I find many weak spots in it." The seasoned musician, highly regarded composer, and friend of Dvořák took young Dawson to task for repeatedly using 6/4 chords at the beginning of measures, often omitting the root of the chord, and also suggested a more effective form for word inflection for the vocalist to carefully express the text. Noting that the work had promise and offering encouragement for improving the composition, Burleigh offered a complimentary close to the letter: "As it is now, it has no commercial value, altho' it has many effective points. With kindest regards and all good wishes, I am Very Truly yours."[29] Dawson's diligence in heeding Burleigh's suggestions was later made evident in 1923 when the Wunderlichs Piano Company of Kansas City, Missouri, published the work.[30]

In the spring of 1922, following a year of teaching music at Kansas Vocational College in Topeka, while briefly taking music theory classes at Washburn College, Dawson realized that he needed further study and sought additional instruction in composition. His self-published composition was a vocal solo with piano accompaniment entitled "Forever Thine," and he sold the published copies door-to-door to raise money for additional schooling. While a student at the Horner Institute of Fine Arts in Kansas City, he wrote *Trio in A* for piano, violin, and cello. This was the composition selected for special music played during his graduation from that conservatory in 1925.[31]

While in Kansas City as director of music at Lincoln High School (LHS) between 1922 and 1925, Dawson also began to arrange traditional African American songs for his singers. This choice of subject matter for Dawson's compositions may have been influenced by Dett, Locke, and Aaron Douglas, LHS art instructor. Douglas, who would later go on to achieve widespread acclaim for his art, was firmly invested in the NAACP movement and was an avid reader of *The Crisis* magazine of the organization.

Douglas and Dawson were roommates at the "Colored YMCA" in Kansas City and developed a strong friendship. Perhaps as a result of Douglas and others, Dawson penned arrangements of the spirituals "King Jesus Is A-Listening" and "My Lord What a Mourning." After the LHS choir performed these numbers at a national music conference in Kansas City, music publishers swarmed Dawson, showing keen interest in printing his arrangements. An article appeared in *The Musical Leader*, April 9, 1925, several days after the close of the Music Supervisor's National Conference (the forerunner of Music Educator's National Conference, currently known as the National Association for Music Education). The author expressed praise for the choir's singing and for the arrangements:

> The colored classes from Kansas City took high honors in the singing during two afternoons. A prominent supervisor left Convention Hall Wednesday afternoon after hearing one of the colored choruses, remarking that the singing was so divinely beautiful he would hear no other that day in order that he might carry the spell as long as possible. Thursday afternoon the great American poet, Edward Markham, commented in terms of high admiration for their work. One musician said, "I have seldom been so moved, and I am fairly critical, though I hope never blasé. I never thought the chord of the dominant seventh could have wrung so much emotional response from me, but it was so, the way those young voices with an unearthly purity and sweetness wrought it."[32]

Dawson hoped to continue developing the genre of the Negro spiritual, what he called Negro folk songs, allowing these songs to express a true Black language free from stereotypes. As a student at Tuskegee, Dawson became intrigued by Dvořák's convictions regarding the root of American music, and he worked to understand and extend the respected composer's intent. Eileen Southern stated that "Dawson was directly inspired by Dvořák's views on nationalism in music."[33] He was interested in composition that used the organic folk idioms of his people and would later compose and arrange a number of these folk songs as well as write a major symphonic work that emphasized these "plantation" motifs. Dawson was fascinated by the folk songs hummed and sung by African Americans in the community where he lived. He listened intently to the many variations of the different tunes sung by his mother and the church choirs. In particular, a concert of African American folk songs, sung by the Jubilee Singers of Fisk University, spurred his excitement for this unique, indigenous music. Dawson's interest in this music was further heightened while he was a student at Tuskegee Institute. The Institute founder, Booker T. Washington, had placed great emphasis on these folk songs. The "plantation melodies," as Washington called them, were an important part of all formal and informal singing activities at the school. At Tuskegee, Dawson gained firsthand knowledge of this music through singing the songs in the Institute Choir and during assemblies, studying the compositional techniques of African American composers who set the tunes, and listening to the melodies repeatedly.

Although many, both Black and white, referred to this body of folk music created by the enslaved as "spirituals," and later by some as "Black spirituals," Dawson adamantly refused this nomenclature. He objected to using the word "Black" to describe the music, explaining his belief that the basic elements of music consist in vibration rather than pigmentation. He preferred the word "Negro" for its Latin roots, explaining that the word, at least at that time, was used in all the Romance languages to refer to people of African descent. Furthermore, he contended that "spiritual" was a nickname given to the songs by the white people who first notated many of them. John Lovell explained: "If you talk with Dawson, the first thing he will tell you is that the songs in question are not spirituals; they need another name for they carry not narrowly religious overtones, but the universal implications for human life."[34] He outlined his theory of the Negro folk songs—including a clear definition of and prescribed approach to interpreting and performing this subset of folk music—in an article in the March 1955 issue of *Etude*. Dawson defines songs in this genre as "group expressions" that convey "the emotions and experiences of the Negro slave in the United States."[35] Dawson believed that the purpose of these songs was not for audience entertainment; rather, the songs, if approached correctly, should reveal the spirit of God contained in the music and serve as a holy blessing to both performer and listener.[36]

THE ORIGINS AND FUNCTIONS OF
AFRICAN AMERICAN SPIRITUALS

Arthur Jones's *Wade in the Water—The Wisdom of Spirituals* discusses how African American spirituals are influenced by the role that music and movement played in African life before the advent of slavery. Those who were enslaved "brought with them a richly textured heritage that included singing and dancing as daily activities" that were "interwoven into everyday routines." Such song and dance were "expressions of a worldview in which communion with the spirits and with tribal sisters and brothers (those living as well as those dead) was not only desirable, but necessary for life, as much as food and water."[37] While instruments could be heard during celebrations and in the daily life of African tribes, singing as a group was a staple of functional cultural activities. The song lyrics were sometimes improvisatory and were often "highly poetic," using "imagery and figures of speech" and "often employing creative metaphors comically or playfully to comment on the behavior of fellow tribesfolk." The practice of cleverly embedding commentary in song would appear during slavery when "slave owners would . . . be ridiculed in poetic, metaphorical call-and-response verses, frequently unaware that they were being made fun of." Jones located the origin of "this kind of 'secret' communication through song" in the African musical tradition.[38]

Another important role music played in African culture was to provide a connection to community both horizontally and vertically. Establishing a sense of kinship with those living, those who had died, and those who were yet to come was achieved and expressed through the mediums of music and dance. Thus, for Africans of different tribes arriving on American shores following capture, and without access to a common language, the bond of kinship was established through music in the form of singing and dancing.[39]

Over time, enslaved people merged a variety of African musical traditions with the culture of the American South, where they had been forcibly relocated. This blending led to the development of a unique musical genre. James B. Kelley defines spirituals as:

> the poetic articulation of black desires for freedom expressed through the syncretism of early African American religion, the creative mixing of the African belief systems that many blacks had brought with them on the slave ships with the Christian belief systems that were first introduced to or imposed on many of them in the New World.[40]

In the antebellum period, enslaved Africans were often allowed to attend church by either standing outside the open back door or by occupying the inside balcony. Bible texts heard during sermons were often explicated in the verses of spirituals that, sometimes, added interpretations or applications to current life situations. Lydia Parrish suggested that in some of these compositions, enslaved people would use language from the Old Testament as a stand-in to refer to life in their homeland.[41] Over time, however, some enslaved people began to find solace in some elements of Christianity, finding parallels between their own enslavement and that of biblical characters, and taking comfort in the Bible's depiction of a loving God.[42] Enslaved preachers supplemented licensed ministers in secret prayer meetings and all-night sings emphasizing passages in Exodus that focused on Hebrew captives striving for freedom from bondage, thereby providing hope for Black congregants.

Spirituals—or as Dawson called them, Negro folk songs—are the unique compositions that developed out of the enmeshment of African musical traditions, Christianity, and the experience of slavery. Lovell suggested that the earliest examples of a song in this genre existed by 1767, although musicologists and ethnomusicologists challenge the validity as incorporating elements from older camp meeting songs.[43] Dawson's view was that contemporary musicians who seek to authentically arrange and perform Negro folk songs must possess a clear understanding of the context in which the songs originated, including an awareness of the role these songs played in the lives of the enslaved.[44] The consensus among scholars is that spirituals were likely both authentic religious expression and a means of communicating coded information that white captors would not be able to understand.[45]

In a foreword to *Negro Slave Songs in the United States* by Miles Mark Fisher, historian Ray Allen Billington wrote that Fisher's work indicated "that [spirituals] revealed the innermost thoughts of the slaves on religions, slavery, relations with their masters, aspirations for the future, and all the multitudinous problems faced by a people held in bondage." Billington also pointed out that Fisher had revealed that "Negroes, through their songs, were able to develop a vocabulary and means of expression that was entirely their own." The ability to express themselves in this manner, bypassing cognition by whites, was a "degree of intellectual freedom" and a feeling of superiority.[46]

While Eileen Guenther asserted that intentions behind the lyrics of spiritual were fluid, varying according to circumstance and locality, scholars nevertheless identify several likely, overlapping purposes of spirituals: to provide an outlet for emotional expression of the desire for deliverance from slavery; to transmit secret messages to other enslaved people without detection from slaveowners; and to aid in escaping conditions of slavery.[47]

Melva Costen indicated that singing spirituals during enslavement was not only a demonstration of the understanding of theology but also a tool through which to survive and possibly emerge from bondage—to be free.[48] She posited that spirituals create conditions in which African Americans can begin to understand their identity, and explained that the poetic expression of the lyrics led "to a sense of well-being, a strong sense of hope in hopelessness, strength of endurance, commitment to freedom and democracy."[49] Writing about his experience in slavery, abolitionist Frederick Douglass, corroborated Costen's views. He noted that singing spirituals was a way to collectively express a desire for freedom as well as an opportunity to momentarily feel unrestricted through making music. Despite their suffering, he wrote, he and other enslaved people "were, at times, remarkably buoyant, singing hymns and making joyous exclamations, almost as triumphant in their tone as if we reached a land of freedom and safety." When they sang of their longing to reach Canaan, for example, he revealed that he and his brethren in fact "meant" to express their longing "to reach the *north*—and the north was our Canaan."[50] He also wrote about a spiritual with the lyrics:

> *I thought I heard them say,*
> *There were lions in the way,*
> *I don't expect to Star [sic]*
> *Much longer here.*
>
> *Run to Jesus—shun the danger—*
> *I don't expect to stay*
> *Much longer here.*[51]

This song was a particular favorite of the enslaved people with whom Douglass worked and lived, and he explained that it "had a double meaning. In the lips of some, it meant the expectation of a speedy summons to a world of spirits; but, in the lips of *our* company, it simply meant, a speedy pilgrimage toward a free state, and deliverance from all the evils and dangers of slavery."[52]

Booker T. Washington echoed Douglass's sentiments about the way spirituals allowed for feeling and expressing a desire for freedom. He noted, "Most of the verses of the plantation songs had some reference to freedom." This was strategic on the part of the enslaved, as white captors could interpret their lyrics about freedom in a way that supported a Christian longing for the afterlife. Yet, over time, the enslaved "gradually threw off the mask . . . and were not afraid to let it be known that the 'freedom' in their songs meant freedom of the body in this world."[53]

Both Washington and Douglass, in writing about the expression of freedom in spirituals, highlight the way that the biblical concepts in these songs lent themselves well to multiple interpretations. Another role of the spiritual in the life of the enslaved, then, was to exploit the metaphorical language of Christianity, using it to communicate covertly with other enslaved persons. Lovell emphasized the convenience of using Christian texts as a "system capable of direct language and undercurrent symbolism at the same time."[54] Given the important role that religion played in the lives of white enslavers, the religiosity of the spiritual allowed the enslaved to safely "sing what they could not say."[55]

As in the examples of Frederick Douglass and Booker T. Washington, without an overt admission of the individual's intent of the meaning behind the lyrics sung, one cannot be certain of any coded message being expressed. Unequivocal specificity of a universal intent is not assured and cannot be generalized across a population. One can only imagine or surmise the plethora of possibilities. With this in mind, there is still a great deal of scholarly work devoted to what Guenther refers to as "unlocking the Biblical code" within spirituals. Lovell refers to these religious ciphers as "symbolism in spirituals," while Rebecca Raber calls many of these songs "Coded Message Spirituals."[56] Table 1 is a compilation of the suggestions from three analysts for approaching the lyrics of spirituals. The table is a starting point to imagine the wide variety of possible meanings of an individual or group lament at being enslaved through the cathartic singing of a spiritual. Specific assignation of intent is not exact, and observers should be encouraged to interpret suggested possibilities, as well as to develop others.

The same coded-language tactics that the enslaved might have used to communicate in spirituals would appear in later musical compositions by African Americans. The origins of blues music of newly freed African Americans that began to emerge in the 1890s, and flowered in the era of Jim Crow laws in the early twentieth century, contained lyrics that might have attempted to convey meaning communicated through the same "mask and symbol" phrase Jones uses to describe possible expression through the spiritual.[57] Blues historian Scott Baretta suggested that blues words that expressed difficulties with spouses or families might have provided a way to covertly comment on the frustration with Black Codes and, later, Jim Crow laws. Years earlier the creative use of religious text to possibly convey one's desires for release from bondage in life was continued following emancipation when one form of slavery had been substituted for another—in the guise of the sharecropping system. Blues and the African tradition of singing and dancing provided catharsis for both performer and listener in that both media

TABLE 1. POSSIBLE MEANINGS OF WORDS IN SPIRITUALS

Words/Terms	Possible Meanings
Heaven, Canaan, Promised Land, Gospel Feast, Mansions, Kingdom	freedom, the northern states, Canada, Africa, Heaven, or...
Hell, Egypt, Babylon, Winter	being sold further south (possibly the greatest horror for the enslaved), slavery, death, sin, or...
Deliverance, Being Redeemed, Baptized, Good Religion	freedom, escape, religious conversion, or...
Jubilee (Leviticus 25:8–10)	emancipation, freedom, escape, or...
Heroic Figures: Moses, Daniel, Elijah, Ezekiel, Jonah, Hebrew Children, Peter, Paul, Silas, Lazarus, Noah, Jacob, Gideon, Joshua, Nicodemus, the Israelites	ordinary men and women enslaved with an extreme desire to be free, those heroes that sought to achieve deliverance from tribulation, or...
Evil Figures: Satan, Pharaoh, Egyptians, Rich Man Dives, Pharaoh's Army, Patrollers	slave traders, white enslavers, slave trackers, or...
Water: Jordan River, Red Sea, Rivers, Baptism, Rain, Fountains	Ohio River, Atlantic Ocean (return to Africa), any river that posed a barrier to freedom, crossing a body of water to freedom, or...
Transportation: Chariot, Ship, Train, Wheels, Wings, Shoes, Walking, Running, Flying, Jacob's Ladder	methods of movement used to escape to freedom, the Underground Railroad, or...
Possessions: Shoes, Robe, Crown, Harp, Bells, Trumpet, Wings	symbols of: traveling, devotion, praise, freedom, or...
Place: "Drinking Gourd," Canaan, "Streets of Gold," Promised Land, Pearly Gates, Jordan River	the North Star, Canada, "Free States," escape routes, or...
Jesus, or King Jesus	Savior of humankind, conductors on the Underground Railroad, owners of safehouses, or...

(Eileen Guenther, In Their Own Words: Slave Life and the Power of Spirituals (St. Louis Mo: Morningstar Publishers, Inc., 2016), 358. John Lovell, Jr., "The Social Implications of the Negro Spiritual," The Journal of Negro Education 8, no. 4 (October, 1939): 642. Rebecca Lynn Raber, "Conducting the Coded Message Songs of Slavery: Context, Connotations, and Performance Preparation," PhD diss., (North Dakota State University, 2018), 19.

voiced the human response to life's hardships.[58] As with specific meaning of coded words in spirituals, the exact identification of a social complaint in blues songs cannot be confirmed unless overtly stated by the performer. Such blatant or forthright voicing of complaints would have been extremely dangerous at the time.

While there were many more quotidian topics that might be covertly conveyed through spirituals, these songs were often useful in communicating about and aiding in escape from slavery. Sarah Bradford, the early biographer for Harriet Tubman, wrote that because those in bondage were not allowed to talk in groups, they might sometimes express plans to flee slavery using phrases from spirituals. Tubman possibly used spirituals to cue travelers to prepare to leave the plantation, all within earshot of enslavers by using known verses or improvising lyrics. Although there is no actual evidence, the song, "I'm bound for the promised land," for example, might have included improvised lyrics to indicate the timing and who would be leading the escape.[59] Along the journey, Tubman could have sung cloaked lyrics to alert those she had placed in hiding that it was safe to emerge from cover. Bradford explains that Tubman possibly sang "Go Down, Moses" in order to indicate that safe, trusted assistants had arrived to help those enslaved who were escaping.[60]

Other spirituals could have contained information that scholars believe helped guide the path of those who had escaped slavery and were seeking refuge in the North. Some suggest that the spiritual "Follow the Drinking Gourd" might have served as a reminder to those escaping slavery to follow the North Star. Unfamiliar with the geography of their environs, and unable to travel by day, runaways depended on the North Star, also known as Polaris, for direction. Finding Polaris was easier when recognizing it among the stars forming the Big Dipper. It is said that the enslaved and others referred to the Big Dipper as "The Drinking Gourd." This spiritual was one among many that might have offered the enslaved practical help in their escapes.[61]

Scholars suggest that many phrases and lyrics found in spirituals—such as "Make my way up to heaven on the other side"—possibly referred to assistance offered runaways in the form of a suggested safe walking path providing secure overnight lodging, or food and drink, that became known as the Underground Railroad. The use of train imagery abounds in these songs. Singing the question "Can I Ride?" in spirituals, for example, may have provided a way to reflect on whether one was prepared to undergo the risks involved in being a runaway, whereas lyrics such as "No second-class . . . no difference in the fare" and "There's room for many-a more" were means of expressing encouragement to escape.[62] Singing "The Gospel train's a-comin'" may have been a way to alert the community that a contingent of travelers was preparing to escape to freedom. While not an actual train, but guised in biblical reference, understanding of the metaphor of the Underground Railroad would have probably eluded white people.

Three of the references in Table 1 refer specifically to the Underground Railroad, and three signify that the direction of escape was to the north. The Underground Railroad was a means for captive men and women to escape to complete freedom, usually in Canada, via a network of assistance from both Blacks and whites. Many myths and legends exist in folklore concerning the Underground Railroad, as well as the method, route, and assistance utilized by the pairs, groups, and individuals who attempted to escape from slavery. Most important in eliciting the truth concerning the Underground

Railroad is that the assistance in escaping occurred only after runaways reached a Free State. "It was only after they [the enslaved] escaped from the South under their own steam that they might run across abolitionists and Underground Railroad agents, themselves often black, who could give them a helping hand."[63]

Indeed, abolitionists such as Frederick Douglass, William Lloyd Garrison, and others made it widely known that those escaping slavery would be fed and guided. However, the runaways had to make it to the source of food and assistance. Responsibility for getting to the help offered by staunch abolitionists was placed on those willing to risk the dangers involved in getting to a Free State. Despite the low success rate and risk of severe bodily harm or death, thousands made the attempt. Free Black writer Henry Bibb in 1853 made manifest the realization that "self-emancipation is now the order of the day."[64] In other words, to be free one had to engage in a DIY project: "do-it-yourself!"

On a surface reading, lyrics about water or rivers in a spiritual refer to the purification of baptism, but it is likely that these also alerted enslaved people to the dangers of escaping slavery. Some suggest that "Wade in the Water" was a means of warning runaways that slave trackers using bloodhounds would be thrown off the pursuit if the escapee entered a body of water. As noted in Table 1 above, references to the Jordan River could have indicated the Ohio River or some body of water that might be the final barrier to freedom in the North for many of the enslaved. Successful crossing of the Ohio River enabled the enslaved to move from the Border State of Kentucky into the Free State of Indiana or Ohio. Phrases such as "Jordan River is chilly and cold / it chills the body but not the soul" might have been an encouragement to persist in determination to be free, regardless of the obstacles. The lyrics of "Deep River" could also have made reference to crossing the Ohio with the words "my home is over Jordan." Anticipation of a better life might be expressed in the words "promised land," "go to the gospel feast," or "where all is peace." Much debate exists over the meaning of the desire expressed in the text of some spirituals to cross over into "campground," yet there is some agreement that the text might suggest the setting for a camp meeting or a type of conclave located in an area away from the planation. Such a secret site could enable African Americans to freely express themselves.

Dawson insisted that one possess a historical understanding of the institution of slavery in order to best compose and perform spirituals, or Negro folk songs, in a contemporary context. In particular, he believed that their proper interpretation hinges on an understanding of the role that religion played for enslaved African Americans. According to Dawson, many of the enslaved felt a oneness with Jesus Christ, who bore no malice toward his persecutors. These enslaved people drew a parallel between Christ's peaceful submission to persecution that eventually led to his victory over death and their own suffering and hoped-for deliverance from slavery. Just as Christ refused to speak ill of those who tortured and killed him, Negro folk songs, in Dawson's view, contain not even a word of hate against white captors. Religion became the vehicle through which many enslaved could express and realize their hope for deliverance from the evils of servility, discrimination, violence, and death. The songs—which Dawson called religious texts—combine melody and harmony to express these beliefs and provide the enslaved with physical and spiritual catharsis.[65] He further asserted that the "Negro" dialect present in many folk songs was a purposeful artistic innovation by the enslaved rather than a "crude attempt to pronounce Anglo-Saxon words." He argued that Black Americans instinctively modified the "harsh and guttural sounds" of English "to satisfy the preference for soft and euphonious vocables characteristic of native African speech." By using "ah" for "I," the diphthong is eliminated. Supplanting an aspirated "th" with "de" makes a more pleasant sound. Choosing "wid" in lieu of the ending "th" sound achieves enhanced clarity. Dawson further explained the different pronunciations of "de" as similar to the use of the "the" in cases of a succeeding vowel or consonant.[66]

The history of slavery on the North American continent, as well as these complex, nuanced beliefs, guided Dawson's choices as composer, arranger, and conductor of Negro folk songs. Lawrence Jackson asserted that Dawson hoped to challenge racial discrimination by creating art that drew on his African roots. Dawson embedded unembellished Negro melodies into masterful works that used the whole suite of Western compositional devices available to him at the time.[67] This strategy resulted in many compositional successes as well as a great deal of criticism throughout his life as a composer.[68]

DAWSON'S EARLY PUBLISHING CAREER AS CHORAL COMPOSER AND ARRANGER

While early interest in publishing Dawson's spirituals seemed high at the time, noted publishers such as Oliver Ditson and others did not follow through with interests in printing Dawson's works. H. T. FitzSimons and Gamble Hinged Music eventually published several of Dawson's works, but by then he was working for both companies. The first of Dawson's works published was "King Jesus Is A-Listening," copyrighted in 1925 by the H. T. FitzSimons Company of Chicago. It seems that Mr. FitzSimons, owner of the publishing company, had heard William Dawson's Lincoln High School Choir in concert during the Music Supervisors National Conference in April 1925, in Kansas City. Dawson's preference for the term "Negro," as opposed to Black, is seen in this first publication, as it bears the subtitle "Negro Folk Song," instead of spiritual. FitzSimons was impressed by the choir's performance of the music and wanted to publish some of Dawson's arrangements.[69] The FitzSimons Company was so pleased with the response to this publication that they soon published more of Dawson's arrangements. "I Couldn't Hear Nobody Pray" received a copyright in 1926,[70] while "Talk about a Child That Do Love Jesus" was copyrighted in 1927.[71] Both were printed as a part of FitzSimons's Aeolian Choral Series. In 1980 Dawson rearranged "Talk about a Child," and it was rereleased by FitzSimons.

Dawson set a text by Vernon N. Ray entitled, "Go to Sleep," for vocal solo and for choirs of SATB (Soprano, Alto, Tenor, Bass), SSA (Soprano I, Soprano II, Alto), and TTBB (Tenor I, Tenor II, Baritone, Bass) voices that was published by FitzSimons in 1926. However, Alice Tischler's 1981 listing of Dawson's works indicated that this one was out of print. A copy of the piece exists in the list of shorter works as a part of the William Dawson papers in the Rose Archives at Emory University.[72]

While FitzSimons claims to be Dawson's first publisher, the Remick Music Corporation, who bought out Gamble Hinged Music Company, soon had another of his arrangements copyrighted and published, in 1927. The Remick publication "Jesus Walked This Lonesome Valley" was written specifically for the Tuskegee Institute Choir and its director, Mrs. Jennie C. Lee, known as "Mother Lee," whom Dawson had so admired while a student at the institute. The arrangement was listed under sacred music among selections in the Remick Choral Library Series and was called a spiritual, perhaps due to the belief that the choral piece might sell better or be recognized more quickly if listed under spiritual as opposed to Negro folk song. The song was arranged for several different voicings, including SSA, SSAA (Soprano I, Soprano II, Alto I, Alto II), SATB, and TTBB. Later published by Warner Brothers Publications, which purchased Remick, it bears the inscription to Mrs. Lee and the Tuskegee Choir and notes the copyright date by Remick of 1927.[73]

In 1927 Dawson wrote a three-movement Sonata for Violin and Piano that blended themes from Negro folk songs with the effects of jazz harmony. David Yarbrough asserted that "the sonata was a work in which Dawson explored the expressive and technical and idiomatic qualities of the violin."[74] Given that Dawson commenced work the next year on the symphony that would eventually be completed in 1932 and premiered on the national stage in 1934, it is possible that the sonata was an interim endeavor that served as preparation for his dream of writing an extended work for orchestra.⁷⁵ The *Sonata* for Violin and Piano, however, does not appear on the list of accomplishments Dawson compiled during his lifetime.⁷⁶

Soon after the publication of "Jesus Walked This Lonesome Valley," Remick prepared to publish another Dawson folk song. "You Got To Reap Just What You Sow," copyrighted in 1928, was published under Remick Choral Library Series and is listed on the front cover under the heading "Spirituals," along with other spiritual arrangements by Harold Decker and Noble Cain, both white men. Some pieces are listed as being arranged by Dawson, while others are attributed to him as though he composed or discovered them. When asked about these arrangements, Dawson said that he approached each piece as a composer. Some arrangements incorporate more original elements than others that are more straightforward notations of existing melodies; these more original works significantly alter the original song's melodic and harmonic structure, giving the piece an entirely new identity. "You Got to Reap Just What You Sow" is set for men's, women's, and mixed (SATB) voices. Similar to "Jesus Walked," "You Got to Reap" was subsequently published by Warner Brothers Publications. These two songs were printed together under the heading "Two Spirituals for Male Chorus." In the dual-song publication, "You Got To Reap . . ." appears with a dedication to Paul Robeson, one of the outstanding singers of African American spirituals during the 1920s. This inscription, however, does not appear in the original publication. Both songs include piano accompaniment.⁷⁷

Dawson's arrangement of "My Lord, What a Mourning" was published by the FitzSimons Company and copyrighted in 1927. One way Dawson's arrangement differs from H.T. Burleigh's setting is the use of "Mourning" rather than "Morning." The stained-glass window in the Chapel at Tuskegee, which portrays eleven beloved Negro folk songs, depicts one that is titled, "My Lord, What a Mournin'" and was the inspiration for Dawson's word choice. This and several other settings by Dawson were recorded by the Robert Shaw Chorale on the 1958 album, *Deep River and Other Spirituals*.⁷⁸

Dawson's employer, the Gamble Hinged Music Company, published his setting of Louise Imogen Guiney's poem, "Out in the Fields," in 1929. The inscription printed above the title reads, "In Memory of my Beloved Wife, Cornella," in honor of Cornella who died early in their marriage. "Out in the Fields" is set for vocal solo, mixed and female voices and can be accompanied by piano, orchestra, or wind ensemble.⁷⁹ The Gamble-Hinged Music Company also published Dawson's setting of the Allen Quade poem "The Mongrel Yank" in 1930. Quade's work was taken from the *Chicago Tribune*, and Dawson, in interviews, explained that the meaning of "mongrel" is "A

Yankee of many races." Set for male voices with baritone solo, the piece is the boast of a soldier who proclaims himself a proud American of multicultural ancestry that roams the world. Dawson's affinity for the poem and his decision to set the words to music may have been related to his conviction that the term "American" embraced the diversity of people who came to the United States giving its citizenry a unique and vivid flavor.[80] As was his custom in his later years to rework previously scored compositions, Dawson made changes to "The Mongrel Yank" forty years later, changing the title to "The Rugged Yank." In addition, Dawson reworked voicings by trading notes between the sections and stretching cadences over several measures to enhance chordal cadential points and increase the drama of the piece. The Kjos Music Company published the work in 1970.[81]

Before leaving Chicago to direct the organization of and serve as administrator for the School of Music at his Alma Mater, Dawson received several awards for his compositions. One such award came from department store mogul, Rodman Wanamaker. Wanamaker was a man of many interests that included golf, aviation, and music. In an effort to promote the talents of African American composers, Wanamaker established a nationwide music composition contest "to create a platform that exclusively elevated black composers." The compositions encouraged the use of Black music idioms scored in a classical style.[82] Deadline for submission was July 15 of each year with prizes often awarded in December of the same year.[83] According to a December 23, 1929 letter from The Robert Curtis Ogden Association (RCOA) in the Philadelphia John Wanamaker Store to W. E. B. Du Bois at the NAACP publication *The Crisis*, the contest began three years prior, in late 1926 or early 1927.[84] In 1930, the Rodman Wanamaker Music Contest was held at the annual convention of the National Association of Negro Musicians and was organized by the RCOA, a group comprised exclusively of African Americans. The association awarded various prizes, totaling $1,000.00, in different classes of competition.

In the 1930 Wanamaker Contest, William Dawson received first prize of $150 in Class One for the song "Jump Back, Honey, Jump Back," his homage to the poetry of Paul Laurence Dunbar. He was also awarded first prize of $150 for his instrumental work "Scherzo," in Class Two.[85] Dawson worked to compose music that Black performers could identify with and present with dignity, just as *Clorindy*'s original composer, Cook, did years before. Recall that "Jump Back, Honey, Jump Back," is a setting of the Dunbar poem "A Negro Love Song." Marva Carter, historian and authority on the life and works of Cook, noted the significance of the poem's depiction of "a realistic courtship scene" between African American people "rather than a burlesqued, unrealistic encounter." According to Carter, this shift from degrading to respectful portrayals of Black courtship "signaled the slipping of the minstrel mask."[86] With *Clorindy*, Cook intended to "finally begin to shape the black stage persona to their own purposes, trimming away the demeaning stereotypes that were staples of white dominated minstrel shows or using them satirically in complex multilayered performances."[87] Dawson's choice to enter this song demonstrated his participation in a movement to provide Black performers with compositions that afforded them dignity. Entering the Rodman Wanamaker Contest in 1931, Dawson again took first place, earning $150 in Class One with his song "Lovers Plighted."[88] That prize money increased substantially just one year later when Florence Price won the Wanamaker Contest for her piano sonata and for her *Symphony in E Minor*; the prizes were $250 and $500 respectively.[89]

Dawson's exciting settings of what he called Negro folk songs delighted many audiences and gained overwhelmingly positive responses. Yet not everyone was impressed. Lawrence Jackson indicated that a scathing critique of Dawson's arrangements of spirituals appeared in the *New York Times* in February 1933, following the Carnegie Hall debut of the Tuskegee Choir. The article denounced Dawson's renditions "as failing to capture and reproduce, with a single exception, the Negro folk idiom."[90] The debate concerning how to use African American folk music materials in contemporary compositions would rage on, impacting the reception of Dawson's symphonic work. Nevertheless, he and others continued to arrange spirituals in creative, often dense compositional dressing that included ostinato, a "stacking" of repetitive motifs, textured layering of voices and instruments, counterpoint, a variety of rhythmic accent marks, and other devices. Following Dawson's lead, Moses Hogan, Rollo Dillworth, Keith Hampton and many others continued to set the melodies and lyrics of African American songs more than a century after their creation in the back doors of churches, their balconies, and out in the fields surrounding the plantation.[91]

COMPOSITION, PERFORMANCE, AND RECEPTION OF DAWSON'S SYMPHONIC WORKS

While he was in Chicago studying with Dr. Thorvald Otterstrom, Dawson began work on a symphony utilizing themes found in the folk music of African Americans. Directly influenced by Dvořák, Dawson wanted to do what the Czech composer did not do. Specifically, Dawson desired to use the authentic folk music of African Americans as the inspiration and foundation for an extended symphonic work that would be crafted and written within the guidelines of European composers in the late nineteenth-century nationalist style. Research revealed that Dvořák had only been inspired by the primal song of African Americans and had merely hinted at Black folk themes in his *New World Symphony*. Dawson, on the other hand, wanted to build his symphony entirely out of those themes and motives. Marva Carter related the story that when the Detroit Symphony Orchestra came to the Chicago World's Fair in 1933 to perform Dvorak's *Symphony No. 9 in E Minor*, "From the New World," William Dawson attended the concert. Yet, he was crushed when the commentator indicated that the work was based on Native American themes. Years later he retold his reaction in a recorded interview and recalled the wound incurred as a result of the announcer's remarks:

> And I cried and got up and walked out. That hurt me, because I knew; I know what's in the symphony. America doesn't know these folk songs, and I said to myself, "If I'm successful to complete a symphony based on the music of the 'Negro,' I'm going to title it, 'Negro Folk Symphony'—they can't remove that title."[92]

Dawson had studied many different styles of composition, including that of Schoenberg. The twelve-tone process of Schoenberg seemed to Dawson to be a cerebral, mathematical exercise and not at all the manner in which one could achieve an effective exposition and development of African American musical idioms; nor did he want to limit the power and excitement of Negro music to modern jazz settings. Instead, Dawson believed the rich, sonorous nineteenth-century romantic-symphonic style seemed best suited for his musical ideas.[93] As Jackson wrote, "Dawson also believed in the hierarchy of form from earthy folk expression to the classical orchestra, and that the leavening interventions of classical form were necessary to yield the highest return to raw Black folk material."[94]

Dawson completed his symphony in 1932 before the Tuskegee Choir sang for the opening of Radio City Music Hall. In the *American Business Survey* April 1933 review of the choir's performance at this opening, the writer mentioned Dawson's symphonic composition, stoking William Dawson's burgeoning musical reputation and providing a teaser for the 1934–35 concert season of the Philadelphia Symphony Orchestra. Tucked in between praise for the singers from Tuskegee, the author wrote that Dawson was not only director of a school of music and a preeminent writer and arranger of African American folk music but also a composer of symphonic works. The reporter for the *American Business Survey* went on to describe the great enthusiasm and praise for Dawson's symphony given by those who had the opportunity to hear excerpts. So much was the ballyhoo for the new work that the reporter announced Leopold Stokowski had promised to premiere the composition with the Philadelphia Symphony Orchestra in the following season, which the author considered the finest symphonic ensemble at the time.[95] The reporter, however, wrongly indicated that Dawson was the first Black composer to have ever written a symphony using African American music.[96] William Grant Still's *Symphony Number 1 in A-flat Major*, also known as *Afro-American Symphony*, was completed in 1930 and premiered in 1931 by the Rochester (New York) Philharmonic Orchestra with Howard Hanson conducting. Still's symphonic work utilized blues progressions and rhythmic idioms from popular African American music in the long-established symphonic format. Still utilized the twelve-bar blues progression in the first movement, chromatic chord progressions in a "spiritual" style in movement two, and motifs based on shouting "Hallelujah" in the third movement but eschewed a usual V-I chord progression in the final movement, choosing instead an F to D♭ interval resembling Dvořák's scoring in the *New World Symphony*. For each movement Still selected quotes from the works of Dunbar just as Cook had for use in the earliest African American musicals.[97] While both composers utilized organic Black cultural materials in creating extended musical compositions, Dawson's symphony, in contrast, used exact melodic excerpts from the folk music of Black Americans and drew more on the bond of African heritage. Dawson asserted that Still's *Afro-American Symphony* "was not based on the materials that I used."[98]

Dawson's work was entitled *Negro Folk Symphony* and was subtitled *The Missing Link*. Dawson, in interviews, explained his idea that "a link was taken out of a human chain when the first African was taken from the shores of his native land and sent into slavery." Hence, the first movement is called "The Bond of Africa." The missing link is represented by a motive played by the French horn, sounded in the introduction. This important musical idea recurs in the two successive movements and is the thread that unites the movements of the work. Of the two main themes in the opening movement, the first is original material, while the second is based on the Negro folk song "Oh, M' Lit'l' Soul Gwine-A Shine." The second movement, "Hope in the Night," uses various techniques to accomplish programmatic effects. For example, the movement opens with three gong strokes, suggesting the Christian concept of the holy Trinity—God the Father, Jesus the Son, and the Holy Spirit—which guides man's fate. A steady harmonic backdrop utilizing pizzicato strings depicts the wearisome life of slaves in bondage for over two centuries. Instrumental color and dynamics reflect the slaves' desire for freedom yet reinforce the helplessness of their plight. Tolling bells bring a mood of grief and lament that is followed by the return of three gong strokes and the dying away of the drums that sound a monotonous cadence. Two other Negro folk songs form the subjects for movement three, which is titled, "O Le' Me Shine!" The settings of the melodies, "O Le' Me Shine Lik' a Mornin' Star" and "Hallelujah, Lord, I Been down into the Sea" provide the delightful mirth that exudes from the finale.[99]

Dawson traveled to Philadelphia for the initial rehearsal of his symphony and successive preparation for the first hearing of his extended work. Stokowski broke with tradition and allowed Dawson to conduct the orchestra in the first exposure to the work, known in music circles as sight-reading. In other words, the musicians were playing the music for the first time, without having previously perused the written music notation. Dawson related his initial reaction to hearing an orchestral ensemble perform his composition.

> Mr. Stokowski rehearsed [the symphony] every day. The first rehearsal I was lost. It didn't sound like a thing, and I didn't know what was wrong. So, afterwards I went to Mr. Stokowski and I said, "I've done everything that I know and it doesn't sound like anything." So, he smiled and he said, "Here, have a drink of vodka and forget your troubles." He said, "That's why we always like for the composer to come in a day or so after we have rehearsed." So, the next morning, I went to the third balcony, as far away as I could, so that I could hide or get out. And, it sounded better. So, the next day I came down to the second balcony and it sounded even better. And then the third day [it was] like the sun was coming out and I got down on the first floor. I was willing to be seen then! And so that was my first experience. And to do something like this you score it for a 110-piece orchestra, then you extract the parts and you have them bound and hinged before you hear one note, and then it's put before the men. Now, if you have heard wrongly, then you see what you have done. You've wasted all of your money, all of your time, it doesn't sound like anything. So, the men in the Philadelphia Orchestra just fell in love with the work and the audiences, and they said we don't know where you learned it—but you learned it . . . it was a grand experience.[100]

The world premiere of Dawson's symphony took place on Wednesday evening, November 14, 1934, at the Academy of Music in Philadelphia. Just as the *American Business Survey* reviewer foreshadowed, the Philadelphia Symphony Orchestra performed the work, conducted by Leopold Stokowski.

Jackson indicated that the officials at Tuskegee Institute went "behind the scenes" to ensure the music was performed by a world-famous conductor and orchestra, thus gaining the limelight.[101] Others think that Tuskegee's meddling and maneuvering might have been meant to overshadow the earlier 1931 premiere of the William Grant Still work *Afro-American Symphony*, the first extended instrumental work by an African American. Jackson pointed out, however, that Stokowski was known to be a maverick, often selecting works of unknown composers around the globe to broaden the horizons of listeners. That Stokowski committed to programming the *Negro Folk Symphony* for the Philadelphia Orchestra was probably more than Dawson dreamed was possible. The symphony's debut garnered notoriety for Tuskegee Institute, and president Moton expressed his gratitude to Stokowski in a telegram, writing: "We send you a deep and heartfelt thanks."[102] For some, the debut represented a poignant moment for sharing African art with American symphony audiences, as "Stokowski told the press that Dawson had the ancient voice of Africa transferred to America."[103]

The audience received the music with such excitement that they broke with custom and applauded after each movement, although many say that it was Stokowski who, uncharacteristically, turned to bow after each movement. Others claim that Stokowski merely turned to graciously acknowledge the enthusiastic outburst of the concertgoers. When the last note of the symphony sounded, the crowd again broke into thunderous applause and cheering. Stokowski took bow after bow, eventually retreating into the wings of the stage and reappearing with Dawson. The Maestro shook hands with the young composer again and again to the continuous uproar of the audience. Stokowski, realizing the value of the work and its audience appeal, chose to play Dawson's symphony on the Philadelphia Symphony's weekly radio broadcast two days later. The regular concerts were broadcast nationwide over the CBS radio network. The symphonic work was repeated on the orchestra's Saturday evening concert.[104]

The *Negro Folk Symphony* had its New York debut in Carnegie Hall on Tuesday, November 20, 1934. The *New York Times* critic Olin Downes attended, and his review of the concert appeared the following morning. Downes related that Stokowski, who was fond of premiering new works, had programmed three compositions new to the New York audience for the concert presented that previous evening. American composer, Harl McDonald's first work, *The Santa Fe Trail*; American composer, William Dawson's *Negro Folk Symphony*; and Mexican composer, Manuel Ponce's *Chapultepec*; were heard before Ravel's *Spanish Symphony* completed the concert. The *Times* reporter noted that the audience saved its enthusiasm for Dawson's symphony and related that "the end of the concert saw a majority of them remaining to applaud long and lustily, and to call Mr. Dawson back to the stage several times."[105] While Downes criticized some of Dawson's handling of the melodic materials, he praised Dawson's treatment of folk melodies. He found the work too long and disparaged Dawson's use of canons, but he was impressed that the composer did not merely quote folk melodies but developed the motifs into a solid melodic line to produce a dramatic feeling. Within the melodic speech, the reviewer recognized a "racial sensuousness" within "barbaric turbulence."[106] In a review for the weekly magazine the *New Yorker*, Robert A. Simon also commented on Dawson's symphony. Simon was surprised by the reaction from the staid concertgoers whom he referred to as "lethargic luminaries" and "the gelid gang." Apparently, the music was so effective that the crowd began applauding prior to the final chords. He reduced some of the impact of the crowd's enthusiastic response, however, with an indication that the pre-applause had occurred in previous concert programs when the audience mistook noisy brass interjections for the finale. Levity aside, Robert Simon was impressed with Dawson's musicianship and creativity in combining aesthetic, cultural, and historical materials.

> Mr. Dawson, obviously an extraordinarily equipped musician, doesn't indulge himself in the self-consciousness which comes on most composers when they write with racial materials. His symphony is agreeably free from messages, lessons, and sermons. It is strangely enough, music in which well-defined themes are developed skillfully and the orchestra handled with complete assurance. When Mr. Dawson wants to be dramatic, as he is at the end of his second movement, he makes his point directly and sharply. When he wants a clangorous climax, he knows how to bring it off without abandoning himself to plain noise.[107]

Simon, like Downes, indicated a need for shoring up the symphony and related that Stokowski had even suggested a tightening of the score to Dawson. Simon's article finished with the opinion that, while contemporary intellectuals would possibly not embrace Dawson's work with passionate enthusiasm, there was a place for composers whose musical output was not solely intended to please and impress other composers. Readers were encouraged to take note of Dawson and to look for his further musical creativity. Dawson did continue to produce choral arrangements of original African American melodic material but did not go on to write many other extended instrumental works.[108]

In April 1935, a few short months after the Philadelphia Orchestra premiered the symphony, the Birmingham, Alabama Symphony Orchestra, just three years into operation, chose to perform Dawson's extended instrumental work.[109] Jackson called the symphony's decision a triumph in the time of Robert Moton's tenure as president at Tuskegee. "This was the kind of victory . . . that Tuskegee hoped to bring to the South—patient high-class mainstream excellence that was too prime to be ignored."[110]

The public, who either attended or heard about the performances of Dawson's *Negro Folk Symphony*, seemed to believe that the artistic work represented a step toward achieving racial equality through the composition of outstanding music by African Americans. Carter reported that reactions in the form of articles in the media, telegrams, and personal letters flooded Dawson with congratulations and praise. Herbert Hennagin, editor of the *Kansas City Herald*, recognized the immense personal achievement and asserted that Dawson's work had been a leap forward in promoting the cultural awakening of African Americans. While Edna Kalish, a musician from Baltimore, lamented that Black Americans had been free for only seventy short years, she marveled that Dawson had elevated his race artistically to new heights.[111]

Dawson continued to receive criticism for his particular style of composing intermingled with statements of praise for his symphonic work. Historian Hildred Roach related that Dawson felt the demand to justify his compositional style and to refute the claim that his work was merely an imitation of other composers. Imitation was not Dawson's intent in writing the *Negro Folk Symphony*. He wanted to use well-known and respected historical African American musical material within the established format of a symphony to honor the heritage and experiences of African Americans. At the time, Dawson replied to his critics that he was attempting to "be just myself, a Negro. To me, the finest compliment that could be paid my symphony, when it had its premiere, is that it unmistakably is not the work of a white man. I want the audience to say 'only a Negro could have written that.'"[112] Roach questioned why it is that other composers, such as Milhaud and Ravel, were not similarly called to defend their compositional style, noting that these musicians were free to write music in any chosen style. Despite negative reviews from some music critics, newspaper reporters, and musicians, no one could deny the enthusiastic response to and creativity of Dawson's symphonic work.[113] Indeed, the greater response to Dawson's symphony was quite positive. The composer related to the author of this book some of the comments he received, saying that "many thought it was 'delightful,'" and several thought it "made good use of Negro folk tunes and rhythms." Furthermore, one mentioned that Dawson's "orchestral scoring was artful and tasteful," and another thought "the work was imaginative and fresh."[114] Perhaps the greatest tribute following the *Negro Folk Symphony* premiere came not from a large metropolitan daily newspaper but from William Dawson's own hometown paper, the *Anniston Star*: "Dawson's triumph seems to verify a statement that repeatedly has been made by the *Anniston Star*—that the first genuinely great American music would be written by a Negro."[115] Their review underscores the beliefs of Dvořák, Krehbiel, and others concerning the roots or basic elements of a "national" music of the United States.

Yet others felt that by using white, Western compositional styles, Dawson—and other African American composers like him, such as Still, Burleigh, Hall Johnson, and Edward Boatner—was more interested in gaining personal recognition from white society than in authentically representing African music.[116] Author and intellectual Zora Neale Hurston criticized African American male composers for superficially infusing Black folk music within white musical forms.[117] In an angry letter to the president of Fisk University in 1934, Hurston took the African American composers to task, accusing them of taking quality organic Black cultural materials and converting them to substandard white music. All such efforts, it seemed to her, were done in hopes of being considered an "Artist" by white society.[118] Hurston was born in Macon County, Alabama, only eleven miles north of the county seat of Tuskegee in the small town of Notasulga. However, from the age of three, she was reared in Eatonville, Florida. Eatonville, in Orange County in the center of the state, was the first all-Black incorporated town in the United States, successfully pioneered and established by freedmen in 1887, where, ten years later, her father became mayor.[119] While Hall Johnson argued to Hurston that "the world was not ready for Negro music unless it was highly arranged," Hurston, who grew up in a town led by Black leaders and entrepreneurs, fiercely defended the sanctity of pure African American music.[120]

Others criticized the racial authenticity of Dawson's symphonic work, indicting him for intentionally striving to be like white composers and for leaning heavily on European masters. Lawrence Jackson reported that "Dawson . . . was accused of brushing lightly over Negro melodies with the giant white brush of Dvořák." The *Pittsburgh Courier*, for example, reported that "the symphony was reminiscent of Dvořák and other white composers' symphonies and that it appears well garbed in Caucasian dress."[121]

In rebuttal, Dawson maintained his position and the decision to use the compositional techniques of classical musicians. He proudly embraced his

African American heritage yet was also intrigued by and steeped in a musical education of European traditions. He proclaimed boldly:

> I believe in God as the father of mankind; I believe in my race; I believe in myself; I believe in humanity. I believe that a composer should write music which is a part of his spiritual and moral self rather than from those outside influences which are not a part of his own experiences.[122]

Dawson also defended the use of African American folk materials as the basis for expanded works of art that would "put [folk materials] on the world map," as Dvořák had done both with Bohemian/Czech motives. Dawson argued that even Dvořák had used Black folk material for the themes in the *New World Symphony*, exclaiming: "That is my language! It is the language of my ancestors, and my misfortune is that I was not born when that great writer came to America in search of material."[123] Ultimately, he challenged Black composers to "stop aping white writers and simply put forth the thing that rises within them without thinking of the popular reception it would receive."[124]

Yet despite the praise Dawson received, as well as the success in bringing his symphony to the South, Dawson did not go on to create more large, extended compositions. Jackson recognizes that "as early as his February 8, 1933, Carnegie Hall concert, his execution of the spirituals and his wielding of classical techniques turned into a site of bracing criticism and ... might have had something to do with difficulty in writing later major works."[125] Perhaps due to this critical climate, the *Negro Folk Symphony* was his only major work during his sixty-year sojourn in Tuskegee, and it premiered in the first five years of his employment at the institute there.[126]

DAWSON'S TRIP TO WEST AFRICA AND REVISIONS TO THE NEGRO FOLK SYMPHONY

Intent on authentically conveying the voice of Africa in his *Negro Folk Symphony*, William Dawson renewed his efforts to visit the western part of the continent. Since he was fourteen years old, he had been intrigued by Africa and could finally realize his dream to visit several countries in 1952. He set off for West Africa in November of that year to study indigenous folk music of individuals and tribes. Dawson asked Tuskegee for a sabbatical and remembers thinking, "If they didn't give it to me, I was going to quit my job and go to Africa."[127] Dawson took a portable reel-to-reel tape recorder with which to record African folk music. He explained:

> I had the first tape recorder that was made in America that was run by battery. I heard about it. I went to New York and had a show, and the company built the first one and sent it to me in Tuskegee and got there two weeks before I left. And so I went down in the woods, had some of the boys take drums, get a half a block away and beat them. I could pick it up.[128]

Armed with the new recording device, Dawson packed his bags and set off for the African continent. Ever one for detail, Dawson kept copious notes in a travel log, carefully documenting his experiences en route to and during his sojourn in Africa.[129]

In the mid-afternoon on Friday, November 14, 1952, William Dawson arrived at Idlewild Airport (now John F. Kennedy Airport) in New York City and boarded a Pan American Airways "Strato" Clipper to start his journey to Africa. Soon, he would realize his lifelong dream. The plane departed at 4:00 p.m. but got only as far as Cape Breton Island. Due to landing gear trouble, the plane had to return to New York. After changing to another aircraft, the passengers and crew set off a second time. The plane developed electrical difficulties causing the aircraft to return to Idlewild Airport once again for repairs. Following an hour delay on the ground, the flight took off and was able to complete the original flight plan.[130]

Dawson was impressed with the super-propeller, double-decked plane and must have quoted information located in the seat pocket: "The fastest, most luxurious air liner in the world. Service deluxe!!"[131] Indeed, the Boeing 377 Stratocruiser set new standards for long-range air travel that provided sleeping berths, room to get up and walk around, and an opportunity to take the spiral staircase to the lower floor to enjoy a drink in the lounge that could comfortably seat up to fourteen passengers. Early models were crafted around the B-29 bomber of World War II fame, but later aircraft more closely resembled B-50 Superfortresses. The new planes possessed the speed of the most recent bomber and added a pressurized cabin, which was new for commercial travel. Smoking was permitted during the flight.[132]

Dawson wrote, "Flying at 15,000 feet altitude," in the margin of his travel log soon after take-off but later penned, "Flying at 19,000 feet." The normal operating altitude of the Boeing 377 was between 15,000 and 25,000 feet, with a maximum of 33,000 feet. After a refueling stop in Shannon, Ireland, and a two-hour delay to repair the generator, the plane flew at 10,000 feet to reach London, England. Dawson commented, "Plane had 12 or more 'beds,' crew most polite, grand service, all sorts of 'nick-nacks,' drinks, good food."[133]

Sightseeing and concerts filled Dawson's four-days in London. He made two visits to Westminster Abbey, marveled at St. Paul's Cathedral, toured London Bridge, Tower Bridge, and the Tower of London, as well as the Old Curiosity Shop. However, he listed in great detail the November 16 program performed by the London Philharmonic in Royal Festival Hall, and the Vienna Philharmonic program performed in Royal Albert Hall on Monday, November 17. Twice during his London visit, Dawson noted that he wrote cards and a letter to "home folks and friends."[134]

Arriving at the London airport for a 10 a.m. flight to Paris on Wednesday, November 19, Dawson wrote, "Raining as usual!" As there were challenges in New York, the departure to Paris was delayed two hours, this time due to heavy snow in France. He noted that the passengers consisted mostly of tourists from Spain. Dawson related that one traveler was quite jolly and sang Spanish songs during the ride from the airport into central Paris. Despite the rain that replaced the snow during the ensuing days, Dawson enjoyed sightseeing and meals before attending High Mass at the Cathedral of Notre Dame on Sunday, November 23. Impressed, Dawson penned, "Music from the Choir and two organs was inspiring." That same evening, he attended a performance of *Samson et Dalila* by Camille Saint-Saens at the Grand Opera House, yet he seemed more awed by the edifice: "The interior of the building is grandeur and splendor personified."[135]

Two days later, Dawson attended a lecture-recital by Nadia Boulanger on Igor Stravinsky's music at the American Students and Artist Center located at 261 Boulevard Raspail. The virtuosic organist, noted conductor, and influential professor of composition was an admirer and friend of Russian composer Stravinsky during his sojourn in Paris that spanned the 1920s and 1930s.[136]

Dawson not only felt privileged to meet Boulanger after the performance but thrilled to meet for the first time as well her student Howard Swanson. Swanson, an African American born eight years after Dawson, encountered racial discrimination and a struggle for economic stability in early life. Yet he dedicated his life to always making music.[137] Continued sightseeing, shopping, Thanksgiving dinner with some American friends, a performance of the opera comique *Manon* by Jules Massenet, as well as the writing of more cards to family and friends dominated Dawson's time in Paris through Saturday evening.[138]

Forgoing the description of aircraft and altitude, Dawson reported his departure from Paris on Sunday, November 30, with brief stops in Bordeaux and Casablanca before arrival in Dakar, Senegal, the following morning at

7:30 a.m. Obviously, he got little sleep on the flight, as he indicated he took a three-hour nap upon arrival in the Hotel Terminus Sud. After two days of sightseeing, Dawson complained bitterly that Dakar was extremely expensive. "Inflation worse here than in Paris. Everything cost twice as much . . . 200 francs in Dakar worth 100 in Paris."[139]

Leaving Senegal at 7 a.m. on Thursday, December 4, Dawson traveled to Freetown, Sierra Leone arriving at 3:30 p.m., met by officials and faculty from Fourah Bay College. Later that afternoon, Dawson began recording music sung by students at the school that he termed "native and Creole songs." The call-and-response singing of the students was a cappella (without accompaniment) with harmonic choral singing evident. Much of the other music, however, contained highly rhythmic drum accompaniment and a soloist with a choir repeating an ostinato phrase. Over the next seven days, Dawson met tribal chiefs, heard concerts of local orchestra groups, experienced cultural dance demonstrations, discussed African drumming with experts, and attended services at King Memorial Evangelical United Brethren Mission.[140]

Traveling to Port Loko on Friday, December 12, Dawson recorded rhythmic drumming of indigenous instruments similar to tom drums and rattles. The polyrhythmic drumming seemed almost jazzlike in that instruments improvised over an accompaniment like a solo. Sightseeing, dinners with officials, and concerts at Fourah Bay College filled the following five days.

At 7:00 a.m. on Thursday, December 18, Dawson arrived at the Air France terminal to catch a flight to Robertsfield Airport, located just outside Monrovia, the capital of Liberia. Due to the late arrival of the flight, Dawson did not land until 3:00 p.m. Once in Monrovia, Dawson was met by the secretary of state, a member of the State Department of Education, and the president of the University of Liberia for an evening of dining and conversation. Following two days of sightseeing, Dawson ventured out from Monrovia on December 21 for a visit to the Suehn Industrial Academy and Mission to hear an entire morning of music of the Gola Tribe. Dawson was invited to speak during the midday church service, then, in the afternoon, continued listening to songs of the Gola and Bassa Tribes. He recorded and wrote down rhythmic and melodic lines. He also recorded several pieces presented by three singers and a drummer from the Krahn tribe and noted the unique style. In the evening, children from the academy performed for Dawson. He enjoyed their songs and dances: "One about the pencil that could write and write, and one about the monkey impressed me very much."[141]

As the days progressed toward Christmas Day and into January 1953, Dawson traveled to Suakoko, Gbarnga, Salala, Saniquellie, and other cities/villages. He listened to and recorded the music of members of many African tribes, including Vai, Mende, Gola, and Bassa, as well as students and individuals. Sounds he heard included: highly rhythmic drum accompaniment with a soloist and choir repeating ostinato phrases, call-and-response a cappella, verse/chorus singing, and choral singing in harmony, with hand clapping.[142] On New Year's Day, Dawson wrote that he "walked about the city of Monrovia listening to the various tribes sing and drum their music. The air was simply filled with music!"[143]

After spending a fortnight in Liberia, Dawson boarded a Pan American flight on January 10 at 2:00 a.m. bound for Accra, Gold Coast (now Ghana). The plane was to have departed at 9:30 a.m. the previous morning, but Dawson only wrote in his travel log, "Several hours late!" Because the flight arrived in the capital city at 5:30 a.m., Dawson went to the Lisbon Hotel, ate breakfast and waited for what he thought was an appropriate hour to make contact with his host at Achimota College, music professor Robert A. Kwami.[144] Dawson recorded performances at Achimota College on both January 13 and 15 that presented vocal solo singing without accompaniment as well as choral singing in harmony accompanied by polyrhythmic drumming and other unpitched percussion instruments.[145]

Having boarded a West Africa Airways flight, the "Ashanti Flyer," Dawson was off to Kumasi, Gold Coast, on January 16. There the guest of Ephraim Amu, head of the Music Department at the College of Technology, Dawson was treated to concerts of the college singers and percussionists that day and from the January 20–23. The choral singing was performed a cappella, with many sections that paired the two women's voices in alternation with the two men's voices, followed by an almost contrapuntal sharing of the melodic/rhythmic motive between SATB voices. The SATB choral performances revealed beautiful singing in harmony, yet the TTBB men's choir demonstrated rich, warm vocalization. One folk song was exceptionally impressive in mixed-meter (multiple meter signatures within the same composition), and the SATB arrangement of "Go and Sin No More" was much like a spiritual. On Sunday, January 25, Dawson visited with the Ewe dancers and learned of the importance of certain instruments to accompany the rhythm of their various dances.[146]

Despite holding a ticket on the January 29 Air France flight from Accra, Dawson's departure was delayed two days due to overbooking. After visiting the immigration office to request an extension to his stay in the country, he secured a reservation at the Lisbon Hotel in Accra. During his lengthened visit, he was witness to the funeral celebration of a paramount chief of the Gans tribe. During this elaborately expressive event, many dancers consisting of old and young women, men, and boys performed with approximately ten instrumental ensembles.[147]

Finally, on February 1, Dawson was aboard an Air France flight that stopped for an hour in Lome, French Togoland (now Togo), before continuing on to Cotonou, Dahomey (now Benin). That afternoon and the following day, Dawson recorded the dancing and singing of various local tribes. Of specific interest was the first song that began with a simple rhythmic accompaniment of sticks under a vocal solo of disjunct melodic movement with spoken comments from another vocalist. Successive songs contrasted with intricate polyrhythmic accompaniment of variously sized drums and other unpitched percussion instruments. Vocalizations were a mixture of conjunct and disjunct melodic contour, as well as call (solo) and response (harmony) with clapping.[148]

Again, an Air France flight took Dawson on to Lagos, Nigeria, on February 3. Due to a damaged microphone on his reel-to-reel tape recorder, he was precluded from further recordings until repairs could be completed, on February 9. Then he taped several selections by the Calabar Choral Party. Despite the few recordings in Nigeria, similarities can be made with the music captured on tape from the previous African countries.[149]

A week later, Dawson returned to Accra, Gold Coast (now Ghana). Over the next eight days, he met with various tribes, shopped, dined, and conferred with friends from Achimota College, as well as shipped home art objects and furniture. The final date under which Dawson detailed his activities is February 18. February 24, 1953, however, is the last date penned in the travel log. Dawson did not record the return date/time and flight information in the otherwise detailed account of his journey to the African continent.[150]

For the next thirty-seven years, William Dawson positively gushed when reminiscing about his visit to Africa. He commented that musical expressions could happen at any time of the day or night, and he sought to experience every note. Dawson was enthralled with the rhythm of West African music and recalled his enthusiasm nearly twenty years later: "You find these basic rhythms, and they're terrifically complex. . . . I just wish I could have gotten inside some of them who had come up in that culture to see how he looks at the world and how he feels. I have been reared in another culture, but that is an advantage."[151]

As a result of his research in Africa, and not at the urging of Leopold Stokowski and newspaper reviewers in 1934, Dawson rewrote several sections of the *Negro Folk Symphony*. Southern explained that Dawson hoped to "[infuse] it with the spirit of the African rhythms he had heard there."[152] More specifically, Dawson researcher/scholar Gwynne Kuhner Brown indicated, "He revised [the *Negro Folk Symphony*] following a 1952–53 research trip to six West African countries, particularly by giving a more prominent role to a slightly enlarged percussion section."[153]

Articles about William Dawson in the *New Grove Dictionary of Music and Musicians*, *The International Dictionary of Black Composers*, and other sources indicate that the revision of Dawson's symphony was completed in 1952.[154] However, noting the busy schedule of activities the composer reported in his detailed Africa travel log, and the fact that he was actually an ethnomusicologist in his zeal to experience Trans-African music and dance over a three-month sojourn on the continent, it seems highly unlikely that the revision of his symphony occurred in 1952. Dawson's revised *Negro Folk Symphony* was probably completed in late 1953 or even later.

Eager to let the world hear the new rhythmic energy, Dawson again sought a conductor and once again secured the talents of Stokowski. Dawson's rescored symphony was the first work recorded in June 1963 by the American Symphony Orchestra, founded a year earlier by Stokowski. The new ensemble soon established itself as a rival to the New York Philharmonic Orchestra. Showing a deep interest in works by contemporary composers, Stokowski stirred public interest in many American composers, especially Charles Ives. It is no wonder, then, that the maestro agreed to record Dawson's revised *Negro Folk Symphony* only a year after the orchestra was organized. Stokowski was so enamored with the work that he wrote:

> Dawson has succeeded in portraying the aspect of American life which is both vital and personal. I believe this work to be a distinct achievement in American music. He has voiced the spirit of his people struggling in a new land; the ancient voice of Africa transferred to America and here expressed through the medium of the white man's most highly developed instrument, the symphony orchestra.[155]

Since its premiere, the *Negro Folk Symphony* has been performed in many cities throughout the nation by symphonic groups made of amateurs and professionals alike. Dawson's symphony has also been recorded by several well-known orchestras. The 1992 recording by the Detroit Symphony Orchestra was possibly the last for nearly thirty years. In June 2020 the ORF Vienna Radio Symphony Orchestra released a new recording of the *Negro Folk Symphony* that garnered early plaudits. Tom Huizenga, in a review for National Public Radio, indicated that the performance "has plenty of elegance and fire." Huizenga also offered insight into the reasons the symphony might not have more performances, revealing that there never seemed to be enough copies of the score and that some individual parts were not correct. He recommends that a worthwhile project for a willing publisher would be to correct and reprint the symphony so that it might be more widely performed.[156]

Carter contends that the most logical reason the *Negro Folk Symphony* has not been performed with regularity in the years since its premiere is that it contains the term "Negro" in its title.[157] Conversely, William Grant Still's *Afro-American Symphony* is more widely performed.[158]

William Dawson received a commission from the Columbia Broadcasting System (CBS) in 1940 to compose an orchestral work that would be featured on the radio program "American School of the Air." The piece Dawson wrote was entitled *A Negro Work Song*, and its premiere performance was aired over the CBS radio network on February 20.[159] Dawson indicated that the piece was based on the folksong "Stewball," and included the melodic notation and lyrics on the front cover of the manuscript. According to folklore, the racehorse Stewball was born in "Californy," but all the jockeys swore he flew there in a storm.[160] In a discussion of the work, Brown lamented the brevity of the piece but lauded the display of creativity:

> Although the piece ends somewhat abruptly after four and a half minutes, (doubtless due to the commission's specifications), it is thematically distinctive and appealingly orchestrated. Interestingly, its harmonic language owes more to jazz than that of any of Dawson's other works.[161]

The piece is scored for piccolo, two flutes, two B♭ clarinets, two oboes, English horn, two bassoons, three horns, three trumpets, three trombones, tuba, timpani, cymbals, side drum, violins, violas, violoncellos, and basses, and calls for a cello solo.[162]

Two years later, on March 6, the CBS Orchestra broadcast another performance of the work, conducted by Bernard Herrmann. The work was performed subsequently in Virginia by the Richmond Symphony Orchestra and in Alabama by the Birmingham Symphony Orchestra in 1951 and 1952, respectively. In 1954 *A Negro Work Song* was chosen to be performed at the American Music Symposium, held at the University of Virginia, Charlottesville. William Haaker conducted the Virginia Symphony Orchestra in the concert.[163]

DAWSON'S CONTINUED CAREER AS
CHORAL ARRANGER AND COMPOSER

Following *A Negro Work Song* in 1940, Dawson's compositional output was largely choral works. In her volume about Black American music, Roach questioned Dawson's apparent withdrawal from the composition of extended musical forms but did not venture a full explanation. While he did write music for full orchestra, chamber ensembles, trios, piano, and other solo instruments, Roach notes that the majority of Dawson's compositional output was choral and that his was "generally of the Romantic style, using tonal centers, various overlapping and syncopated rhythms."[164] One obvious reason for his focus on choral music may have been that his administrative duties at Tuskegee allowed him time only to conduct the choir. Although he taught courses in composition and orchestration, worked with the instrumental conductors, and conducted choral works with orchestral groups, he was involved mainly with choral ensembles.

As Dawson commenced his tenure as director of the School of Music, he took advantage of the steam press available at Tuskegee Institute as a part of its industrial training program. When G. Schirmer, a well-known and well-respected publisher, rejected Dawson's arrangements of spirituals submitted for publication, he was not dismayed or angry but determined to succeed. Dawson's friend John Haberlen elucidated that the composer's eventual solution to publishing choral works was to establish his own press. Beginning in the 1930s, the Tuskegee Press hired an engraver from New York and utilized the steam press at the institute to print Dawson's music. By taking control of the publishing end of the business, Dawson sent a message to other composers to publish and copyright their own music creations and in so doing increase personal profit to nearly half the proceeds in lieu of the meagre 10 percent offered by publishers. Dawson would secure a copyright for a choral arrangement and then have copies of the music printed by the steam press.[165]

The Tuskegee Choir Series was born in 1934 with the publication of "Oh, What a Beautiful City." Commemorating their first concert tour to New York City to open Radio City Music Hall in 1932–33, Dawson dedicated the arrangement "to the Tuskegee Choir and their patron, Mr. S. L. Rothafel (Roxy), at Radio City, N.Y." and set the piece for unaccompanied voices. Dawson also had the choir perform the work on the 1933 Carnegie Hall recital.[166] "Soon Ah Will Be Done" was written during Dawson's first year at Tuskegee and performed in a concert to commemorate the fiftieth anniversary of the founding of Tuskegee Institute, in April of 1931. The piece was also sung by the Tuskegee Choir in a 1933 White House concert for President Herbert

Hoover. Arranged for a cappella choirs of mixed and men's voices, "Soon Ah Will Be Done" was finally published in 1934 and is still quite popular.[167] The only arrangement copyrighted in 1937, "Ain-a That Good News," was an a cappella number for mixed, men's, and women's voices, and was dedicated by William Dawson "To my Friend Dr. Robert Russa Moton, President Emeritus, Tuskegee Institute." "Ain-a That Good News," was selected for performance at an American Composers Concert given at Eastman School of Music in 1941.[168] Dawson set and copyrighted the familiar "There Is a Balm in Gilead" in 1939 and dedicated it to Dr. G. Lake Imes, an administrator at Tuskegee Institute and Dawson's close friend. The settings are for unaccompanied mixed, men's, and women's voices.[169] Dawson's arrangement for mixed voices has the distinction of being one of the two African American spirituals found in W. W. Norton Company's 1978 edition of *Choral Music*. The other work, "Listen to the Lambs," was arranged by Robert Nathaniel Dett and was part of the Tuskegee Choir's repertoire.[170]

Dawson added two Negro folk song settings to the Tuskegee Choir Series in 1942: "Steal Away"[171] and "Ezekiel Saw de Wheel."[172] "Steal Away" is the better known of the two folk tunes, but Dawson's "Ezekiel" has been more widely performed. Dedicated to Dr. John Finley Williamson and the Westminster Choir in Princeton, New Jersey, "Ezekiel" is an exciting setting that begins with a simple statement of the melody, quickly followed by a rich harmonization of the theme, which is sung by four-part men's voices. The women then enter for a brief development of the main idea. After a tenor soloist sings two verses, the refrain is heard again. This time, a group of four altos, two first tenors, and two baritones sing an ostinato accompaniment on the syllables "doom-a-looma," and "wheel-in-a," creating a marvelous effect of a turning wheel, gyrating underneath the melody. The piece ends up on a rousing B♭ chord, with the first tenors on a "G," providing a touch of dissonance for an exciting finish.

Dawson's unique choices for "Ezekiel" were influenced by his rich experience with a variety of African American music, including what he heard and created during his time on the Chautauqua circuit. Longtime Dawson friend Haberlen related Dawson's explanation of the specific origin of the "dooma-looma" syllabic idea. While touring in the northern United States on the Chautauqua Circuit between 1918 and 1921 with the Tuskegee Quintette, the members of the ensemble would invent melodic and textual rhythmic motifs they would insert into their performances as they went along the circuit. "Dooma-looma" was created during one of these journeys.[173] Repetitive circular background chants were documented as early as 1863 in which "one singer would rapidly repeat a phrase underneath the main melody."[174]

Furthermore, African American male quartets in Alabama, especially the Blue Jays in the 1920s, regularly employed ostinato phrases in which "the group does not respond to the leader . . . but maintains an independent undersong, the primary function of which is to sustain and propel the rhythm."[175] By the 1940s the background chant came to be known as "vocal percussion."[176] Dawson creatively blended these elements—group improvisations from his past, vocal percussion, ostinato phrases—to compose the rhythmically complex "Ezekiel."

Dawson published four new vocal arrangements in 1946, making it a memorable year. The first piece, "Behold the Star," is a Christmas setting employing mixed chorus, soprano and tenor solos, as well as echo chorus. The soprano soloist sings the first two verses supported by the choir. The tenor soloist sings his part from off-stage above the choir's hum. This is answered by an abrupt tempo and dynamic change with "Allelujah, Behold the Star!" The last fourteen measures of the arrangement are sung by twelve voices, just off-stage.[177] The second setting, "Hail Mary!" is arranged for mixed and men's voices and is dedicated to Allen Irvine McHose.[178] McHose was professor of music theory at Eastman School of Music in Rochester, New York, from 1931 until 1962, and was the author of books on the counterpoint of eighteenth- and nineteenth-century composition, as well as sight-singing and melodic dictation. One can easily understand Dawson's choice of dedication, given his penchant for counterpoint. The third song that emerged in 1946 is probably the most familiar of all the folk songs of African Americans: "Swing Low, Sweet Chariot." Dawson first set the well-known melody for mixed and men's voices, then wrote an arrangement for women's voices that was copyrighted in 1949.[179] "Ev'ry Time I Feel the Spirit," another lively tune, was also set for all three voicings in 1946.[180]

Dawson wrote and published an especially sensitive setting of "Mary Had a Baby" in 1947. The edition for mixed voices[181] includes a beautiful soprano solo. This popular arrangement bears a dedication to noted conductor and arranger Robert Shaw.[182] "Little Boy Chile," describing the birth of Christ, was also published in 1947 for mixed voices.[183] "There's a Lit'l Wheel A-Turnin' in My Heart" is an animated setting for unaccompanied mixed voices that was printed in 1949.[184]

Dawson's 1952–53 trip to West Africa influenced his subsequent publications. In 1955 the Tuskegee Institute Press published Dawson's SATB rendition of a rhythmic song "Adawura B Me" by Ephraim Amu, head of the music department at the College of Technology in Kumasi, Gold Coast (now Ghana). Serving only as editor for the piece, which was also included in the Tuskegee Choir Series, Dawson indicated on the introductory page that a translation of the title means "The Gong Gong says beat me." A Gong is a rhythm instrument important in West African music. The highly rhythmic a cappella piece begins with staggered entrances of the four voices, much like counterpoint, with passages that are polyrhythmic. Dawson explains that the work "sets forth graphically an onomatopoetic effect of the *Adawura* and the small *Mmremma* drum when they are beaten together simultaneously in an African ensemble."[185] Though published by Remick in 1955, the piece does not appear to have been printed again. However, one copy resides with Dawson's papers in the Emory University archives.

Following his resignation from Tuskegee Institute in 1955, Dawson sought to have his works published by an established commercial music publisher. He contracted with the Neil A. Kjos Company to continue publishing the Tuskegee Choir Series. The Kjos Company became the sole selling agent for all Dawson choral works that were originally published by the Music Press at Tuskegee Institute. Even after his retirement, Dawson continued to compose and arrange choral works. While most compositions were new works, several of the subsequent Kjos publications were Dawson's older settings of Negro folk songs. "I Wan' to Be Ready," though published in 1967, was one of the pieces the Tuskegee Choir recorded in 1955. This spirited arrangement was dedicated to Dawson's second wife, Cecile.[186] "Zion's Walls," published in 1961 by Kjos for mixed voices and soprano solos, utilizes the repetitive phrase "God's gonna build up Zion's walls."[187] Dawson's revised version of "The Mongrel Yank" was published in 1970 by Kjos Music Company under a new title, "The Rugged Yank."[188] Using the repetitive, accented recurring phrase "ka-o, ka-o, ka-o" Dawson wrote "In His Care-O" and published the piece in 1961 for mixed and male voicings. "Feed-A My Sheep," set for mixed, men's and women's voices, was published by Kjos in 1971. "Slumber Song" published in 1974 is set for four voicings: SATB, TTBB, SSA, and SA.[189] Some of Dawson's later works were arrangements of pieces outside the Negro folk song genre. In 1968, for example, he arranged the "Pilgrim's Chorus" from Richard Wagner's opera *Tannhäuser* for men's voices.[190] One of Dawson's last arrangements is a setting of the familiar tune "Londonderry Air." He selected the sensitive words of Edith Sanford Tillotson's poem "Before the Sun Goes Down."[191] Along with publishing new works, Dawson continued to rewrite and maintain copyrights of his earlier compositions throughout his final days.

In addition to the works listed above, archival research revealed the existence of quite a few unpublished manuscripts, most of which can be found among Dawson's papers in the Stuart A. Rose Archives and Rare Book Library at Emory University in Atlanta, Georgia. Five compositions not yet published and possibly unknown to musicians and scholars are mentioned here.[192]

First among these unknown compositions is a special choral arrangement of a spiritual Dawson called "Hallelujah" for the concert celebrating the Tuskegee Institute's fiftieth-anniversary Jubilee in April of 1931. The piece was performed by the Tuskegee Choir but was never published, yet a complete manuscript of the work is available in the Emory archives. The program notes indicate:

> The work, written for this occasion is based on a familiar "spiritual." It is designed for choral uses and is given a formalized treatment to make it suitable for any occasion where the mood of jubilant elation is to be expressed. The words of the chorus are a formalized version of the original sentiment in language long familiar to Negro congregations. The work is given its first public rendition tonight.[193]

The text was written by G. Lake Imes, who served in many administrative roles at Tuskegee Institute during his tenure at the school.[194]

The second of the unpublished works, without a surviving manuscript, is also an arrangement of a spiritual. Dawson composed "Seeking for the City" for the on-campus concert that originated from the Tuskegee chapel to honor the issuance of the Booker T. Washington stamp in April of 1940. The Tuskegee Choir sang "Seeking for the City" during the commemoration festivities that were broadcast over the NBC radio network.[195] Uncharacteristically of the usually meticulous composer who kept myriad copies of correspondence and multiple copies of his published music, a copy of the work could not be found in either the Emory or Tuskegee archives.

Dawson's only solo work for piano and orchestra, titled "Interlude," is described in detail by Strong in the *International Dictionary of Black Composers*. The five-minute work for keyboard is romantic in style in three movements. While Strong does not expound on the orchestral accompaniment, copies of both the piano part and orchestral score can be found among Dawson's papers in the Rose Archives at Emory University.[196] The symphonic accompaniment is scored for two flutes, two oboes, two bassoons, four horns, three trumpets, three trombones, tuba, timpani, cymbals, bells, violin, viola, cello, double bass.[197]

The piece "Break, Break, Break" by Dawson is missing from his published oeuvre to date. Soon after William Dawson's ninetieth-birthday celebration on campus in 1989, Dan Williams, archivist in the Hollis Burke Frissell Library at Tuskegee University, included a photocopy of this unknown choral work as a part of a packet he sent to the author of this book. The work, whose text is a poem by Alfred Lord Tennyson of the same title, is for mixed chorus, tenor and bass soloists, and includes organ and piano accompaniment (the piece is also scored for orchestra). The manuscript is in Dawson's own handwriting with an Opus No. 4 marking underneath his name as composer, yet no specific date of composition is written. The emotional poem explores themes of loss, the fleeting nature of life, and the inability to retrieve happiness of previous days. In Tennyson's case, the passing of Arthur Hallam, a good friend, inspired the verse, which causes one to contemplate the loss in Dawson's life that may have prompted the musical setting of the stanzas. Dawson had lost his mentor, Booker T. Washington, his first wife, Cornella, and his parents, along with others. Yet the manuscript gives few clues as to the significance of the words to Dawson.[198] While the tempo alternates from slow to allegro consistently throughout, the piece begins marked *Grave*, and the manuscript bears Dawson's own penciled-in settings for the great, swell, and choir, as well as a dynamic marking of *fortissimo* in the pedals. Throughout the piece the voices occasionally enter in canonic fashion; there are instances of men singing together followed by women singing as a duet, and the tenor and bass soloists take turns. The tenor's role, however, is far more important. In typical Dawson compositional tradition, the dynamics and tempo are carefully marked with precise effects using both horizontal and vertical accents with an indication for a sforzando in several places. At the key change in the middle of the work, marked *pianissimo*, Dawson indicates the voices should be *sotto voce* and further adds "in an undertone" in parentheses. Symphonic scoring for the work includes piccolo, flute, two oboes, two clarinets in B♭, two bassoons, three horns, two trumpets, three trombones, violins, violas, cello, and bass.[199]

The recent discovery of an undated manuscript entitled "Oppression" for small orchestra in one movement, located among Dawson's papers at Emory University, might provide a slight answer to the questions that continue to arise as to why Dawson did not continue to produce extended symphonic compositions. He did, in fact, write several unpublished and unknown works for orchestra. "Oppression" is scored for two flutes, two oboes, English horn, two B-flat clarinets, bass clarinet, two bassoons, four horns, two trumpets, three trombones, tuba, timpani, chimes, gong, cymbals, four harps, two first violins, two second violins, two violas, cello, and bass.[200]

Dawson's final published composition appears to be "Dorabella," in 1981 by the Kjos Music Company. Dawson said the piece for male voices was: "Written as an especial tribute to Bruce Montgomery for his twenty-five years as director of the University of Pennsylvania Glee Club."[201] Following the premiere of the piece a year earlier, Staff Writer for the *Philadelphia*

Inquirer, Samuel L. Singer, wrote an article celebrating Montgomery's work and the piece written in his honor.

> Montgomery, truly a Renaissance man as conductor, composer, librettist and singer with many stage credits, received tributes from Gov. Thornburgh and a host of others. Not the least of the honors was the world premiere of "Dorabella," written for the occasion by American composer William L. Dawson.
>
> The glee club had offered to commission the work from Dawson, but the Composer instead made it a gift, out of friendship for Montgomery, and even paid his own way from Alabama. "Dorabella: is a humorous work, to a poem Dawson wrote, about married life, from "her pumpkin pie, and the apple of her eye" to "bread and butter." With piano accompaniment, it is a rather demanding work that the glee club sang with spirit and flexibility under the composer's direction.[202]

Columnist Samuel Singer had previously reviewed a concert by the Tuskegee Choir under Dawson's direction with an article that appeared in the *Philadelphia Inquirer*, May 29, 1946.

Other musical sketches, arrangements, and compositional fragments for voices and instruments by the composer exist in the William Dawson papers housed in the Rose Archives at Emory University. A list can be found in Appendix A.

Throughout a life span of ninety years, William Dawson did compose works that were not related to or based on Negro folk songs. Yet the major thrust of his compositional creativity was a manifestation of his pride in his African American heritage. Despite Jim Crow laws that firmly established barriers of racial discrimination through segregation, social injustice, and terrorism, Dawson remained committed to reach his goal of becoming a musician and composer. In final confirmation of the manifestation of Dawson's strong racial pride, K. Robert Schwarz, research assistant at the Institute for Studies in American Music at Brooklyn College, wrote on May 2, 1990, just seventeen days before the composer's death, "When viewed from today's perspective, composers like Dett, Price, Still, and Dawson cannot help but appear heroic. They fought back against the racism of their country, and of their chosen profession, and time has been their vindication."[203]

Chapter 5

DAWSON THE PEDAGOGUE

1921–90

DAWSON THE TEACHER

One of William Dawson's most prominent traits was his relentless desire for education. From his initial choice to run away from home to pursue education at Tuskegee Institute, to his graduate work in music, to his trip to West Africa for self-study of indigenous musical traditions, his quest for learning was a lifelong driving force. His beliefs about the awarding of academic degrees reflect Dawson's attitude about learning. Many graduates, as well as those who leave school prior to the completion of a program or degree, assume an attitude of finality and close the door on further learning. Yet Dawson held that "there is no such thing as a dropout!" Despite one's exit from formal educational institutions, learning does not cease; rather, life itself is an ongoing process of education, and one's experiences and encounters continuously add valuable knowledge and allow one to evolve and grow. Dawson's own continued search for knowledge afforded him opportunities not only to develop his musical skills but also to equip him to teach others. He believed that it is not possible to "teach teachers to teach." Rather, a person becomes equipped to teach others only by engaging in a wide variety of learning opportunities. Therefore, he held that prospective teachers, especially those in music, need rich experiences working with music in many different ways.[1]

This belief reflected Dawson's own educational and pedagogical trajectory. Not only had he studied the theoretical aspects of music at Tuskegee and other institutions, but he added to his knowledge of vocal repertoire by studying voice and singing in the choir. He broadened knowledge of orchestral music by studying each instrument individually. He also composed, arranged, and conducted the Tuskegee Band. Some of his most rewarding musical growth was achieved through singing with the Tuskegee Quintette, an ensemble of five men. Ensemble singing provides strength to all participants, as each member contributes an important part of every chord that is formed. Further, the students gain invaluable experience rehearsing and performing a wide variety of music in a small ensemble. This practical preparation, he believed, is necessary for those who wish to teach music. Just as each music student in college is required to study applied music, where concepts of music are directly associated with one's own instrument, the music education major should have many choral experiences, including small ensemble participation where musical concepts can be applied firsthand. Students, then, can learn all facets of choral tone in a small ensemble.[2]

Through his experience conducting numerous school, church, and community ensembles, Dawson came to believe that: "The conductor is everything!" The conductor, he asserts, is responsible for every activity in which the group engages. He believed that from deportment to diction, from intonation to interlude, the director molds the group to personally preconceived specifications. Continuous study of musical styles, coupled with experience in choral groups, which applies that knowledge in actual performance, is vital in preparation for conducting. The effective conductor, according to Dawson, also needs to be able to give a personal example, when necessary, during the rehearsal period. An accurate model is frequently more helpful than excessive explanation. In order to demonstrate vocally and to shape choral sound carefully by instructing students on proper breath management and good vocal production, prospective choral conductors need extensive voice study. Much of the learning about how to conduct must occur individually, as "the conductor must grow himself." Dawson also said, "The best thing is to perform under a good conductor." Experience with a variety of conductors provides opportunity for building an eclectic philosophy of conducting.[3]

Dawson's extensive experience led to the development of his personal choral pedagogy, which has two main features: the teaching of sight-singing and the use of dynamic rehearsal strategies. Both features were born out of his emphasis on accuracy. Clyde Owen Jackson was a choir member and student at Tuskegee Institute, beginning in 1945. Jackson recalls, "Dawson insisted on accuracy. He was like that in everything. He was neat. You couldn't come in late to a rehearsal because he would lock the door. He would give written exams on music."[4] Dawson rarely refused chorus participation to anyone who had limited or nonexistent sight-reading skills. He endeavored both to teach those who could not sing at sight and to strengthen those who demonstrated that skill. Every member of the chorus was required to bring a "harmony pad" to rehearsals, a small blank booklet. Students wrote pitches in the notebook and sang intervals, as sight and sound were paired in the teaching process. Students were also required to write and sing all major and minor scales. Through the emphasis on sight-reading skills development, Dawson was working to make each person an independent singer. He also weaned his singers from having a strong dependence on the piano. In this way students became confident independent singers, capable of producing fine intervallic and intonational discrimination. Jackson attested to the emphasis on sight-reading skills, as well as Dawson's disciplined approach to music. He explained that "once you passed sight-singing, you got a letter to put on your sweater, just like athletes."[5]

Yet Dawson's students did more than "just sing!" Because of his unique approach to the rehearsal time, each singer learned that they were an integral part of the ensemble, which required them to attentively listen to and think about the music. A choral rehearsal period was viewed as a time to work for creation rather than recreation. Because Dawson was interested in having the students learn as much as possible about music, he worked to keep every choir member alert during rehearsals. While working with a particular section, Dawson encouraged other voice parts to compare the section being sung with their individual parts. Students would listen for phrases, harmonic modulation, cadential effect, canon, programmatic writing, and other structural aspects of the piece being studied. It was not uncommon for Dawson to call on individuals to report on what they had heard while he was attending to a choral challenge. Not only was this approach good for maintaining classroom management, it disciplined the students to be constantly attuned to what was occurring in the music. Total engagement sharpened their aural skills considerably, helping students to grow musically as well as vocally. One portion of each rehearsal was devoted to vocal production and dynamic contrasts. In addition to focused work toward vocal development in the warm-up period, students were taught to interpret dynamic markings. Much of Dawson's choral music contains intense dynamic contrasts that are similar to an orchestrally derived effect, thus considerable time in rehearsal was spent on dynamics.[6]

Often looked upon as a strong disciplinarian and a hard taskmaster, Dawson demanded the best from others and drove himself mercilessly. Of the many of us who knew and worked with him, perhaps Robert O'Meally, literary scholar and expert on the life and work of Ralph Ellison, best describes Dawson's teaching style: "I was always aware of Dawson's presence as a very demanding artist; one very demanding of himself and others, and very aware, too, of his role as a teacher."[7] O'Meally's description of Dawson reveals an aggressive martinet whose teaching was based on a model most people today would call "old-fashioned." While the teaching style seemed dominated by fierce gruffness, the ultimate intent was not to be adversarial toward the pupils but to alert the students that the instructor cared deeply for the learners, hoping that the final product of their efforts would be the "perfectability of mankind . . . at least when it comes to the arts."[8] O'Meally explained that Dawson would often throw objects at students just to underline his point.[9] Ellison frequently referred to the "discipline of the artist," something he, as a student, learned under William Dawson's tutelage. Acknowledging Dawson as an authoritarian did not detract from the man's influence and effect. In fact, Ellison praised Dawson by saying, "Through his dedication to art, he has made it possible for me to be as dedicated and disciplined about literature."[10] Dawson taught the arts through attention to discipline, the dogged, relentless pursuit of perfection of aesthetic skills through the repeated practice of fundamentals. Again, pointing to Dawson's aura as a disciplinarian, Ellison evoked the image of someone who would "take you to the woodshed."[11] O'Meally related that Dawson didn't intend the woodshed as a place of punishment, but rather, a place to instill the discipline of striving for artistic excellence through breaking down a passage to build mastery through repetition.[12]

Dawson applied the same high standards to himself as he did his students. Nephew Milton Randolph Jr. notes that Dawson was highly disciplined, not only physically by rising each morning to perform deep knee bends and push-ups but also mentally through continuing to study and learn each day. Artistically, Dawson never seeming quite satisfied with his own creativity and sought to continually perfect his output. In so living his life, William Dawson also sought to instill this mind-set in those with whom he came in contact and to encourage creative expression.[13] Dawson's tenacity to reach perfection through choral performance by means of tyrannical teaching was evidenced by taunting jibes hurled at singers. John Haberlen relates quotes made by Dawson during rehearsals of the composer's own works. As a demanding conductor he could be intimidating if one didn't realize his ulterior motive was to lead the choir to create art within a time frame. If too many singers were looking at their music instead of watching him, he would utter, "Don't look at the notes, they're just notes, you know. Make music with me!"[14] The polyrhythmic intricacies of Dawson's composition "Ezekiel Saw de Wheel" often presented a challenge for choirs. In several rehearsals he admonished choir members with the barb, "Don't pat your foot, you disturb my rhythm!"[15] And if a particular choral ensemble was not performing up to par, Dawson would upbraid the group with, "Music is my food, don't poison me with your bad performance!"[16]

Dawson never seemed quite satisfied with performances of his works by others and would often take a choir to the "woodshed" to provide the discipline needed to achieve success. At the Inaugural Mississippi ACDA State Convention in April of 1986, for which William Dawson was the invited "headliner," he caught the Long Beach, Mississippi, High School Choir coming off stage following the performance of one of his spirituals and took them to the choir room to further "school" them concerning his artistic intentions. Dawson's purpose was to prepare the young for leadership in their life and time. Regardless of the current social and political climate, Dawson adamantly, relentlessly, and effectively strove to enable students to experience perfection in the arts.[17] O'Meally insisted that "Dawson intended to have it. He would pull excellence out of you!" The passage from Ralph Ellison's *Invisible Man* that declares, "The things that hurt you helped you," may have referenced William Dawson. As a teacher, he would go to great lengths to help students.[18]

Despite his gruffness, as a teacher Dawson was always interested in the educational growth of his students. He welcomed any student who came to him in search of musical education, honoring and remembering teachers from his past, such as Regina Hall, who had reached out to help in his own quest for learning. He challenged the students to learn and to be the best they could be by setting unwavering student goals with clear, high standards. Dawson firmly believed that it was satisfying to achieve a goal in part because of its universality; students proved to themselves that they were able to meet a standard that existed for all, not just a chosen few. He felt no qualms about giving a student a grade of "incomplete." Dawson did not care if it took a student two months or two years; he kept working with that student to achieve the established learning goal. Unskilled students were placed in special groups for extra help. Dawson found that in working with these students, the most effective learning assessment was derived through conscientious teacher observation. His continual observations led to analysis of student problems and eventual progress, which enabled William Dawson to become an effective and outstanding music educator.[19]

DAWSON THE CONDUCTOR "IN DEMAND"

Dawson eventually gained national recognition for his composing and conducting from the fame of the Tuskegee Choir and the success of his major symphonic work, the *Negro Folk* Symphony, debuted by Leopold Stokowski and the Philadelphia Orchestra. This notoriety led many to extend invitations to Dawson asking him to conduct ensembles and adjudicate music festivals and competitions. As early as 1939, Dawson was invited to be guest conductor for a state high school honors choral clinic featuring his choral works. This first invitation was to direct the Oklahoma All-State High School Chorus in Tulsa. Dawson was not able to accept many of these guest-conducting appearances in the 1930s and 1940s due to his duties at Tuskegee Institute and his concert journeys with the Tuskegee Choir. As a result, he was not able to accept a second invitation until early December of 1946. The subsequent guest-conducting opportunity was a unique opportunity for Dawson, because the chorus was composed of choral directors from the state of New York School Music Association. The group rehearsed for three days and sang in a concert as a special feature of the convention held at the Eastman School of Music in Rochester.

In April 1948 Dawson was guest conductor and adjudicator for the North Carolina State Choral Contest and Festival in Durham. A year later, on April 22, Dawson appeared as guest conductor for the Kentucky All-State Chorus in Louisville. A month later Dawson conducted the combined junior and senior high school choirs of Schenectady, New York, in the program entitled, "Music for Unity," which was the title of the annual music festival. Three years later he was asked to return to Schenectady for the Music in Unity event, this time to conduct a choir of five hundred voices. On May Day, 1955, just prior to his resignation at Tuskegee, Dawson again accepted an invitation to Schenectady.[20]

A year following his retirement from the institute, Dawson was selected by the State Department of the United States government to serve as a cultural emissary to Spain. There, he spent July, August, and September of 1956 conducting choirs and presenting choral clinics. The goals of the trip were explained in an unclassified report from the American Embassy in Madrid by Antonio Gonzales de la Peña, who was Dawson's host. The overriding aim of Dawson's journey to Spain was cultural exchange. The second aim of William Dawson's sojourn in Spain was to visit cultural arts centers to make political and arts connections to promote cultural understanding and sharing. Peña expressed a desire for Spaniards to learn of the beauty and meaning of African American spirituals and for Dawson to promote and share the genius of Spanish composers, most specifically, Tomás Luis de Victoria. Of special interest was the opportunity for a native American composer of color to share the interpretation of his own personal choral compositions through rehearsal and performance in the cathedrals of Spain.[21] Dawson indicated that the plan for the concerts in Spain was to divide the program into two parts; the first part featured the choral music of Victoria and very specifically and carefully stated that the second part was "devoted to the religious folk songs of the American Negro, which are commonly referred to as "spirituals." Dawson noted that the rehearsals were intense, sometimes lasting well beyond 10 p.m., even stretching until midnight. In addition to group rehearsals, he had time to work with the singers who were chosen to perform the solos in his compositions.[22]

According to Peña's narrative, Dawson's arrival on the Iberian Peninsula signaled the first time a musical cultural exchange such as this had occurred in Europe. The reverse of having a Spaniard conduct the music of Spanish composers with American choirs was also proposed in the project description, but no evidence in later years can be found to corroborate the event. Peña's report indicated that his hope was to continue musical exchanges between the United States and Spain on a yearly basis, which would lead to a valuable artistic exchange.[23]

Dawson's visit and work in Spain were highly acclaimed from both an artistic and human standpoint. According to Peña, the choral performances conducted by Dawson were considered technically perfect and unsurpassed in beauty. The Spanish people were impressed by his indefatigable spirit and personality. From his early work with the choristers in San Sebastian through his final engagement with the choral ensemble of the Empresa Bazan at El Ferrol in the Cathedral of Santiago, audience and participants left with unforgettable memories. Peña noted that many concertgoers drew comparisons between the expressive beauty of Dawson's historic Negro folk songs and the *Responsorious* of Victoria. The Spanish people were impressed that Dawson could compose, arrange, and conduct Negro folk songs and also direct with much feeling the polyphonic music of sixteenth-century Spanish composer Tomás Luis de Victoria. Having previously associated only blues and jazz with African American musical output, the Spanish concertgoers were truly inspired by the pure melodies of Black cultural music, insisting the songs must have been inspired by heavenly choirs. Some were led to exclaim: "I did not know there could be in America such music!"[24]

Peña did admit, however, that there were religious leaders and members of church choirs who were reluctant to invite William Dawson for the musical cultural exchange. It is not clear whether the reticence was due to Dawson's skin color or to objections to welcoming African American music into historic cathedrals. Nevertheless, Dawson won them over with the "spirituality" of his music, his compositional technique, and personal warmth. Upon the conclusion of each choral workshop and concert, participants eagerly asked him to return and to send more of his vocal compositions for their pleasure and performance.[25]

Dawson conducted a special concert, given by Orfeon Donostiarra of San Sebastian in the Basilica at Loyola, a highlight of the celebration in honor of the four hundredth anniversary of the founder of the Company of Jesus, Saint Ignacio of Loyola. The director of the Orfeon Donostiarra, Maestro Gorostidi, wrote a farewell to Dawson that extolled the composer's humble, simple, and modest work with the people there. The maestro was in awe that Dawson worked so diligently for the perfection of the delivery of text, nuance, accent, and dynamics—all accomplished by maintaining a calm, peaceful demeanor. Gorostidi told his singers that if he had to ever leave as conductor, he could not find a better replacement than William Dawson. Gorostidi encouraged each choir member to shake hands with the guest conductor and reveal that he had won not only their hearts but also their praise and thankfulness.[26]

The cultural exchange was a most memorable event, and the Spanish citizens admitted the effect was above and beyond expectations. Peña explains:

The ineffaceable mark which Dawson has left on hearts and on memories is greater than we had expected, and he has the deep satisfaction of having discovered a new world, the world of Victoria's universal music which he wishes to make known in America, thus being, so to speak, a new "Columbus." So here we have two worlds, which have met again and which together have found new horizons.[27]

Dawson was equally touched by his experience in Spain, as expressed by his heartfelt thanks at the close of his report to the US embassy in Spain:

This mission has enriched my own experience immeasurably as I have been privileged to know at first hand the high standards maintained in the centers of Spanish art in all its aspects. . . . It has been highly gratifying to note the response of the people of Spain among all classes to the particular forms of American music which it was my privilege to present to them, and the spontaneous and genuine sympathy with which they interpreted the religious folk music of the American Negro.

I return home with the feeling that these two great countries . . . have been brought closer together by this bond of musical art which springs from the same source, a profound experience of religious devotion which makes all men kin.[28]

Following his return to the United States in the fall of 1956, Dawson was frequently engaged as a guest conductor. For the first eighteen months after his exchange in Spain, he prepared for and appeared as guest conductor of bands and choral groups in New York and Michigan. In New York he appeared in Syracuse in December of 1956, Schenectady in April of 1957, White Plains in November of that same year, and Rockland County in March of 1958. The music supervisor of Pontiac, Michigan, schools invited Dawson to direct the Eighth Annual Vocal Clinic in November of 1957.[29]

Dawson received a high honor in the fall of 1958 when he was selected to conduct the Fisk University Choir of Nashville, Tennessee. Since the inception of the choral performing ensembles at Fisk, there had been few African American guest conductors of the Jubilee Singers and the choir. Dawson was proud to be one of the African American musicians chosen to direct this group. During his one-year stay, Dawson conducted the choir in a performance of the Hector Berlioz oratorio *L'enfance du Christ*. The group under Dawson's direction also presented the Samuel Coleridge-Taylor cantata *Hiawatha's Wedding Feast* as a part of the Thirtieth Annual Festival of Music in the School's Memorial Chapel. While working at Fisk, Dawson was reunited with his longtime friend Aaron Douglas, who, as a part of the Harlem Renaissance, was often referred to as the Father of African American Art.[30] Once again, both men were teaching on the same faculty as they had done nearly twenty-five years prior in Kansas City.[31]

Dawson's popularity in New York was evidenced by his third invitation to be guest conductor of the All-State Choir at the New York State School Music Association's (NYSSMA) Annual Conference.[32] Following the convention in early December of 1960, the New York *School Music News* reported that six hundred students had been selected to appear in the various ensembles that rehearsed and performed during the conference. The report praised Dawson and asserted that, under his direction, the All-State Choir sounded the best it ever had. The reporter wrote:

> The All-State Choir, directed by William Dawson, was probably as inspiring (and inspired) a chorus as we have heard. For the first time in our experience, the audience rose in tribute to the fine leadership of this choral master conductor. The spirituals: LISTEN TO THE LAMBS and EVERY TIME I FEEL THE SPIRIT carried an emotional story to the audience (as well as the chorus) that reached the realm of divinity. It was a thrilling moment.[33]

In the next two years, William Dawson made guest-conducting appearances in Minnesota, Washington, DC, Virginia, Maryland, and Pennsylvania. The highest honor paid to Dawson in 1961 was to conduct the Conference Chorus of over four hundred voices at the Eastern Division Convention of the Music Educators National Conference held in the nation's capital. In December of 1962, he was again invited to the NYSSMA conference, this time at the Concord Hotel in Lake Kiamesia, New York.[34]

The Massachusetts Music Education Association asked Dawson to conduct their All-State Chorus March 21–23 of the following year in Springfield. R. C. Hammerich, reporter for the *Springfield Republican*, noted the favorable audience reaction to Dawson's chorus. Approximately 2,500 teachers and parents of all-state ensembles heard the final concert of the 184-voice choir after sixteen hours of rehearsal that occurred over two and a half days. While the reporter indicated that all the ensembles should be commended for fine performances, he noted that the audience clearly favored Dawson's All-State Choir by offering its most enthusiastic response. In a very short time, Dawson had gained the trust and willingness of the group and molded the All-State Choir into a tight-unit capable of both nuanced singing and producing an enormous sound.

The choir performed six numbers, all from memory, and sang mostly a cappella. Hammerich noted that "every eye was on the conductor's expressive hands and the big sounds rolled and billowed and the feathery sounds floated through the auditorium. Dawson's control over the dynamics of this group was uncanny."[35] Following the appreciative concert ovation from those in attendance, Dawson left the stage, whereupon the All-State Choir themselves broke into thunderous applause while the audience stood in tribute.[36]

Two years passed before Dawson was once again on the guest musician lecture, conducting, and performance circuit. Invited as guest conductor of the Texas Southern University Choir, an HBCU in Houston, Dawson rehearsed the ensemble March 11–12, 1965, and presented a concert the final evening. Five days later, serving as guest lecturer on the President's Lecture Series at South Carolina State College, an HBCU in Orangeburg, Dawson spoke on March 17 of the origin, importance, and effect of African American Music upon the music climate in America.[37]

Not only was Dawson invited to direct large choral groups, but he was much in demand as guest orchestral conductor, especially in performances of his *Negro Folk Symphony*. The first was during the Annual Music Symposium at the State University College at Fredonia, New York (now known as SUNY-Fredonia), May 15–18, 1965. Dawson was invited to lecture during the conference and to conduct the University Orchestra in a performance of his *Negro Folk Symphony* during the second half of the concert program.[38] Dawson was next asked to conduct his symphony with the Kansas City Philharmonic Orchestra on January 29, 1966. This invitation was a memorable one for Dawson, given his history with the city. John Haskins's review of the performance in the *Kansas City Star* describes an enthusiastic response to the *Negro Folk Symphony*, the work written by one of their own, a former Kansas City resident. The reporter noted that the enormous crowd attending the third concert of the Philharmonic season spilled over into the side aisles, an excess which would surely have alarmed the state fire marshal. Despite having been written nearly thirty years prior, Dawson's *Negro Folk Symphony* performance marked the premiere presentation by the orchestra and was conducted by the composer, which produced enthusiastic ovations before and after. Haskins pointed out that Dawson had revised the work following his sojourn in Africa in the 1950s which solidified the thematic unity and essence of religious folk songs of Negroes enmeshed in the Romantic style. All told, the newspaper reporter concluded that the turns of phrases and use of orchestral color and instrumentation were particularly compelling under Dawson's the direction.[39] An article by music critic Haskins that appeared in the *Kansas City Star* six months later reflected on the Kansas City Philharmonic music season and expressed continuing praise for Dawson's composition. Having first noted the peaks and valleys of the season, Haskins proclaimed, "Composer-Conductor William Dawson, leading his *Negro Folk Symphony*, made both a musical and extra-musical impact."[40] Almost immediately following the Kansas City debut of his symphony, Dawson traveled to Hampton, Virginia, for a guest choral-conducting appearance at the famed Hampton Institute, the alma mater of his mentor, Booker T. Washington. Dawson conducted the Concert Choir during the Hampton Institute Fine Arts Festival held on campus March 3 and 4, 1966. Later that month his *Negro Folk Symphony* was performed by the Atlanta Symphony Orchestra.[41]

After the Atlanta performance, Dawson began preparing for a huge celebration at Fisk University in May.[42] Fisk University, the HBCU in Nashville, Tennessee, celebrated its Centennial Anniversary in April and May of 1966. Dawson was selected to conduct the Nashville Symphony Orchestra in a concert that closed the celebration. Louis Nicholas reported in the *Nashville Tennessean* that the idea to close the Fisk Festival's centennial year with an ambitious program devoted solely to Black composers could not have been a more fitting conclusion to the festivities and lamented that the chapel was not filled to capacity. Nicholas expressed satisfaction at the invitation of William Dawson, noting the composer's eminence, but upbraided the planners for undertaking such an ambitious program that included only two rehearsals of the Nashville Symphony with a guest conductor. With plenty of rough spots, the reporter lamented, the less-than-perfect performance was nevertheless received more favorably than an overperformed piece that needed little rehearsal. Despite the performance flaws, Nicholas observed that Dawson was clear with his interpretation and evoked eloquent moments from the ensemble during the less technical passages. Regardless of the performance's imperfection, it was spirited. Nicholas wrote:

> Dawson's *Negro Folk Symphony* is a richly romantic work, cyclic in form, lushly orchestrated, not concerned with being fashionable, but with being honest and sincere, and expressive of the spirit of the Negro.
> There is great beauty in the melodies (several Negro spirituals are used), and much interest in the greatly varied rhythms which are African inspired. This is a most appealing work.[43]

Werner Zepernick's review in the *Nashville Banner* failed to mention the Centennial Celebration, but he did note that the size of the orchestra had to be reduced due to the limited space in the Fisk Chapel. According to his review, Dawson was a focused conductor whose clear, concise beat matched the intensity of his feeling about the piece. Despite the enthusiasm and energy Dawson brought to the podium, Zepernick confirmed the *Tennessean*'s report that the performance was not stellar in some passages, but he complimented Dawson's conducting nevertheless:

> Dawson is a no-nonsense conductor who goes about his business with energy and enthusiasm. His feeling about the music is as concise and clear as his beat, and his forces seem to feel secure under his guidance. More rehearsal time would be benefited the ensemble, which was ragged in places.[44]

Zepernick praised the lush sounds and unique, well-developed themes of Dawson's symphony. The audience demonstrated its appreciation and admiration by giving Dawson a standing ovation at the close of the concert.[45]

Just two days later, Dawson hurried from Nashville to appear as guest conductor of St. Croix's Annual Festival of Art and Music in the United States Virgin Islands.[46] Later in 1968, Dawson was the featured conductor of the combined forces of the Talladega College Choir and the Mobile, Alabama Symphony for a performance of the oratorio "The Ordering of Moses" by Robert Nathaniel Dett. This concert marked one of the events surrounding the college's centennial anniversary and was an especially significant honor for Dawson. Talladega College was close to his hometown of Anniston, and the school had been the alma mater of one of his uncles.[47]

Two highlights in William Dawson's career occurred in 1969 and 1970. First, he was selected to serve as guest conductor for a performance of Dett's "The Ordering of Moses," one of several concerts given as part of the Golden Jubilee Convention of the National Association of Negro Musicians. Held in August of 1969, the oratorio was presented in the St. Louis, Missouri, Kiel Opera House. A year later Dawson flew to Quebec Province, Canada, as consultant for a workshop taking place during the 1970 Choralies Internationales Canadiennes. The clinic occurred at Laval University in Quebec City.[48] Also during this time period, he presented several choral workshops for the Neil Kjos Company, beginning in 1968 in Park Ridge, Illinois, as visiting composer/conductor for the fifteenth annual event. Later, Dawson was featured conductor at a series of Kjos workshops for teachers in New York City; Philadelphia; Arlington, Virginia; Detroit; Columbus, Ohio; and Chicago.[49] Additionally, he was chosen to be a part of a Human Relations Education Workshop in Schenectady, New York. In that capacity Dawson spoke to elementary teachers of the city's school system in May of 1969. He was also a part of the twenty-fifth annual festival of "Music for Unity." This marked the eighth time Dawson had been selected as conductor of the festival.[50] In February 1970 Dawson was invited to be lecturer-consultant on African American music at Atlanta University in Atlanta, Georgia. One year later he traveled to the US Virgin Islands in a similar capacity. He spoke on "Contributions of the Negro in the World of Music" at the College of the Virgin Islands in St. Thomas. Dawson returned to the Virgin Islands in November of 1971 to deliver the keynote speech at the Afro-Caribbean Music Conference held under the auspices of the college.[51]

While the years 1973–74 were lean in terms of conducting engagements, Dawson accepted an invitation to return to Kansas City in June of 1975. The University of Missouri-Kansas City (UMKC) Conservatory of Music extended a request for Dawson to present a choral workshop from the 23rd through the 27th. His alma mater, the Horner Institute of Fine Arts, had merged with the Conservatory of Music at UMKC, and the workshop invitation was viewed as a homecoming.[52] At the time of the "homecoming" in Kansas City, Dawson was nearing his seventy-sixth birthday and showed absolutely no signs of slowing down the pace of his active life. While she did not always travel with her husband, Cecile Dawson was a part of the celebration in Missouri. Mrs. Dawson grew up in the city and graduated from high school there in the 1920s. The officials at UMKC were gracious hosts and proudly extended hospitality and praise to the couple during their time on campus.[53]

Dawson's calendar was always full with nationwide appearances during the years 1975–81. In several copies of Dawson's "Highlights of the Life and

Career of William L. Dawson," reporting abruptly stops on page 16 with a guest conducting event in November of 1978 in Moline, Illinois.[54] Mysteriously, pages 17 and 18 are missing in most of those documents, but those two pages have been discovered recently among Dawson's papers in the Stuart A. Rose Archives at Emory University. Impressive "highlights" from the sixteen intervening years include: conducting the Alabama African American All-State College Choir in 1979, and guest conductor of three different choirs in 1980: the Georgia All-State High School Choir, the Notre Dame University Glee Club, and the Auburn University Concert Choir. While Dawson lived five months into 1990, the highlight document ends on page 21 with the mention of his participation in a music reading festival held in Kansas City, September 26, 1981.[55]

My own experience with William Dawson began in the spring of 1979, and I remember working with his busy schedule to make visits to his home to conduct interviews over the next two years. My aim was to document Dawson's life up to that moment, and following the completion of my dissertation, I kept in touch sporadically. While his engagements continued, it is likely that Dawson began to curtail the number of appearances he made each year beginning in the early 1980s. His incredible career, however, continued to place him in high demand for his expertise as an icon of choral music and a bastion of composition. Still well respected as a clinician, conductor, and featured speaker, Dawson was often asked to share his thoughts on the folk music of African Americans for the American Choral Directors Association (ACDA) National, Division, and State Conventions.[56]

In February 1984, at the ACDA Southern Division Convention in Atlanta, Georgia, Dawson utilized the Morehouse College Glee Club, conducted by Wendell Whalum, as a demonstration choir, to discuss the style and performance of his own compositions.[57] In April of 1986, I invited Mr. Dawson to be the headliner for the first-ever state convention of the Mississippi Chapter of the ACDA at the University of Mississippi in Oxford. Dawson remained in great demand, despite his being an octogenarian. It took him several weeks to check his booking dates and personal calendar to confirm availability and accept the invitation. The fact the Dawson was the headliner for the 1986 Mississippi ACDA meeting stands in contrast to the situation fifty years earlier. When William Dawson's Tuskegee Choir performed in Starkville, Mississippi, at Mississippi State College, now Mississippi State University, Blacks were treated very differently. At the bottom of the advertisement flyer for the 1936 performance were these words, "Balcony reserved for Negroes."[58]

Less than two months before his death, on March 10, 1990, William Dawson was honored at the ACDA Southern Division Convention in Birmingham, Alabama, with a "Salute to William Dawson in Honor of His 90th

Birthday." He conducted the Festival Chorus in his arrangement of "Ev'ry Time I Feel the Spirit," followed by a concert of five of his choral works conducted by Brezeal Dennard: "Ain-a That Good News," "Hail Mary," "There's a Lit'l Wheel A-Turnin' in My Heart," "There Is a Balm in Gilead," and "Soon Ah Will Be Done."[59]

DAWSON IN RETROSPECT

Dawson set his sights early on becoming a musician and teacher and succeeded despite having to face many, many obstacles. He chose to faithfully and consistently tread the path of persistence throughout his lifetime. His path was one that included great challenges, marked by obstacles of resistance to him due to his race. Dawson's peaceful persistence enabled him to sharpen his skills and go to places previously unavailable to African Americans. Fortunately, his accomplishments and achievements also opened doors that would have been otherwise closed. In reality, Dawson's great yearning for an education was indeed a driving force in his life. He viewed every experience as an opportunity to learn and to increase his ability to deal with any number of challenging situations, especially those that existed only because of the color of his skin. Engaging in and succeeding in lifelong learning enabled William Dawson to reach closure on what he set out to accomplish in life.

His vast experiences as a student at Tuskegee enabled him to accept teaching positions in Topeka and Kansas City. Those early years of instruction added to his musical expertise, which was further supplemented by collegiate study in music theory and composition. The musical knowledge and erudition he gleaned through many educational experiences provided the capabilities necessary to structure and direct the music education of others.

To organize and direct a school of music was an awesome task, made even more difficult due to economic depression in the United States during the 1930s. Still, Dawson worked diligently to provide a comprehensive music education for the college students at Tuskegee Institute. A stern disciplinarian with a caring spirit who never turned any singer away from his choir drew students to him. Yet the international economic situation took its toll, and the School of Music's enrollment dropped considerably by 1940. Undaunted, Dawson adjusted and tried to offer the best musical experiences to meet the changing student needs. His intuitive vision enabled him to plan and provide effective course offerings and useful degree plans.

William Dawson's extensive music background enabled him to effectively mold the sound of the Tuskegee Institute Choir effectively. Under his brilliant direction, the Tuskegee Choir rose to national fame in a few short years.

Through singing at myriad important functions throughout the Eastern United States, the choir distinguished itself and brought notoriety to both the school and its outstanding conductor. During his tenure, the Tuskegee Choir sang on all three radio networks, NBC, CBS, and ABC, as well as on CBS and NBC television networks. For many years Dawson's choir had the distinction of having sung on the air for continuous half-hour programs, longer than any other choral group. This broadcast exposure, coupled with numerous concert journeys, enabled the Tuskegee Choir to touch many hearts with their beautiful music.

William Dawson's compositional skills preserved the historical significance of a body of African American folk music and enhanced the Tuskegee Choir's reputation. His music-writing ability also helped him achieve a personal goal of writing a symphony based on themes found in the folk idioms of Black Americans. Dawson's compositions made his name distinctive in American music history.

Following his resignation from Tuskegee Institute in 1955, William Dawson was able to accept more guest-conducting invitations, lecture engagements, and workshop leadership assignments for over thirty-five years. Pursuing a lifelong dream, he researched the indigenous cultural music of Africa in 1952–53, was sent to Spain on a cultural exchange mission in 1956, and was frequently invited to conduct choral groups in Canada, the Caribbean, and throughout the United States. Retirement did not slow Dawson's rapid pace. He continued to compose at his home in Tuskegee, Alabama, and prepare for the many music engagements he accepted each year.

William Dawson, a demanding, yet sensitive man was an outstanding scholar, a skilled pedagogue, a gifted composer, and an exceptional lecturer. Above all, he was a teacher whose influence spanned nearly seventy years and who remained vital through the end of his days. Students under his tutelage attest to his greatness. Author and former student Ralph Ellison autographed a copy of his book *Invisible Man* for William Dawson and wrote the following tribute to his teacher: "To William Dawson: who before I knew him inspired me, and who after I came to Tuskegee taught me, by example, the discipline of the artist."[60]

Ellison insisted that because of mentors such as Dawson and others, he was more than prepared to intuit beyond the surface understanding of discrimination and segregation. Directing even more praise for the impact of William Dawson on his life, Jackson quotes Ellison in further tribute:

> I rode freight trains to Macon County, Alabama during the Scottsboro trial because I desired to study with the Negro conductor/composer,

William L. Dawson, who was, and probably still is the greatest classical musician in that part of the country. I had no need to attend a white university when the master I wished to study with was available at Tuskegee. [61]

Ultimately, though, Ellison indicated the musician was creating himself through the process of discipline. Ellison believed William Dawson deserved the credit for the revelation. O'Meally shared Ellison's continued praise with the student's own explanations and added to Ellison's tribute.

"As Dawson reached out through his choir, through his ability to make people who were not really musicians give voice to sublime music, he was doing something else. He was acting as a 'Cultural Hero,' as a living symbol of what was possible." So, by watching Dawson, by imitating him, by disciplining yourself to be like Dawson, they learned from him, generations of students . . . and became themselves. This was whether they became musicians or not, now. You knew from Dawson that if you were going to become a teacher of math that you had to have Dawson's values there. If you were going to become a doctor or a lawyer or whatever it was, you wanted something of that fervor and drive for excellence in your work.[62]

Ellison's initial written tribute to his mentor William Dawson, penned in a personal copy of *Invisible Man* given to the conductor/composer, was quoted earlier in this chapter. Years later, Ralph Ellison expanded the accolade:

Dear Bill, you first became an inspiration when I was still in high school. Two years later I rode freight trains to study with you at Tuskegee. Now some 50 years later you remain for me, as for countless others, a model and guide whose art, genius, and sheer integrity still inspire my striving for excellence. Thanks for performing your elected role so superbly. For by doing so, you not only pointed the way, but affirmed our faith in the transcendent possibilities of art.

God Bless You,
Ralph W. Ellison[63]

Tuskegee Institute Bulletin 1914-15
Volume 9 #2

Catalog listing of the C Preparatory Class at Tuskegee Institute, Dawson's second year. (Tuskegee University Archives, Tuskegee University)

TUSKEGEE NORMAL AND INDUSTRIAL INSTITUTE 148

Austin, Henry .... Chicago, Illinois
Andrews, Daniel .... Arabi, Georgia
Bachelor, Robert Benjamin .... Muskogee, Oklahoma
Barnes, Alma .... Athens, Georgia
Boswell, Mary Etta .... Evergreen, Alabama
Battles, James Davis .... Dublin, Georgia
Bentley, John Thomas .... Covington, Georgia
Bernam, Samuel .... Glancy, Mississippi
Bevans, Victor Alexander .... Nassau, Bahama Islands
Biggers, Nellie Bell .... Hardaway, Alabama
*Brooks, Albert .... Tuscaloosa, Alabama
Brown, William Wilson .... Mobile, Alabama
Black, Larnie .... Waverly Hall, Georgia
Brown, Richard Allen .... Richmond, Alabama
Bunkley, Christopher C. .... Vicksburg, Mississippi
Burrell, William Henry .... Templeman Crossroads, Virginia
Burney, Hattie May .... East Tallassee, Alabama
Burt, Howard .... Atlanta, Georgia
Carleton, John William .... Lafayette, Alabama
Casterman, Arwood .... Sicily Island, Louisiana
Chapman, Bettie Salivia .... Grove Hill, Alabama
*Christian, Bertha .... Camp Hill, Alabama
*Clinton, Lawrence .... Chicago, Illinois
Clowney, John .... Tryon, North Carolina
Cobb, Esker Samuel .... Andalusia, Alabama
Combs, Otis .... Lake City, Florida
Cotton, McGalop .... Baton Rouge, Louisiana
Cummings, Elius Leroy .... Agricola, Georgia
Daniels, Lee Home .... Hammer, Alabama
Davis, Mabel .... Fort Valley, Georgia
Davison, Rosa .... Eclectic, Alabama
*Dawson, Bashie .... Genoa, Florida
Dawson, William Levi .... Anniston, Alabama
Day, Mary Eliza .... Sayre, Alabama
Doak, John Algenon .... Birmingham, Alabama
*Dove, John .... Sylvarena, Mississippi
Drewry, Prince .... Montgomery, Alabama
Dunn, James .... Eutaw, Alabama
Dye, Alexand .... Elberton, Georgia
Evans, Jefferson Davis .... Newbern, Alabama
Farmer, Charles .... Anniston, Alabama
Felton, Charles .... Tysonville, Alabama
Fletcher, Rosa Belle .... Meadow Station, Virginia
*Flowers, Glover .... Sun, Mississippi

*Part of Term

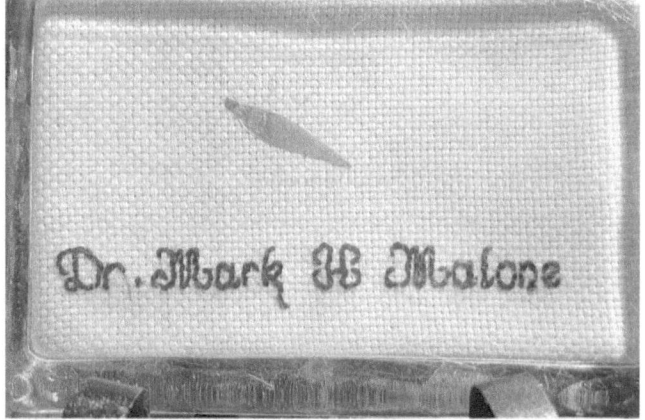

Petal from the funeral wreath of Booker T. Washington (who died November 14, 1915), given to Mark Hugh Malone by William Levi Dawson. Photo by Mark Hugh Malone. (From the personal collection of the author)

William Levi Dawson in Student Cadet Uniform, c. 1918. (William Levi Dawson Papers, Stuart A. Rose Manuscript, Archives, and Rare Book Library, Emory University)

William Levi Dawson with trombone, c. 1920. (William Levi Dawson Papers, Stuart A. Rose Manuscript, Archives, and Rare Book Library, Emory University)

William Levi Dawson in band uniform with trombone, c. 1920. (William Levi Dawson Papers, Stuart A. Rose Manuscript, Archives, and Rare Book Library, Emory University)

William Levi Dawson's pocket diary, February 26, 1921. (William Levi Dawson Papers, Stuart A. Rose Manuscript, Archives, and Rare Book Library, Emory University) Photo by Mark Hugh Malone.

William Levi Dawson and Aaron Douglas, Faculty Page, 1924 Lincoln High School Yearbook, Kansas City, Missouri. (Lincoln High School, *Lincolnian*, Kansas City, MO, 1924, faculty page)

Regina Hall, Horner Institute of Fine Arts Summer Bulletin, 1925. (University Archives, University of Missouri–Kansas City)

William Levi Dawson, director of Band and Orchestra, 1924 Lincoln High School Yearbook, Kansas City, Missouri. (Lincoln High School, *Lincolnian*, Kansas City, MO, 1924, Music Department page)

Orchestra

L. H. S. Band

Members of the Chicago Civic Orchestra, 1929–1930 season. (Tuskegee University Archives, Tuskegee University)

TUSKEGEE INSTITUTE CHOIR
AND MALE CHORUS

William L. Dawson, Conductor
ONLY CONCERT APPEARANCE
AFTER RADIO CITY
• PROGRAM OF
NEGRO FOLK MUSIC

CARNEGIE HALL
57th Street and 7th Ave.
Wednesday Evening
Feb. 8th at 8:30 o'clock

100 VOICES

1. STEAL AWAY .... arr. by Dawson
   GO DOWN MOSES .... arr. by Burleigh
   I'LL NEVER TURN BACK NO MORE .... Dett
2. OH, WHAT A BEAUTIFUL CITY .... Dawson
   (Dedicated to Samuel Rothafel—"Roxy")
   NOBODY KNOWS DE TROUBLE I SEE .... arr. by Dawson
   GOOD NEWS .... arr. by Dawson
3. LOST IN THE NIGHT .... Christiansen
   SUN DOWN (Londonderry Air) .... arr. by Dawson
   LISTEN TO THE LAMBS .... Dett

INTERMISSION •

4. SYLVIA .... Speaks
   I'M IN HIS CARE—O .... Dawson
   (By Request)
   ABSENT .... Matcalfe
   SOON AH WILL BE DONE WID DE TROUBLES OF DE WORL' ... Dawson
   MALE CHORUS
5. STUDY YOUR PRAYER .... arr. by Dawson
   I HEARD OF A CITY CALLED HEAVEN .... Johnson
   GREAT DAY .... arr. by Dawson

TICKETS: 55c, 83c, $1.10, $1.65, $2.20.
Box Seats, $2.75 and $2.20.
NOW on sale at Box Office.
Recital Management:
NBC ARTISTS SERVICE
George Engles, Managing Director
711 Fifth Avenue : : : New York

Tuskegee Choir program, Carnegie Hall, New York City, February 8, 1933. (Tuskegee University Archives, Tuskegee University)

Fiftieth
Anniversary Celebration
1881-1931

Tuskegee Normal and Industrial Institute

UP FROM SLAVERY
A FESTIVAL OF NEGRO MUSIC
giving
An Illumination of the Mind and Mood of the Negro in his Journey through Slavery to Freedom out of Sorrow through Hope to Joy . . . . . .

INSTITUTE CHAPEL
Monday, April Thirteenth
7:30 p. m.

The Quartet, The Boys' Glee Club, The Girls' Glee Club, Children's House Chorus, and The Band

WILLIAM L. DAWSON, *Director of Music*
Assistants: Portia Washington Pittman, Adelaide Towson Foster, O. Lexine Howse, Emily Moore Neely, Alberta L. Simms, and Cadet Major Phillmore Hall

Tuskegee Institute program from the Fiftieth Anniversary Concert, entitled, "Up from Slavery," April 13, 1931. (Tuskegee University Archives, Tuskegee University)

The cover of the inaugural program of the Opening of Radio City Music Hall in New York City, December 1932. (Tuskegee University Archives, Tuskegee University)

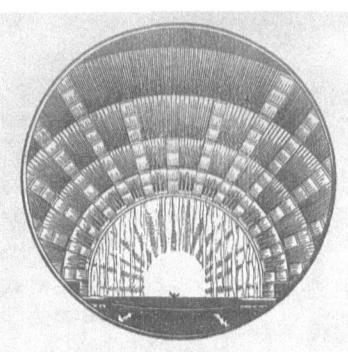

RADIO · KEITH · ORPHEUM
PROUDLY PRESENTS
THE INAUGURAL PROGRAM
OF THE
RADIO CITY MUSIC HALL
UNDER THE PERSONAL DIRECTION OF

Roxy

RADIO CITY
IN ROCKEFELLER CENTER

THE PROGRAM

The Entire Performance Conceived and Supervised by "ROXY,"
Director-General of the Radio City Music Hall and the RKO Roxy Theatre

1. "HYMN TO THE SUN,"
   from Rimsky-Korsakoff's "Le Coq d'Or"
   CAROLINE ANDREWS, Soloist
   The great "Contour Curtain," first of its kind in the world, was constructed under the Ted Weidhaas patents by Peter Clark, Inc. Operated by thirteen motors, its flexible contours open new vistas in the field of stage decoration.

2. MINSTRELSY

3. THE RADIO CITY MUSIC HALL ROXYETTES
   Directed by RUSSELL MARKERT

4. DE WOLF HOPPER

5. WEBER AND FIELDS

6. FRAULEIN VERA SCHWARZ *of the Staats-Oper, Berlin*
   Who is making her first appearance in America at the invitation of "Roxy"
   "LIEBESWALZER," from "Wiener Blut," Johann Strauss
   Specially arranged by Leo Bloch

7. BERRY BROTHERS, *Dancers*

8. IMPRESSIONS OF A MUSIC HALL
   (A) THE WALLENDAS, *Continental Aerialists*
   (B) THE KIKUTAS, *Oriental Risley Act*

9. IN THE SPOTLIGHT
   EDDIE AND RALPH

10. THE RADIO CITY MUSIC HALL BALLET
    PATRICIA BOWMAN, *Premiere Danseuse*
    Choreography by Florence Rogge. Music by Maurice Baron

11. THE MAN WITH THE MICROPHONE
    TAYLOR HOLMES, *the Distinguished Comedian*

12. THE TUSKEGEE CHOIR · WILLIAM L. DAWSON, *Director*
    (A) "BEAUTIFUL CITY" . . . William L. Dawson
    (B) "GOOD NEWS" (traditional) Arr. by William L. Dawson
    This is the first appearance of this celebrated choral organization in New York, who come from Tuskegee Institute specially for this engagement.

13. RAY BOLGER, *outstanding young American Dancing Comedian*

14. THE MAN WITH THE MICROPHONE

15. HARALD KREUTZBERG
    Assisted by Margaret Sande, The Radio City Ballet Corps and Male Dancers, presenting, for the first time anywhere
    "THE ANGEL OF FATE," *A Dramatic Dance Scene*
    Choreography by Harald Kreutzberg. Music by Friedrich Wilckens.
    The Angel of Fate, descending from Heaven to perform his work on earth, visits a rural feast. Displeased at the gayety, he places the Mask of Death upon the King's face. Later, meeting an innocent maiden, the Angel finds, to his sorrow, that she becomes sophisticated through his teaching, and too becomes a victim of the Death Mask. On a battlefield the Angel dances with a mask symbolic of modern warfare. The soldiers, following the Angel's example, lift their masks to their faces, and die. In the final scene, the Angel, his tasks on earth completed, ascends once more to Heaven.

16. DOCTOR ROCKWELL

17. NIGHT CLUB REVELS
    RAY BOLGER, PATRICIA BOWMAN, BERRY BROTHERS, JOSIE AND JULES WALTON, DOROTHY FIELDS, AND JIMMY McHUGH
    (Miss Fields, daughter of Lew Fields, is making her first stage appearance.)
    THE RADIO CITY MUSIC HALL ROXYETTES, BALLET CORPS, CHORUS
    "HEY, YOUNG FELLA!" by Dorothy Fields and Jimmy McHugh
    "MAD MOMENTS" . . . by Harry Revel and Mack Gordon
    "RIDING HIGH" . . . by Harry Revel and Mack Gordon

The inside page of the inaugural program of the Opening of Radio City Music Hall in New York City, December 1932. (Tuskegee University Archives, Tuskegee University)

Newspaper picture of the Tuskegee Choir at the Empire State Building in New York City, February 3, 1933, originally published in the *Kansas Plain Dealer*. (Tuskegee University Archives, Tuskegee University)

Concert program featuring band and choir conducted by William Levi Dawson, August 27, 1929, during an audition for selection to perform in the 1933 Chicago World's Fair. (Tuskegee University Archives, Tuskegee University)

William Levi Dawson and the Tuskegee Choir on the stage at Carnegie Hall, New York City, February 8, 1933. (Tuskegee University Archives, Tuskegee University)

Photo: William Levi Dawson and Leopold Stokowski examining "Negro Folk Symphony" score.

"I am happy to introduce this composition to the American audience because I believe it to represent two distinct American achievements in American music. It is a work of national importance. It is not only musically impressive in itself, but primarily because of its distinctly American character, Dawson has succeeded in eloquently portraying that aspect of American life which he has seen, and lived, and felt, most profoundly. It is a work which is both vital and personal."

by Leopold Stokowski

****

William Levi Dawson and Leopold Stokowski study the score of the *Negro Folk Symphony*. (Tuskegee University Archives, Tuskegee University)

Available - - -

The recording of *William Dawson's Negro Folk Symphony* by Leopold Stokowski and the American Symphony Orchestra on Decca "Gold Label Series" records.

LEOPOLD STOKOWSKI
CONDUCTS
NEGRO FOLK SYMPHONY
BY
WILLIAM DAWSON
AMERICAN SYMPHONY ORCHESTRA
DECCA

NEGRO FOLK SYMPHONY

FIRST MOVEMENT
(The Bond of Africa)

SECOND MOVEMENT
(Hope in the Night)

THIRD MOVEMENT
(O Le' Me Shine, Shine Like A Morning Star!)

Negro Folk Symphony brochure, page 1. (Used by special permission of William Levi Dawson)

The World Premiere of The Negro Folk Symphony was given by Leopold Stokowski and the Philadelphia Orchestra.

PRESS REVIEWS AND COMMENTS

NEGRO SYMPHONY HAS SUPERB MATERIAL—"The audience reserved its greatest enthusiasm for the symphony of William Dawson. In essence this music has a dramatic feeling, a racial sensuousness and directness of melodic speech, and a barbaric turbulence."

Olin Downes/
"THE NEW YORK TIMES"

THE CUSTOM OF NO APPLAUSE BROKEN—"The climax of the concert given by the Philadelphia Orchestra in Carnegie Hall last evening came with the performance of the *Negro Folk Symphony* of William L. Dawson, which so moved the fashionable audience that Mr. Stokowski found himself forced to turn and bow at the end of the second movement, a proceeding not generally countenanced in polite hearing of symphonies.

"The reaction was to music full of life, deep feeling, of rich vitality and throbbing with dramatic power of expression. It was tense with emotion, built on several Negro spirituals, the entire work developing the story of the struggle of the Negro, held for long years in darkness, and at last sounding with assurance of wondrous hope, 'O Le' me shine like a morning star.' The climax was thrilling. The work strikes a red letter mark in contemporary musical history."

Henriette Weber/
"THE NEW YORK EVENING JOURNAL"

STOKOWSKI GIVES PREMIERE OF DAWSON'S SYMPHONY—"The Symphony is based on Negro melodies, and the first movement has the subtitle, 'The Bond of Africa,' but Mr. Dawson, obviously an extraordinarily well-equipped musician, doesn't indulge himself in self-consciousness which comes on most composers when they write with racial materials. His symphony is agreeably free from messages, lessons, and sermons. It is, strangely enough, music in which well-defined themes are developed skillfully and the orchestra handled with complete assurance. When Mr. Dawson wants to be dramatic, as he is at the end of his second movement, he makes his point directly and sharply. When he wants a clangorous climax, he knows how to bring it off without abandoning himself to plain noise."

Robert A. Simon/
"THE NEW YORKER"

Negro Folk Symphony brochure, page 2. (Used by special permission of William Levi Dawson)

NEGRO SYMPHONY A HIT—"Without further ado let it be recorded that Mr. Dawson's "Negro Folk Symphony" took the house by storm. It is easy enough to account for this commotion. The Negro themes chosen by the composer are striking in themselves and are employed with skill; the music is vivid with imagination, warmth, drama, and then there is the sumptuous orchestral dress. One is eager to hear it again and again."

Pitts Sanborn,
"NEW YORK WORLD-TELEGRAM"

"Dawson has succeeded in portraying that aspect of American life which is both vital and personal. I believe this work to be a distinct achievement in American music."

"He has voiced the spirit of his people struggling in a new land; the ancient voice of Africa transferred to America and here expressed through the medium of the white man's most highly developed instrument, the symphony orchestra."

LEOPOLD STOKOWSKI

Study Score of Negro Folk Symphony
available from
SHAWNEE PRESS, INC.
Delaware Water Gap, Pa. 18327
Price $5.00

Albums ordered from the Petite Bazaar will be autographed by the composer.

ORDER BLANK
for Symphony

Petite Bazaar
(Mrs. C. N. Dawson, Prop.)
P. O. Box 1052
Tuskegee Institute
Alabama 36088

( ) Stereo DL 710077 .... $8.98
(Insurance, Postage, etc., included in price)

Please send record(s) to:

Name_____

Street_____

City_____State___

Zip_____

Negro Folk Symphony brochure, page 3. (Used by special permission of William Levi Dawson)

ALSO AVAILABLE
ON WESTMINSTER "GOLD SERIES RECORDS"

TUSKEGEE INSTITUTE CHOIR
SINGS SPIRITUALS

Conducted by
WILLIAM L. DAWSON
15 Selections

ORDER BLANK
for Choir Recording

Petite Bazaar
(Mrs. C. N. Dawson, Prop.)
P. O. Box 1052
Tuskegee Institute
Alabama 36088

( ) WGM $7.00
(Insurance, Postage, etc., included in price)

Please send record(s) to:

Name_____

Street_____

City_____State___

Zip_____

Negro Folk Symphony brochure, page 4. (Used by special permission of William Levi Dawson)

William Levi Dawson, a drawing by Aaron Douglas, 1935. (William Levi Dawson Papers, Stuart A. Rose Manuscript, Archives, and Rare Book Library, Emory University)

William Levi Dawson at the piano, pose 1, 1936. (William Levi Dawson Papers, Stuart A. Rose Manuscript, Archives, and Rare Book Library, Emory University

Tuskegee Choir Flyer for concert at Mississippi State College, Starkville, Mississippi, April 22, 1936. (Tuskegee University Archives, Tuskegee University)

The Tuskegee Choir

of the World Famous

Tuskegee Normal and Industrial Institute
Founded by Booker T. Washington

SPRING CONCERT TOUR
April and May 1936

MISSISSIPPI STATE COLLEGE
MONDAY, APRIL 20, 1936

Wednesday, April 22, 1936 · · · 8:00 p.m.
Admission — 20c & 40c
Balcony Reserved for Negroes

THE TUSKEGEE CHOIR
William L. Dawson, *Conductor*
Alvin J. Neely, *Manager*   R. S. Darnaby, *Secretary*
Tuskegee Institute, Alabama

William Levi Dawson at the piano, pose 2, 1936. (William Levi Dawson Papers, Stuart A. Rose Manuscript, Archives, and Rare Book Library, Emory University)

Tuskegee Choir advertisement for radio concerts on CBS, 1946. (Tuskegee University Archives, Tuskegee University)

WAPI
"The Voice of Alabama"

Presents the World-Famous

Tuskegee Institute Choir

Over the Coast-to-Coast Facilities of the

Columbia Broadcasting System

Sundays, February 3, 10, 17, 24, 1946

9:30-10:00 A. M., CENTRAL STANDARD TIME

From the Chapel on the campus of Tuskegee Institute, **Tuskegee, Alabama**, WAPI will present to Columbia's nation-wide audience the moving spirituals of the world-famous Tuskegee Institute Choir each Sunday morning in February, 1946, 9:30-10:00 A. M., Central Standard Time. Surrounded by the famous "singing windows" of the **Chapel**, Dr. William L. Dawson directs his own arrangements of immortal **songs**.

A PUBLIC SERVICE FEATURE

of

WAPI AND THE COLUMBIA BROADCASTING SYSTEM

Newspaper picture of protesters at the Tuskegee Choir concert at Constitution Hall, Washington, DC, June 15, 1946. Originally published by *Black Dispatch*. (Tuskegee University Archives, Tuskegee University)

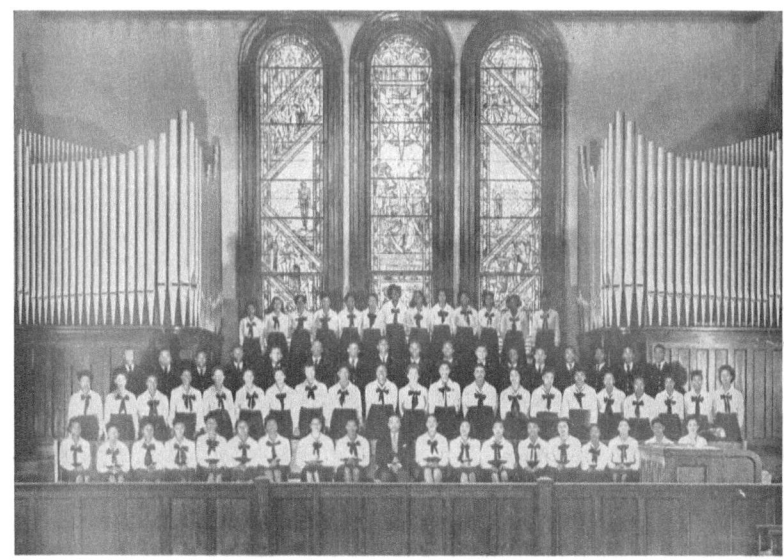

Tuskegee Choir announcement of appearance on the *Edgar Bergen and Charlie McCarthy Show* on radio, February 6, 1950. (Tuskegee University Archives, Tuskegee University)

William Levi Dawson with portable tape recorder in Nigeria, West Africa, 1953. (William Levi Dawson Papers, Stuart A. Rose Manuscript, Archives, and Rare Book Library, Emory University)

William Levi Dawson in Loyola, Spain, 1956. (William Levi Dawson Papers, Stuart A. Rose Manuscript Archives, and Rare Book Library, Emory University)

William Levi Dawson portrait, 1960. (William Levi Dawson Papers, Stuart A. Rose Manuscript Archives, and Rare Book Library, Emory University)

William Levi Dawson's 90th Birthday celebration program front cover, September 24, 1989. (Tuskegee University Archives, Tuskegee University)

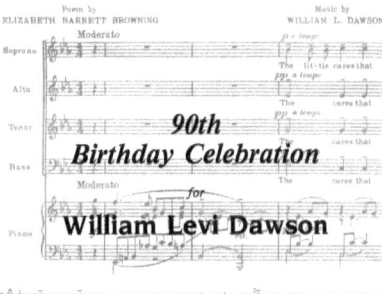

William Levi Dawson Memorial Service program front cover, May 5, 1990. (Tuskegee University Archives, Tuskegee University)

Stained glass window in the Tuskegee University Chapel. Photo by Mark Hugh Malone. (From the personal collection of the author)

William Levi Dawson's gravesite in the Tuskegee University Cemetery. Photo by Mark Hugh Malone. (From the personal collection of the author)

Appendix A

CHORAL AND ORCHESTRAL COMPOSITIONS AND ARRANGEMENTS

TABLE 2. PUBLISHED CHORAL WORKS BY WILLIAM LEVI DAWSON				
Title	Voicing	Accompaniment	Copyright	Publisher
Ain-A That Good News	SATB TTBB SSAA	a cappella	1957	Kjos*
Before the Sun Goes Down	SATB	piano	1978	Kjos
Behold the Star	SATB	a cappella	1948	Kjos
Dawson Spirituals, Vol. 1	SATB	a cappella	2002	Kjos
Dawson Spirituals, Vol. 2	SATB	a cappella/piano	2002	Kjos
Ev'ry Time I Feel the Spirit	SATB TTBB SSAA	a cappella	1946	Kjos
Ezekiel Saw De Wheel	SATB	a cappella	1942	Kjos
Feed-A My Sheep	SATB TTBB SSAA	piano	1971	Kjos
Hail Mary	SATB TTBB	a cappella	1946	Kjos
I Couldn't Hear Nobody Pray	Solo SATB (out-of-print)	a cappella	1926	Fred Bock Music** (original publisher-FitzSimons)
In His Care-O	SATB TTBB	a cappella	1961	Kjos
I Wan'To Be Ready	SATB TTBB SSAA	a cappella	1967	Kjos
Jesus Walked This Lonesome Valley	SATB TTBB SSAA SSA	piano	1927	Out-of-Print (original publisher-Remick and Warner Brothers)
King Jesus is A-Listening	SATB TTBB SAB SSA (out-of-print)	a cappella	1925	Fred Bock Music (original publisher-FitzSimons)
Lit'l Boy Chile	SATB	a cappella	1947	Kjos
Mary Had A Baby	SATB TTBB	a cappella	1947	Kjos
My Lord What a Mourning	SATTB	a cappella	1927	Fred Bock Music (original publisher-FitzSimons)

Title	Voicing	Accompaniment	Copyright	Publisher
Oh, What A Beautiful City	SATB	a cappella	1934	Kjos
Out in the Fields	SATB SSA	piano, orchestra, wind ensemble	1957	Kjos
Pilgrim's Chorus, from Wagner's Tannhauser	SATB TTBB (out-of-print)	a cappella	1968	Kjos
Slumber Song	SATB TTBB SSA SA	piano	1974	Kjos
Soon-Ah Will Be Done	SATB TTBB	a cappella	1934	Kjos
Steal Away	SATB TTBB	a cappella	1942	Kjos
Swing Low, Sweet Chariot	SATB TTBB SSA	a cappella	1946	Kjos
Talk About A Child That Do Love Jesus	SATB	piano	1927	Fred Bock Music (original publisher-FitzSimons)
The Rugged Yank	TTBB	piano	1970	Kjos
There Is A Balm in Gilead	SATB TTBB SSA	a cappella	1939	Kjos
There's A Lit'l Wheel A Turnin' In My Heart	SATB	a cappella	1949	Kjos
You Got To Reap Just What You Sow	SATB TTBB SSAA (out-of-print)	piano	1928	Kjos (original publisher-FitzSimons)
Zion's Walls	SATB	a cappella	1961	Kjos
(Mark Hugh Malone, William Levi Dawson: American Music Educator, Tallahassee, FL: The Florida State University, Unpublished dissertation, 1981.) *Neil A. Kjos Company, 4382 Jutland Drive, San Diego, CA 92117 **Fred Bock Music Company, P.O. Box 10069, Glendale, CA 91209				

Because William Dawson considered his compositions to always be in a state of flux, he frequently made adjustments that would, in his opinion, enhance the quality and presentation of the meaning of the lyrics through his creativity in music. The following list was compiled by the archivists in the Stuart A. Rose Manuscript, Archives, and Rare Book Library within the Woodruff Library at Emory University in Atlanta, Georgia, which is the repository for all of Mr. Dawson's papers and ephemera. The corresponding dates for each composition may indicate subsequent changes or republication dates for each work, and copies are available for perusal by securing an appointment and submitting a formal request for viewing the materials.

Adawura B, Me (The Gong Gong Says Beat Me), SATB, Remick, 1955
Ain'a That Good News! (Female), Tuskegee/T/140, 1974
Ain'a That Good News! (Female), Tuskegee/T140 [color cover], 1975

APPENDIX A: COMPOSITIONS AND ARRANGEMENTS

Ain'a That Good News! (Male), Tuskegee/T104, 1965
Ain'a That Good News! (Male), Tuskegee/T104 [color cover], 1974
Ain'a That Good News! (Mixed), Tuskegee/T103A, 1974
Ain'a That Good News! (Male), Tuskegee/T103A [color cover], 1974
Before the Sun Goes Down (SATB), Kjos Music, 1978
Before the Sun Goes Down (SATB), Kjos Music, 1978
Behold the Star (Mixed), Tuskegee/T111, 1946
Behold the Star (Mixed), Tuskegee/T111, 1973
Dorabella (Male), Tuskegee/T141, 1981
Ev'ry Time I Feel the Spirit (Female), Tuskegee/T126, 1966
Ev'ry Time I Feel the Spirit (Female), Tuskegee/T126, [color cover] 1966
Ev'ry Time I Feel the Spirit (Male), Tuskegee/T125, 1966
Ev'ry Time I Feel the Spirit (Male), Tuskegee/T125, [color cover]1966
Ev'ry Time I Feel the Spirit (Mixed), Tuskegee/T117, 1946
Ev'ry Time I Feel the Spirit (Mixed), Tuskegee/T117, 1973
Ev'ry Time I Feel the Spirit (Mixed), Tuskegee/T117, [color cover] 1973
Ev'ry Time I Feel the Spirit (Mixed) [see Series 10]
Ezekiel Saw de Wheel (Mixed), Tuskegee, T110, 1942
Ezekiel Saw de Wheel (Mixed), Tuskegee/T110, 1969
Ezekiel Saw de Wheel (Mixed), Tuskegee/T110, [color cover], 1969
Feed-A My Sheep (Male), Tuskegee/T133, 1971
Feed-A My Sheep (Mixed, Tuskegee/T134, 1971
Forever Thine, Tuskegee, 1920
Hail Mary (Male), Tuskegee/T113, 1973
Hail Mary (Mixed, Tuskegee/T112, 1949
Hail Mary (Mixed), Tuskegee/T112, 1973
Hail Mary (Mixed), Tuskegee/T112, [color cover], 1973
I Couldn't Hear Nobody Pray, FitzSimons, 1954
I Wan' to Be Ready (Female), Tuskegee/T129, 1978
I Wan' to Be Ready (Male), Tuskegee/T128, 1978
I Wan' to Be Ready (Mixed), Tuskegee/T127, 1967
I Wan' to Be Ready (Mixed w/ piano), Tuskegee/T127-A, 1978
In His Care-O (Male), Tuskegee/T123, 1961
In His Care-O (Mixed), Tuskegee/T122, 1961
In His Care-O (Mixed), Tuskegee/T122, [color cover] 1961
Jesus Walked This Lonesome Valley, Remick, 1927
Jesus Walked This Lonesome Valley, Warner Brothers, 1927
Jesus Walked This Lonesome Valley, Remick, 1950
Jesus Walked This Lonesome Valley, Remick, 1927
Jesus Walked This Lonesome Valley (low), Remick, 1927
Jesus Walked This Lonesome Valley (Mixed), Gamble-Hinged Music, 1927
Jump Back, Honey, Jump Back, Wunderlichs Piano, 1923
King Jesus Is A-Listening (Mixed), FitzSimons, 1925
King Jesus Is A-Listening (Male) FitzSimons, 1957

King Jesus Is A-Listening (SAB), FitzSimons, 1988
King Jesus Is A-Listening (SATB), FitzSimons, 1953
King Jesus Is A-Listening (SSA), FitzSimons, 1946
King Jesus Is A-Listening (SSA), FitzSimons, 1956
King Jesus Is A-Listening (SSA), FitzSimons, 1974
Lit'l Boy Chile (Mixed), Tuskegee/T120, 1942
Lit'l Boy Chile (Mixed), Tuskegee/T120, 1974
Lit'l Boy Chile (Mixed), Tuskegee/T120 [color cover], 1974
Mary Had a Baby (Male), Tuskegee/T119, 1947
Mary Had a Baby (Male), Tuskegee/T119, 1974
Mary Had a Baby (Male), Tuskegee/T119 [color cover], 1974
Mary Had a Baby (Mixed), Tuskegee/T118, 1947
Mary Had a Baby (Mixed), Tuskegee/T118, 1974
Mary Had a Baby (Mixed), Tuskegee/T118 [color cover], 1974
The Mongrel Yank (SATB), Gamble-Hinged Music, 1930
My Lord What a Mourning (high), FitzSimons, 1927
My Lord What a Mourning (low), FitzSimons, 1927
My Lord What a Mourning, FitzSimons, 1954
Negro Folk Symphony [piano study score, marked copy], Shawnee, 1965
Oh, What a Beautiful City (Mixed), Tuskegee/T100, 1962
Out in the Fields, Remick, 1928
Out in the Fields, Remick, 1929
Out in the Fields (Female), Tuskegee/T131, 1957
Out in the Fields (high), Gamble-Hinged Music, 1929
Out in the Fields (high), Tuskegee, 1957
Out in the Fields (low), Gamble-Hinged Music, 1929
Out in the Fields (medium), Gamble-Hinged Music, 1957
Out in the Fields (medium), Tuskegee, 1957
Out in the Fields (Mixed), Tuskegee/T130, 1957
Pilgrim's Chorus, Kjos Music, 1968
The Rugged Yank, Kjos Music, 1970
The Rugged Yank (Male), Tuskegee/T132, 1970
Selections from Tuskegee Choir Series by William L. Dawson, Kjos Music [1965?]
Slumber Song (Female), Tuskegee/T137, 1974
Slumber Song (Male), Tuskegee/T139, 1974
Slumber Song (Mixed), Tuskegee/T138, 1974
Soon-Ah Will Be Done (Male), Tuskegee/T101-A, 1962
Soon-Ah Will Be Done (Male), Tuskegee/T101-A [color cover], 1962
Soon-Ah Will Be Done (Mixed), Tuskegee/T102, 1934
Soon-Ah Will Be Done (Mixed), Tuskegee/T102, 1962
Steal Away (Male), Tuskegee/T109, 1969
Steal Away (Mixed), Tuskegee/T109 [color cover], 1970
Swing Low, Sweet Chariot (Female), Tuskegee/T116, 1949
Swing Low, Sweet Chariot (Female), Tuskegee/T116, 1973

APPENDIX A: COMPOSITIONS AND ARRANGEMENTS

Swing Low, Sweet Chariot (Male), Tuskegee/T115, 1946
Swing Low, Sweet Chariot (Male), Tuskegee/T115, 1973
Swing Low, Sweet Chariot (Mixed), Tuskegee/T114, 1949
Swing Low, Sweet Chariot (Mixed), Tuskegee/T114, 1973
Swing Low, Sweet Chariot (Mixed), Tuskegee/T114 [color cover], 1973
Talk about a Child That Do Love Jesus, FitzSimons, 1927
Talk about a Child That Do Love Jesus, FitzSimons, 1980
Talk about a Child That Do Love Jesus [with organ], FitzSimons, 1980
Talk about a Child That Do Love Jesus (high), FitzSimons, 1927, 1955, 1983
Talk about a Child That Do Love Jesus (low), FitzSimons, 1927
Talk about a Child That Do Love Jesus (low), FitzSimons, 1983
There Is a Balm in Gilead (Female), Tuskegee/T106, 1939
There Is a Balm in Gilead (Female), Tuskegee/T106, 1967
There Is a Balm in Gilead (Female), Tuskegee/T106 [color cover], 1967
There Is a Balm in Gilead (Male), Tuskegee/T106, 1967
There Is a Balm in Gilead (Male), Tuskegee/T106 [color cover], 1967
There Is a Balm in Gilead (Mixed), Tuskegee/T105, 1939
There Is a Balm in Gilead (Mixed), Tuskegee/T105, 1949 [see Series 10]
There Is a Balm in Gilead (Mixed), Tuskegee/T105, 1967
There Is a Balm in Gilead (Mixed) Tuskegee/T105 [color cover], 1967
There Is a Balm in Gilead (high), Tuskegee, 1967
There Is a Balm in Gilead (low), Tuskegee, 1967
There's a Little Wheel A-Turnin' in My Heart, Tuskegee/T121, 1975
There's a Little Wheel A-Turnin' in My Heart, Tuskegee/T121 [color cover], 1975
Two Spirituals for Male Chorus [Jesus Walked This Lonesome Valley and You Got to Reap Just What You Sow] Warner Brothers, 1927
You Got to Reap Just What You Sow (Female), Tuskegee/T144, 1928
You Got to Reap Just What You Sow (Male), Tuskegee/T143, 1928
You Got to Reap Just What You Sow (Mixed), Tuskegee/T142, 1928
You Got to Reap Just What You Sow (Mixed), Tuskegee/T142 [color cover], 1928
You Got to Reap Just What You Sow (in E<flat>), Remick, 1928
You Got to Reap Just What You Sow (in G), Remick, 1928
You Got to Reap Just What You Sow, Remick, 1928
You Got To Reap Just What You Sow, Warner Brothers, 1928
Zion's Walls (Mixed), Tuskegee/T124, 1961

Source: William Levi Dawson Papers, Stuart A. Rose Manuscript, Archives, and Rare Book Library, Emory University.

Musical sketches, arrangements, and compositional fragments for voices and instruments by William Dawson can be found in the Rose Archives. The list below indicates titles not already published or mentioned in print.

SUBSERIES 2.2
Scores—Shorter Works

Adagietto for String Orchestra
Afterglow
All over God's He-bum
Amen
Ansieta (anxiety)
Ansioso (anxiety)
Anybody Here Love My Jesus?
Dance (Juba)
Danny Boy
Dawn (Composition Sketchbook 1)
Do Lord
El Sueño del Infante Jesus (Composition Sketchbook 9)
Go Tell It on the Mountain
God I Need Thee
Go to Sleep
Good Night
I Haven't Seen Daddy (Composer sketches)
In the Hollow of His Hand (Composition Sketchbook 6)
Interlude for Orchestra and Piano
Interlude for Orchestra and Piano [piano score]
The Journey to Calvary
Konju-Raku
Lady Moon (composer sketches)
Liberian National Anthem (arrangement)
Mary Had a Chile (composer sketches)
My God Is So High (composer sketches)
My Heart's A-Flame (fragment)
O, Clap Your Hands
Oh, My Little Soul Gwine Shine like a Star, Hallelujah!, and Oh Le'me Shine
Oppression
Poème Erotique [This score is an arrangement of a piano piece of the same name composed by Melville Charlton (1880–1973) in 1911. Dawson's arrangement is for concert band].
Rise Up, Shepherd an' Foller (composer sketches)
Romance in A for Violin, Cello, and Piano (see also Composition Sketchbook 1)
Ship of Zion (See Composition Sketchbook 6)
Sonata in A, arranged for piano trio (piano part is missing)

Sonata in A, arranged for string quartet (contains the score version of the 2nd movement)
Summertime
Sun Set (tone poem) for concert band with reeds (see also Composition Sketchbook 1)
Till Your Thoughts Are Just for Me (fragment)
Tomorrow May Be Too Late
Tre Giorni Son Che Nina (see Composition Sketchbook 9)
True Religion
Uncle Ben's Step (see Composition Sketchbook 1)
A Vow (fragment)
Were You There?
You Can't Catch Me (arrangement) [This file includes notation for "You Can't Catch Me" by Chuck Berry and "Come Together" by The Beatles, showing similarities between the two songs. Dawson created this comparison as an expert witness on behalf of Big Seven Music, Chuck Berry's music publisher and copyright holder for the song, in an infringement suit against John Lennon.]
You're Tired Chile

UNIDENTIFIED FRAGMENTS AND COMPOSER SKETCHES

Composition Sketchbook 1 (1922?)
Composition Sketchbook 2 (1923?)
Composition Sketchbook 3 (Exercises in Counterpoint, Kansas City, Missouri, 1923–25)
Composition Sketchbook 4 (1923–57?)
Composition Sketchbook 5 (1927?)
Composition Sketchbook 6
Composition Sketchbook 7
Composition Sketchbook 8
Composition Sketchbook 9
Composition Sketchbook 10
Composition Sketchbook 11
Composition Sketchbook 12
Composition Sketchbook 13
Composition Sketchbook 14
Composition Sketchbook 15

Source: William Levi Dawson Papers, Stuart A. Rose Manuscript, Archives, and Rare Book Library, Emory University, 16–19.

Appendix B

AWARDS AND HONORS RECEIVED BY WILLIAM LEVI DAWSON

AWARDS AND HONORS RECEIVED BY WILLIAM LEVI DAWSON[1]

1929 Won the Chicago Daily News Contest for Band Conductors for the 1933 World's Fair
1930 Won Wanamaker Contest prize: Class 1, first prize for a song, "Jump Back, Honey, Jump Back," Class 2, first prize for "Scherzo" for orchestra.
1931 Won Wanamaker Contest prize: Class 1, first prize, for a song, "Lovers Plighted."
1956 April 25: Awarded the honorary degree of Doctor of Music by Tuskegee Institute during its Diamond Jubilee Anniversary Celebration.
1963 November 8: Received an Alumni Achievement Award from the University of Missouri at Kansas City, Kansas City, Missouri.
1967 February 25: Recipient of the University of Pennsylvania Glee Club Award of Merit and Citation at the University of Pennsylvania, Philadelphia, Pennsylvania.
1969 June 22: Honored at the fifth annual "Festival de Musique," sponsored by the Senior Choir of the Abyssinian Baptist Church of New York City. Howard T. Dodson, Minister of Music, presented the plaque on which is engraved this statement: "To William Dawson with Honor for Supreme Achievement in the World of Music."
1971 December 4: Honored by the Tuskegee-Philadelphia Alumni Chapter at its Golden Anniversary Dinner in Philadelphia, Pennsylvania, Saturday, December 4. Ralph Ellison, author of *Invisible Man*, and a former student of Mr. Dawson's was the guest speaker.
1974 January 24–26: Honoree of the Third Annual Workshop on Afro-American Music. (Sponsored by the Music Department of Clark, Morehouse, Morris Brown, Spelman and the Center for African and African-American Studies). Conference Coordinator, Dr. Richard A. Long, Atlanta University, Atlanta, Georgia.
February 8: Guest of Honor at the Second Annual American Music Choral Festival, Dr. Katherine H. Mahan, Chairman, at Columbus College, Columbus, Georgia.
1975 February 20: Performance of his *Negro Folk Symphony* by the Crescent Youth Symphony Orchestra of Greenville, South Carolina, Dr. Robert Cheseboro, conductor. The Honorable Max M. Heller, mayor, and Council of the City of Greenville, South Carolina, conferred the title of Honorary Citizen upon William Dawson at

the concert. The program was designated as an official Bicentennial event by the Greenville American Revolution Bicentennial Celebration Committee. The concert was presented in the Furman University McAllister Auditorium.

March 6–8: Honored by the American Choral Directors Association at its Third National Convention in St. Louis, Missouri: "For His Pioneering Leadership, Inspiration, and Service to the Choral Arts."

April 26: Inducted into the Alabama Arts Hall of Fame. The four 1975 honorees were: actress Katherine Cornell, composer-conductor William Dawson, author William Faulkner, and artist Anne Goldwaite.

May 11: Conducted a concert sponsored by the Mayor's Advisory Council on Art and Culture, and the Baltimore City Schools. Part I was a performance of the *Negro Folk Symphony* by the Baltimore Symphony Orchestra conducted by the composer. Part II was choral music sung by a select high school chorus of 200 voices and an off-stage chorus of 1,400 voices accompanied by a brass ensemble and the BSO. Mayor William D. Shaefer presented Mr. Dawson with the Key to the City and conferred upon him while he was in the city an Honorary Citizenship of Baltimore City. The concert "Let's Make Music Together" was presented to a standing-room-only audience in the Lyric Theatre, Baltimore, Maryland.

December 14: Chosen as the person of honor outside of the Brotherhood of Alphamen by the Tuskegee Institute Alumni and College Chapters of Alpha Phi Alpha Fraternity, Incorporated.

1976 April 2: Honored by the Tuskegee Chapter of Continental Societies, Inc., in Commemoration of the Country's Bicentennial Celebration for "his work and contributions in the Tuskegee area, and in the field of music." A 1976 Service Award plaque was presented.

May 2: Honored by the Tuskegee Institute Chapter of The Links, Incorporated, "for his numerous contributions to music." "Freedom and the Fine Arts" are facets of the organization's program goals. The honoree was presented a pen mounted on a marble base and appropriately engraved.

1977 April 24–26: Honored by Georgia State University and its Department of Music. Dawson guest-conducted the GSU Orchestra, the GSU Concert Choir, the GSU Community Gospel Choir, and the Atlanta Junior College Choir. A plaque received reads: Georgia State University Honors William L. Dawson FOR HIS OUTSTANDING MUSICAL CONTRIBUTIONS AS A COMPOSER AND CONDUCTOR APRIL 26, 1977. On this occasion Dawson was made an honorary citizen of the city of Atlanta, by the Honorable Maynard Jackson, mayor of Atlanta, and in recognition thereof was presented a Certificate of Citizenship. The concert was in the GSU Art and Music Recital Hall, Atlanta, Georgia.

1977 November 8: Made an honorary member and received Certificate of Membership, Phi Mu Alpha Sinfonia Fraternity of America, National Chapter Honorary, November 8, 1977.

1978 May 7: The honorary degree of Doctor of Laws was conferred on William L. Dawson by Lincoln University, Lincoln University, Pennsylvania.

1980   Fine Arts Award, Alabama Coalition for Arts and Humanities at Alabama State University

1981   April 11: Citation from

THE UNIVERSITY OF MICHIGAN SCHOOL OF MUSIC

The Eva-Jessye Afro-American Music Collection
takes great pleasure in recognizing
the distinguished contributions
of
WILLIAM LEVI DAWSON
to the presentation and understanding of the
Afro-American folksong and to American music in general.
We observe and honor these contributions
on this 11th day of April
in the year of our Lord Nineteen Hundred and Eighty One.

April 12: Chosen by the Board of Directors of the Intercollegiate Music Council as the 1981 recipient of the Marshall Bartholomew Award. The award was established by the ICMC. to honor outstanding individuals who contribute significantly to the male chorus movement in memory of the late Marshall Bartholomew. The ICMC Seminar in 1981 was held April 10–12 at the University of Michigan at Ann Arbor.

November 20: The mayor of Philadelphia, Pennsylvania, designated this day "William Levi Dawson Day," and the city's director of cultural affairs presented Dawson with their highest award. A concert of his choral compositions was given by the Mendelssohn Singers at the Academy of Music.

1982   Honorary Doctorate of Music by Ithaca College, Ithaca, New York

1983   Heinecke Award

1989   Inducted into the Alabama Hall of Fame

1990   Honored a second time by the American Choral Directors Association at the March Convention of the Southern Division in Birmingham, Alabama, in celebration of his ninetieth birthday. Awarded an honorary plaque by Georgia State University

Awarded a citation for his distinguished contributions to the understanding of African-American folk song, by the University of Michigan School of Music.

Appendix C

SIGNIFICANT LETTERS, SPEECHES, AND INTERVIEWS REGARDING THE LIFE OF WILLIAM LEVI DAWSON

LETTERS TO DAWSON—
THE TUSKEGEE CHOIR-NBC RADIO BROADCASTS, 1937

1

November 29, 1937

Dear Mr. Dawson:
As radio editor of the New York Daily Mirror permit me to congratulate you on the best job of directing a choral group these ears have ever heard. Your singers are in a class by themselves and I am going to come right out and say so in an early edition of this paper.

Sincerely,

/s/ Nick Kenny,
Radio Editor,
N.Y. Daily Mirror

Used by special permission of Mr. Dawson

2

November 6, 1937
Dear Mr. Dawson:

As the Radio Editor of the Norfolk Virginian-Pilot, this is the first time I have ever taken the time to write a letter to any one program to commend it.

But I should like to say that the Tuskegee Choir is bringing to its listeners a type of musical entertainment I believe is universally understandable and thoroughly appreciated, a sort of sung philosophy that, besides its enjoyableness, certainly should be one means of furthering a better relationship between white people and Negro people.

You may be interested to know that I find many persons here are greatly interested in the Tuskegee Institute Choir programs. The three broadcasts so far evidently created a considerable following in Norfolk despite the fact that Hampton Institute is just across Hampton Roads from us and frequently presents its choir over the radio.

I have only one suggestion for your program. I think it should be timed so that your signing off number, "Deep River," would be allowed at least one full chorus or more and that the announcer's concluding remarks be shortened a little.

With many wishes for your continued success on the air, I am
Yours very truly,

/s/ H. G. Tilghman

Used by special permission of Mr. Dawson

LETTER CONCERNING THE TUSKEGEE CHOIR RECORDING

Dear Miss Barker:
I feel that I must take this opportunity to tell you, after having made our Tuskegee Institute Choir recording with Mr. William L. Dawson, that in all of my musical and recording experience (which you know has been quite extensive), I have rarely had the pleasure of working with as capable a man

as Mr. Dawson. I do not hesitate to say that I think he is perhaps the finest choral conductor in the country, and the skill he exercises in extracting the best from a choral group is quite wonderful.

Kindest regards,

Sincerely yours,

WESTMINSTER RECORDING CO., INC.

/s/ Kurt List
Musical Director

Used by special permission of Mr. Dawson

LETTERS TO DAWSON ON HIS 90TH BIRTHDAY
Government Officials

1

State of Alabama
House of Representatives
Montgomery, Alabama
RESOLUTION
H I R 54

By Representative Clay

COMMENDING WILLIAM LEVI DAWSON
ON THE OCCASION OF HIS
90TH BIRTHDAY CELEBRATION

WHEREAS, Alabama native William Levi Dawson, world renowned conductor and composer, is an alumnus of Tuskegee University [sic] where

WHEREAS, Mr. Dawson who for some 25 years conducted the Tuskegee University [sic] Choir, was the moving force behind the choir's rise to fame through a performance at the opening of Radio City Music Hall and in appearances on a number of nationally televised programs, including those hosted by Ed Sullivan, Kate Smith, Eddie Fisher and others;

and

WHEREAS, among numerous of Mr. Dawson's compositions and arrangements of spirituals, are "Out in the Fields," as well as his well known "Negro Folk Symphony" which was premiered in 1934 by the Philadelphia Orchestra under the direction of Leopold Stokowski; and

WHEREAS, William L. Dawson, a member of the Alabama Music Hall of Fame, has indeed brought great honor to the State and to Tuskegee University [sic], both of which acknowledge with pride his incomparable talent, genius, and achievement; now therefore,

BE IT RESOLVED, That William Levi Dawson is hereby most highly commended; he further is extended sincere best wishes on the occasion of his 90th birthday celebration, at which event he shall be presented with a copy of this resolution.

I hereby certify that the above
Resolution was approved on this
The 1st day of September 1989,
Pursuant to HR 201 adopted in
The 1988 2nd Special Session of
The Alabama Legislature.

/s/ John W. Pemberton, Clerk

Author's personal collection of photocopies, originally sent by Tuskegee University archivist, Dan Williams, immediately following the 90th Birthday Celebration of William L. Dawson.

2

United States Senate
Washington, D.C. 20510

August 17, 1989

Mr. William L. Dawson
c/o Mr. Daniel T. Williams
Hollis Burke Frissell Library
Tuskegee University,
Tuskegee, Alabama 36083

Dear Mr. Dawson:

I would like to join your family, friends, and Tuskegee University in wishing you a happy 90th birthday.

Birthdays are indeed special occasions, and I trust that this one will prove especially memorable for you. You are well deserving of this time of celebration given in your honor. Your talents as composer and conductor make you an asset to our state.

I join with my fellow Alabamians in congratulating you on your 90th birthday, as well as your successful career. I wish for you continued health and happiness.

With kindest regards, I am

Sincerely,

/s/ Howell Heflin

Author's personal collection of photocopies, originally sent by Tuskegee University archivist, Dan Williams, immediately following the 90th Birthday Celebration of William L. Dawson.

3

The WHITE HOUSE
Washington

September 27, 1989

Dear Mr. Dawson:

Happy Birthday! Barbara and I are delighted to add our best wishes to those you have received on this special occasion.

As you reflect upon a full life and distinguished career as a world-renowned composer and conductor, you can find great joy in the contributions you have made to the arts. I applaud your leadership and artistry, which have enriched generations of Americans.

I hope you had a splendid 90th birthday. May every blessing be yours in the year to come.

Sincerely,

/s/ George H. W. Bush

Mr. William L. Dawson
Tuskegee, Alabama

Author's personal collection of photocopies, originally sent by Tuskegee University archivist, Dan Williams, immediately following the 90th Birthday Celebration of William L. Dawson.

LETTERS FROM FORMER FACULTY

1

1211 Old Montgomery Road
Tuskegee, Alabama 36088
August 29, 1989

Mr. William L. Dawson
P. O. Box 1052
Tuskegee Institute, Alabama 36088

Dear Mr. Dawson:

When I came to Tuskegee years ago to work in the Music Department for Tuskegee Institute, one of the duties assigned to me was to assist Mrs. Jennie Cheatham Lee, Director of the Choir and Mrs. Emily Moore Neely, Organist, as Pianist for the Sunday morning service. The Sunday morning prayer opened with "Cast Thy Burden on the Lord"—sung by the Choir.

Little did I know that the playing of the Arpeggios played by me on the piano were being closely observed by a student, whom I came to know in later years as William Levi Dawson, and to this day never fails to remind me of the performance.

As time moved on I became the fortunate "listener" to the music of this talented student who has brought joy to thousands of people, not only at home, but to the world with his music.

Congratulations and Good Wishes from a loyal Friend.

/s/ Adelaide Towson Foster

2

Orrin Clayton Suthern, II
ORGANIST CONDUCTOR
LECTURER IN BLACK MUSIC

September 17, 1989

Dr. William L. Dawson
Tuskegee University
Alabama.

Dear Friend:

How quickly, in some instances, time passes. It hardly seems that fifty years have passed since I arrived on the Tuskegee campus as a member of the faculty of the then School of Music. What an experience for a twenty-two year old youngster about to embark on a career as an organist and teacher. Under your guidance those five years spent at Tuskegee were the foundation for the most rewarding direction which became my musical life.

Although you never got around to writing for the organ your compositions for chorus made up a significant portion of the repertoires of the choruses I had the pleasure of conducting at Florida A and M; Bennett College, Dillard University, and at Lincoln University, Pa [sic] until my retirement.

Congratulations-best wishes-and continued good health.

/s/ Orrin Clayton Suthern, II
Professor Emeritus
Lincoln University, Pa.

LETTERS FROM FORMER STUDENTS

1

RALPH ELLISON
730 Riverside Drive
Apartment 8-D
New York, New York
10031

Dear Bill:

Let me begin with a bit of personal history: I first heard of you during the late twenties (1927, I believe), from a new found friend who had arrived in our community from Kansas City. With great enthusiasm he was describing the wonderful band of his school there, and when I asked him the name of its director he said, "He's a wild son-of-a-gun named Dawson." And when I asked him why he called you wild he said, "Because if those guys make a mistake he'll pick up the first thing handy and go up side their heads!"

Well, I was far more impressed by his description of the excellent performers that you'd made of your young musicians than by his comments on your temper. After all, we had a few hair trigger teachers of our own, I had dreams of becoming a composer, and I was searching for a role-model. Then, in 1931 an older friend who had become a member of the Tuskegee Band returned home and gave me a description of your musicianship, your organizational genius, and your personal style. He described your dress, your manner, your magic on the podium, and the exacting discipline which you demanded (and received) from your musicians. And then as though fate had taken a hand I was soon to hear the Tuskegee Choir during a broadcast from Rockefeller Center. All of which and [sic] left me convinced that if I intended to continue my studies in music it should be under your guidance.

Two years later, being short of the money needed to journey by passenger train, I hopped a freight and arrived at Tuskegee where I became a member of the band and one of your students in the school of music. It was the beginning of a relationship and nothing that I had heard about you proved to be untrue. You were a strict disciplinarian, an inspiring teacher, a stylish dresser, and a magical conductor who transformed choirs of untrained voices into ensembles that phrased and soared like angels. And then to my awe I heard the initial performance of your *Negro Work Symphony* and knew that "Dawson, William L." would be magical words in my life—Yes, and my Kansas City friend was accurate concerning your temper, which proved true when I made a mistake in a harmony class and you threw a piece of chalk at my head!

But most important to me was the fact that you took my artistic ambitions seriously and had assembled a music faculty which did the same. And although it turned out that I would end as a writer rather than a composer, the discipline and encouragement which you provided was far more important in my development than I am able to tell you. For this I thank you, Bill, and my congratulations on this, your 90th birthday!

Sincerely,

/s/ Ralph

Author's personal collection of photocopies, originally sent by Tuskegee University archivist, Dan Williams, immediately following the 90th Birthday Celebration of William L. Dawson.

2

September 15, 1989

Dear Mr. Dawson:

May I congratulate you on having reached your ninetieth birthday, and for your timeless contributions to music which, I am sure, will be the source of enjoyment to those who will hear them for years to come. I was a member of the nineteen-hundred-thirty-two Tuskegee choir that opened the Radio City Music Hall, sang for President Hoover, and President-elect Franklin D. Roosevelt.

Some years ago I retired from the Army Corps of Engineers to pursue a career in Architecture and Building Construction. I subsequently taught Building Construction at the Prince Georges Community College in the State of Maryland. I am presently retired from the District of Columbia Public Schools as an instructor in Architectural Planning and as an administrator in Adult Education. I feel a rare distinction in having been part of a select group that performed under your personal direction.

Again, my felicitations. May you savor the substance of your achievements in these, your golden years.

Respectfully,

/s/ Lionel V. Gordon

Author's personal collection of photocopies, originally sent by Tuskegee University archivist, Dan Williams, immediately following the 90th Birthday Celebration of William L. Dawson.

3

1620 Portal Drive, N.W.
Washington, D.C. 20012
September 24, 1989

Dear Mr. Dawson,

I am happy to have the opportunity to congratulate you on your 90th birthday celebration.

Ever since we first met, you have been a symbol of perfection and accomplishment for me. During my years in your original choir at Tuskegee, it was always evident that you demanded the best of us and never failed to help us achieve that goal. This attitude helped to instill in me the importance of doing my best in all endeavors.

There is no doubt in my mind that your work throughout the years has fostered a greater appreciation on the part of Americans of all races, as well as people of other countries, for African-American music, especially Negro Spirituals. We are particularly thankful to you and proud of you for having made this gift to the world.

As for me, I shall never forget nor minimize the value of the opportunities you gave me to travel with the choir. I still think of the memorable Southern Tour we made, when we were so well received by the many audiences. Needless to say, New York and the opening of Radio City Music Hall will always stand out as the gem of my school career at Tuskegee. Some highlights of this experience were: visiting Hyde Park to sing for President-elect Roosevelt, singing atop the then-new Empire State Building, performing at Carnegie

Hall, and singing with Eugene Ormandy's Philadelphia Orchestra. I remember that you once said, "you will tell your children and grandchildren about these experiences." You were absolutely right—I have!

Not only were you deeply involved with the students at Tuskegee, but also with the community, I remember many times when special programs were being presented, you invited vocalists from the community as well as former choir members to participate with the choir. Lois and I had the pleasure of participating in some of these events.

Through the years since we left Tuskegee I have participated with church choirs in my normal church-going experiences. In my present church, (which is in process of "cultural change,") it has been my pleasure to introduce them to much of your music, which is gradually being integrated into your services.

I am proud to have had the opportunity of knowing you and working with you. I never pass up the chance to let people know that I have sung in your choirs.

God bless you and keep you in health and happiness for many years to come.

Lois joins me in sending our love to you and Mrs. Dawson.

Sincerely,

/s/ Wendell E. Gaillard

Mr. William L. Dawson
808 Bibb Street
Tuskegee, Alabama 36088

Author's personal collection of photocopies, originally sent by Tuskegee University archivist, Dan Williams, immediately following the 90th Birthday Celebration of William L. Dawson.

LETTERS FROM FRIENDS AND COLLEAGUES

1

P.O. Box 2061
FPO New York
September 12, 1989

Mr. William Dawson
Professor Emeritus of Music
Tuskegee University
Tuskegee Institute, AL 36088
Dear Mr. Dawson,

It has been my great pleasure to have known you as a personal friend and neighbor at Tuskegee. The great Tuskegee Institute Choir, which you taught and conducted in the historical chapel there, was an inspiration to all of us who heard you perform the time-honored Negro Spirituals.

My own special memory is that of you and I standing outside your wife's gift shop one fall evening, at sunset. You instructed me to sing the musical scale, after which you rendered your professional opinion. "You have a good voice," you commented.

May God continue to bless you.

Always,

/s/ Muhammad Musa Muslim Abuwi
formerly known as
Marshall S. Cabiness, Jr.
Great-grandson of
Booker T. Washington

2

September 1, 1989

Mr. William L. Dawson, Director
Tuskegee University Choir (1931–35)

Tuskegee University
Tuskegee, AL 36083

HAPPY BIRTHDAY Mr. Dawson:

We all are just passing thru. Some are short gainers, the Martin Luther Kings, John F. Kennedys, and Billie Holidays. Others are middle gainers, the Robert R. Motons, Franklin D. Roosevelts and Duke Ellingtons. And then there are God's chosen long gainers, emissaries of servitude, the Nelson Mandelas, Claude Peppers and William L. Dawsons.

To bask in the shadow of eminence is a luxury available to all and enjoyed by many. My cup runneth over.

Sincerely yours,

/s/ Horace D. Milan
258 E. 47th Street
Los Angeles, CA 90011

Author's personal collection of photocopies, originally sent by Tuskegee University archivist, Dan Williams, immediately following the 90th Birthday Celebration of William L. Dawson.

3

112 Van Nuys Boulevard
Savannah, Georgia 31419

Mr. William Dawson
Tuskegee, Alabama

My Dear Friend, Bill:

My heartiest congratulations upon your 90th birthday! I am sure that my humble expression will join the resounding praises of a vast multitude of your colleagues, your friends, your former students, and your devoted friends around the world on this, your special day!

I recall with great pride the delightful afternoon I spent with you at the Elite Café in Montgomery, when we sat down over a delicious meal to discuss plans for a gala concert. In my meager way, I was seeking to pay a long-overdue tribute to you and your monumental work as a composer in a concert to be presented by the Montgomery Civic Chorale. We were planning to call this program: ALABAMA SINGS. A major portion of the program was to be a group of your own pieces, performed by the Chorale and conducted by you. The date was to be Saturday, October 25, 1980.

You accepted my proposal, and you graciously consented to conduct your own pieces. You made countless tiring trips down to Montgomery to rehearse the Chorale. I shall always remember how my own heart thrilled during those rehearsals as you shared with me and my singers from your rich experiences as a musician, a native Alabamian, and one who understood as no one else the depth of the Black culture of the South as expressed in the beautiful, moving music you loved. As an arranger your work was marvelous; as a composer your music was deep; as a conductor, you were relentlessly demanding, focusing not only on the details of diction, rhythm, intonation and dynamics, but, most importantly, on the very soul of the music. How my singers respected you! The concert was presented as scheduled to a packed house at the Civic Center in Montgomery. Television personality Dan Atkinson narrated, the singers sang their hearts out for you, and the audience rose to their feet in a thundering ovation at the end!

Later I invited you to conduct my church choir at Memorial Presbyterian Church in a performance of your gorgeous "Mary Had a Baby." Again, you graciously consented. As you prepared my choir for the performance, they all fell in love with you, and they gave their all in that performance. Again, the congregations stood for a long ovation. I don't recall ever hearing stuffy Presbyterians applaud like that!

Your contributions to American music are incalculable. Your profound influence upon young music students' lives is immeasurable. You have made the world richer by your long, productive life. You are a giant—a legend in your own time! I applaud you on this happy occasion, thanking God for your great gifts. I am truly proud and humbled to call you my friend. Many, many happy returns!

With warm affection,

/s/ Gene L. Jarvis

Author's personal collection of photocopies, originally sent by Tuskegee University archivist, Dan Williams, immediately following the 90th Birthday Celebration of William L. Dawson.

SPEECH BY A FORMER STUDENT

1

Ralph Ellison's speech before the Tuskegee Alumni Philadelphia Chapter's Golden Anniversary, December 4, 1971.

Here a very great composer, a master of choral music is being honored by a fellow who studied under him, who went to Tuskegee because there was a man named Dawson there. Who, since this seemed to be a part of the tradition, and it actually happens, rode freight trains. It's too far to walk . . . to get to a place where there was musical excellence. Where there was a tradition of music creativity. Most people didn't think about it in those terms, and yet it was there. It was there, I suspect, before Mr. Dawson graduated and returned to work his wonders on the scene. But it was there as a deep tradition, one which bathed each and everything that was done at Tuskegee with the overtones and undertones of a scent of life, which perhaps could not have been expressed except through art.

It was there perhaps out of the sheer desperate need to assert our hopes and our dreams against the complications of living in the South, or for that matter living in America. Being up against definitions of our humanity, which we could not accept and were too busy trying to go where we wanted to go and become what we wanted to become to stop and spend too much time in arguing about it. But the assertion of our own sense of life, the insistent drive to define human hope in the United States, not through avoiding those aspects of reality and especially of our condition, which were brutal and dehumanizing. But to take that, too, as part of the given scene and then determine to go beyond it, not to ignore it, not pretend it didn't exist, but to humanize it, to take it in. To make it connect up to other aspects of living, with the dream, with the sounds of the future. The sounds of hope. We did that through music, that was a tradition, that is a tradition. For by and the slave past which bathes, which enhances the activities of Tuskegee.

Underneath the desire for education, underneath the desire for the possession of more technology, underneath the drive for intellectual competency, is that other thing, that thing that can only be expressed through art.

Now I said its [*sic*] rather odd that a fellow who didn't make it as a musician should be here trying to say something to and about William L. Dawson, but I think just as he reached out through his choir, his ability to make people who were not really musicians give voice to sublime music, he was doing something else, acting as a cultural hero, acting as a symbol, a living symbol of what was possible. And so we came to Tuskegee and so we played in the band and in the orchestra and so we studied, he once threw a piece of crayon at me. And, so you learn that even there life is real, life is honest, life is ambiguous, but, you got certain messages of which you weren't quite sure you were getting.

When Mr. Dawson stood before a choir or the band or the orchestra, you had the sense that you were dealing with realities beyond yourself. That you were being asked to give yourself to meanings which were undefinable, except in terms of music. and except in terms of musical style. But, you also had the sense that with his elegance and with his severity, with his grasp of the meaning of verse, the value that he could draw out of a word and make you draw out of it. The way he could make you phrase could teach you to grasp the meaning of a line of verse to which sometimes he had set to music. Sometimes, Handel. Gave you a sense that through this activity, through this dedication to the arts you were going beyond, and you were getting insight into your other activities.

As I said Tuskegee has been a place of music and it is ironic that through all of the years of its identity as a place of agriculture and industry, it had that other dimension, that dimension of art which went beyond the simple matter of our singing and our playing instruments. Tuskegee during the 30s was one of the major musical centers of the South. It was at Tuskegee that the Metropolitan Opera groups came. It was to Tuskegee that the great string quartets came, that the Philharmonic came. It was not to the University of Alabama, it was not to White schools in the area, but to Tuskegee. It was there that the tradition was. And, I'll tell you something else. It wasn't a new thing when the Tuskegee Choir opened Radio City during the 30s it was only the event through which the broader America, the broader United States became aware of what had been going on there for many, many years.

We live into ourselves. We grow from what went before. What comes after us depends upon what we do in preserving that which we share and which has been handed over into our keeping. I think it's quite important that during the 50th anniversary of the Philadelphia Tuskegee Club that you honor Mr. Dawson and that you impress upon the nation-at-large, that something very, very crucial to the cultural life of the United States and perhaps to the political life of the United States will be lost if we allow the tradition of Tuskegee to go down. I'm not talking now about politics. I'm talking about living examples. I'm talking about musical traditions because what is frequently overlooked, usually overlooked in these days where we talk of discovering our identities, is that there was an identity there all along, and when you see a choir like that, two choirs, one improvised I understand, the other which has been together. When you hear the articulation, when you hear the blending of the voices. That grew out of an identity. An identity based up on struggle with basic realities. A tradition which has been extended, broadened, and enriched by William L. Dawson. A tradition which is made out of musics which our forefathers heard and created out of what was around them and what they brought with them from Africa. But the magical thing about it is that it is not simply an in-group music. This is a definition, an artistic definition of what the American experience is when faced with grace, when faced with a willingness to give oneself to the tragic dimensions of the American experience. This is very precious. The entire nation depends on it because there is not enough of it.

We are very lucky that an artist of Mr. Dawson's statue found his way to Tuskegee at the age of 13. He must have been a little criminal because he ran away from home! But [he] spent many years there and received the basis of his musical training at Tuskegee. Some years ago in speaking with a group of my White colleagues, along with another Tuskegeean, we were talking about the writings of Joyce and Elliott and Pound and all of a sudden Albert Murray said, "Well Ralph, aren't you glad that we discovered these people at Tuskegee and for ourselves." And yes, I was glad, because now I can never read the poetry of those poets without associating it with Tuskegee, without seeing the magenta skies at dusk in summer, without seeing the clock in White Hall.

I must say that I was a fellow who used to wake Dr. Price up when I was there because I was a trumpeter. I used to stand out there early in the morning and blow "first call." And most of the time I put you to bed, too. Their tradition, the place, the associations, the sense of discovering that which is ever new, and the old, and the continuing, the abiding, this is one of the roles of the artist. If you can't spell it out, and some of these things cannot be spelled out in words, but they can be felt, they can be grasped, they can enter you, they can animate your body, and thus animate your mind. This is a great gift. We are very fortunate that such a man as Mr. Dawson.

Has touched so many of our lives. Through his dedication to art, he's made it possible for me, for instance, to be as dedicated and disciplined about literature. I'm sure the same is true for most of you who have been taught by him and touched by him. This is a secret of education which goes beyond grades, which goes beyond even brilliance of mind. This is a secret of the place, and the people, and the times, and that deep art of music, which is far more important to us than such poor critics as I have been able to spell out. If there were a choir here, I would say let us sing, "Let us break bread together." I am not particularly religious. I am claimed by music. I was claimed by William L. Dawson.

"Tuskegee Alumni, Philadelphia Chapter, Golden Anniversary" (Philadelphia, Pennsylvania,) 4, 1971, Side A, William Levi Dawson Papers, Stuart A. Rose Manuscript Archives, and Rare Book Library, Emory University.

INTERVIEWS WITH MR. DAWSON

1 Dawson's responses during an interview on National Public Radio, 1982

Negro folk songs

And so, these songs, they're called spirituals. That's not the right name. They're called plantation songs. That's not the right name. They're called Jubilee Songs. That's not the correct name. The correct name for them are folk songs, and no one person can write a folk song. Suwannee River is not a folk song. Kentucky Home is not a folk song. I doubt if Stephen Foster ever saw the Suwannee River, as he was in Pittsburgh or somewhere. Delius even. People don't know; Delius, the English composer came to Florida and lived among the Negroes. And, you'll find something in some of his things trying to catch this. And, it has been the Europeans who have come and taken hold of this. There's Stravinsky and Milhaud, Ravel. They have taken this music. These are Negro Folk Songs, that's what they are! And, no one person can write a folk song. That's why they call them folk songs. And, I think, for an example, if you remember "Care-O." One person started that. "One day as I was a-walking, down the lonesome road. Well, the spirit spoke unto me and it filled my heart with joy, joy, joy." And, the others pick it up. And they keep on doing this singing and after 10 or 15 or 20 years or more that comes out as that gem. That's true of all folk music. Now the Germans are very, very careful to name what it is. Das ist ein volk lied. That is a folksong! . . . But, if you want to know a people, what the people are, you go to their folk song.

"Interview with William Levi Dawson—The Sunday Show (National Public Radio), 1982," William Levi Dawson Papers, Stuart A. Rose Manuscript, Archives, and Rare Book Library, Emory University.

2 Dawson's responses to an interview in Philadelphia, Pennsylvania, October 8, 1979.

The importance of music in education

Was asked to speak to a "harmony" class at Overbrook High School: "I started with music and I told them that with music, everything at the university could taught if one knew the disciplines well enough. And, I proceeded to ask them questions about the things they were studying. And I tied it up with Geometry, because music contains everything in it—Grammar, Mathematics, Philosophy, Physics, Sociology, you name it, it's in music—literature, history. And, it's really a vital part of our life . . ."

The original Fisk Jubilee Singers/Queen Victoria's Gift/ Jennie Cheatham Lee/Dawson

[Queen Victoria] gave all the young ladies [in the Fisk Jubilee Singers] a diamond ring. I had a teacher, Mrs. Jennie Cheatham Lee—who was the choir director at Tuskegee for 25 years. She had one of those rings from one of the original Jubilee Singers and she wore than ring . . . And she took that diamond out of that ring and had it made into a stick-pin and gave it to me. So a few years ago my wife asked me if I'd give it to her, so I did.

"Interview with William Levi Dawson, Philadelphia, Pennsylvania, October 1979," William Levi Dawson Papers, Stuart A. Rose Manuscript, Archives, and Rare Book Library, Emory University.

3 Interview of Aaron Douglas and Jennie Cheatham Lee ("Mother Lee") by William Dawson, Nashville, Tennessee, May 10, 1953.

Aaron Douglas: I think in this life there are very few things that are more important, more precious than that of friendship. And uh today, I have the opportunity to meet and old friend, really, I should say, my best friend, William L. Dawson. We have struggled along all of these years and I thought we were really together and I was sure of it until he went off to Africa and beat me to an ambition that I've always had from our Kansas City experience when we used to vie with our various arts—he with his music and me with my painting. And then we were both ambitious to get to Africa—we were interested in things African and giving expression in the various arts to something with an African flavor. And so, I am somewhat miffed with him for having beaten me to this great experience.

Another thing that I should say about this day that has given me a great deal of pleasure to be invited by Mrs. Jennie Lee to sit with Bill Dawson, she called him her son, to sit with them in Chapel this morning in the Fisk Jubilee Chapel. It was a great pleasure and I enjoyed it and I appreciated the opportunity to be with two extremely fine musicians and to share the experiences of worship with them.

Jennie C. Lee: My son, William L. Dawson, and it is a pleasure to have him with me on Mother's Day. We also had as a guest in my home the distinguished artist, Aaron Douglas.

"Mother's Day recording with Martha M. Brown, Aaron Douglas, Mrs. Janus C. Lee, [sic] and William Dawson, Nashville, Tennessee, May 10, 1953," William Levi Dawson Papers, Stuart A. Rose Manuscript, Archives, and Rare Book Library, Emory University.

NOTES

INTRODUCTION

1. Vernon Edward Huff, "William Levi Dawson: An Examination of Selected Letters, Speeches and Writings," doctoral diss., Arizona State University, 2013, 2.
2. Huff, "William Levi Dawson," 2.
3. Lynée Lewis Gaillet, Diana Eidson, and Don Gammill, *Landmark Essays on Archival Research* (New York: Routledge/Taylor & Francis Group, 2016), 282.
4. Gaillet, Eidson, and Gammil, *Landmark Essays on Archival Research*, 283.
5. Gaillet, Eidson, and Gammil, *Landmark Essays on Archival Research*, 288.

CHAPTER 1: DAWSON'S EARLY YEARS AND EDUCATION: 1899–1930

1. Mark Hugh Malone, Interviews with William L. Dawson, Tuskegee, AL, March 23, 1979, January 24, 1981, February 7, 1981, February 21, 1981. William L. Dawson and Bess Bolden Walcott, interview by author, Tuskegee, AL, October 10, 1981. When I sent the manuscript of my dissertation to William Dawson for his approval of accuracy, he not only read the document but sought the assistance of longtime Tuskegee faculty member Bess Bolden Walcott to confirm the content. Bolden, a new graduate of Oberlin College in 1908, was immediately hired by Booker T. Washington and remained at the school for fifty-four years but continued part-time service into the 1970s. At Tuskegee, Mrs. Walcott founded and edited two important campus publications, was public relations director, curated the George Washington Carver Museum, started the first African American Red Cross chapter, and was instrumental in securing Tuskegee's placement on the National Register of Historic Places. Mrs. Walcott was a leader in the suffragist movement and was National Vice-President of the Women's International League for Peace and Freedom. Following her death at age 101, she was posthumously inducted into the Alabama Women's Hall of Fame, in 2003. What a joy to meet this incredible woman when she was almost ninety-five years old, and to receive her blessing of historical accuracy.

George Dawson's brother Levi also named a son William Levi Dawson, making the two men with the same name first cousins. Levi's son, who later was referred to as William Levi Dawson, Sr., was born in Albany, Georgia, in 1886 and eventually became a member of the

US House of Representatives from Illinois in 1943. William Dawson Sr. served fourteen consecutive terms in Congress before his death in 1970. Interview with Jennifer Randolph, grandniece of William Levi Dawson (musician), November 18, 2021.

Major content for this chapter came from extensive interviews with William Dawson (as noted above), with many of the details written in a doctoral dissertation completed at Florida State University in 1981. More information has been discovered during recent research, enhancing the original tale, which was at that time the most extensive and seminal work concerning the life and work of William Levi Dawson. Unless otherwise noted by endnote in this chapter, consider the source of the information to be those fascinating and important face-to-face interviews with the amazing subject of this book.

2. Significantly, guitarlike instruments were a part of music-making in West Africa among the griots, who served as singing historians, commenting on social life. In the late 1800s, newly freed African Americans constructed a one-string guitar, called a diddley bow, out of materials at hand to accompany blues music. The lyrics of blues songs were often a lament about life. Dawson may have been inspired to create his stringed instrument as a result of having seen and heard instruments similar to the diddley bow. Scott Baretta and Mark Malone, *The Mississippi Blues Trail and Beyond: Teachers Guide*. Jackson: Mississippi Arts Commission, 2012, 13–15.

3. Booker T. Washington. "Atlanta Exposition Address, 1895," *Black History Bulletin* 68, no. 1 (2005): 18–20; Booker T. Washington, "Atlanta Exposition Speech-September 18, 1895," Booker T. Washington Papers, Manuscript Division, Library of Congress, Washington, DC, https:memory.loc.gov/cgi-bin/query/r?ammem/aaodyssey:@field(NUMBER)+@band(mssmisc+ady0605), accessed December 28, 2021.

4. Booker T. Washington, "Atlanta Exposition Address, 1895."

5. Booker T. Washington, *The Story of My Life and Work* (Chicago: J. L. Nichols, 1900), 59; Frederick Douglass, "Letter to Mrs. Stowe," Frederick Douglass Papers, the University of Virginia, December 2, 1853, http://utc.iath.virginia.edu/africam/afar03agt.html.

6. Booker T. Washington, *The Story of My Life and Work* (Chicago: J. L. Nichols, 1900), 320; Mark Hugh Malone, interviews with William L. Dawson, Tuskegee, AL, March 23, 1979, January 24, 1981, February 7, 1981, February 21, 1981; William L. Dawson and Bess Bolden Walcott, interview by author, Tuskegee, AL, October 10, 1981.

7. Washington, *Story of My Life and Work*, 391–92.

8. Booker T. Washington held honorary degrees from two Ivy League institutions: an MA from Harvard University, awarded in 1896, and the LLD. from Dartmouth College, awarded in 1901. Generally, most recipients of honorary degrees are not referred to with the titles bestowed. Nonetheless, many people, out of respect for the accomplishments and leadership of Booker T. Washington, respectfully and affectionately referred to the man as Dr. Washington.

9. Washington, *Story of My Life and Work*, 391–92.

10. Washington, *Story of My Life and Work*, 391–92.

11. Washington, *Story of My Life and Work*, 391–92.

12. Horner, John. "Graduation Music in 1925," unpublished manuscript, part 3.

13. *Tuskegee Normal and Industrial Institute Bulletin* 8, no. 2 (1914–1915): 148.

14. *Tuskegee Normal and Industrial Institute Bulletin* 8, 148.

It is highly likely that the African student in Dawson's C Preparatory Class was Ponnett Mawalile from Matabele Land, Bulawayo, South Africa.

15. "Interview with William Levi Dawson, Philadelphia, Pennsylvania, October 8, 1979," William Levi Dawson Papers, Stuart A. Rose Manuscript, Archives, and Rare Book Library, Emory University.

16. Donald J. Grout, *A History of Western Music* (New York: W. W. Norton, 1988), 545–46, 635.

17. Hugh A. Orchard, *Fifty Years of Chautauqua: Its Beginnings, Its Development, Its Message, and Its Life* (Cedar Rapids, IA: Torch Press, 1923).

18. With the military-style format for male students, each could earn ranks while on campus. Neely, a graduate of Tuskegee, had attained the rank of captain; interviews with Cynthia Wilson, former archivist at Tuskegee University Archivist (1998–2007), November 16, 2021, at Tuskegee University Archives. Following graduation from Tuskegee in 1909, Neely served as custodian (1909), superintendent of buildings and grounds (1910–19), registrar (1919–30), registrar and Dean of Men (1931–1937), dean of men (1937–1941), executive secretary of the Tuskegee Alumni Association (1941–53); Lanice P. Middleton. *Tuskegee University Cemetery Stories: The Lives That Built a Great American Educational Institution* (Montgomery: NewSouth Books, 2021), 63–64.

19. Booker T. Washington held honorary degrees from two Ivy League institutions: an M.A. from Harvard University, awarded in 1896, and the L.L.D. from Dartmouth College awarded in 1901. Generally, most recipients of honorary degrees are not referred to with the titles bestowed. Nonetheless, many people, out of respect for the accomplishments and leadership of Booker T. Washington, respectfully and affectionately referred to the man as, Dr. Washington.

20. *Burlington Free Press*, "Redpath Chautauqua Opens Auspiciously," *Burlington Free Press*, August 17, 1921, p. 6.

21. W. E. B. (William Edward Burghardt) Du Bois, Letter from W. E. B. Du Bois to Encyclopaedia Britannica, May 12, 1926 (MS 312), W. E. B. Du Bois Papers, Special Collections and University Archives, University of Massachusetts Amherst Libraries.

22. Coleman, Nancy. "Why We're Capitalizing Black," *New York Times Insider* (New York, NY), July 5, 2020, http://nytimes.com/2020/07/05/insider/capitalized-black.html, accessed February 15, 2021.

23. Du Bois, W. E. B. (William Edward Burghardt), 1868–1963. Letter from W. E. B. Du Bois to Encyclopaedia Britannica, February 14, 1929. W. E. B. Du Bois Papers (MS 312). Special Collections and University Archives, University of Massachusetts Amherst Libraries.

24. Nancy Coleman, "Why We're Capitalizing Black," *New York Times Insider* (New York, NY), July 5, 2020, http://nytimes.com/2020/07/05/insider/capitalized-black.html.

25. "LeBron James: LA Lakers star says the unrest in Washington shows 'we live in two Americas,'" *Sky Sports*, https://www.skysports.com/nba/news/36226/12182098/lebron-james-la-lakers-star-says-the-unrest-in-washington-shows-we-live-in-two-americas, accessed February 8, 2021.

26. Marva Carter, "Session 6: 19th and 20th Century Notions of 'The Composer,'" March 4, 2005, DVCAM, 1hr58m, "In Celebration of William Levi Dawson" symposium records,

William Levi Dawson Papers, Stuart A. Rose Manuscript, Archives, and Rare Books Library, Emory University.

27. Mark Hugh Malone, interviews with William L. Dawson, Tuskegee, AL, March 23, 1979, January 24, 1981, February 7, 1981, February 21, 1981; William L. Dawson and Bess Bolden Walcott, interview by author, Tuskegee, AL, October 10, 1981. During one of my visits to interview William Dawson, he gave me a petal from one of the flowers plucked from the funeral wreaths of Booker T. Washington. My wife placed the petal in a paperweight with a cross-stitch of my name. At the time of publication of this book, the petal was over one hundred years old.

28. Mark Hugh Malone, interviews with William L. Dawson, Tuskegee, AL, March 23, 1979, January 24, 1981, February 7, 1981, February 21, 1981. William L. Dawson and Bess Bolden Walcott, interview by author, Tuskegee, AL, October 10, 1981.

29. Milton Randolph Jr., "Session 2: William Dawson, Up Close," March 3, 2005, DVCAM, 2hr36m, "In Celebration of William Levi Dawson" symposium records, William Levi Dawson papers, Stuart A. Rose Manuscript, Archives, and Rare Books Library, Emory University.

30. T. C. Harrington, Official Record of the Proceedings of the Board of Park Commissioners, Kansas City, MO, May 25, 1922, unpublished document in the possession of the Kansas City Parks and Recreation Department.

31. Amy Helene Kirschke, *Aaron Douglas: Art, Race, and the Harlem Renaissance* (Jackson: University Press of Mississippi, 1995), 9.

32. John Horner, "Graduation Music in 1925," unpublished manuscript, part 3.

While conducting research in the Missouri Valley Special Collections of the Central Library of the Kansas City Public Library System, March 9, 2021, I met Dr. John A. Horner, who was working as a volunteer in the archives. He shared with me his familiarity with the Horner Institute of Fine Arts, and his knowledge of Roy Wilkins's writings about William Dawson becoming the first African American graduate of the Horner Institute, and offered a brief unpublished blog that shared his own research on William Dawson. Horner's findings were presented in four segments.

33. "Interview with William Levi Dawson, Philadelphia, Pennsylvania, October 8, 1979," William Levi Dawson Papers, Stuart A. Rose Manuscript, Archives, and Rare Book Library, Emory University.

34. Creative Artists' Workshop, "Talking It Over with Roy Wilkins," *Kansas City Call*, December 13, 1934. Reprinted in *William Dawson: A Umum Tribute and a Marvelous Journey* (Philadelphia: Creative Artists' Workshop, 1981), 5–6. In preparation for the Philadelphia tribute, editor of the special publication, James G. Spady, received material from the honoree William Dawson. Mr. Dawson mentioned that I was nearing the completion of my dissertation, and Spady sent me an autographed copy. The title on the cover of the publication is listed as *The Creative Artists' Workshop presents William L. Dawson Day a Umum Tribute*, but the inside cover is titled as noted in the citation above. The citation of pagination above is supposed, as pages were not numbered. Gwynne Kuhner Brown notes that the editor James G. Spady's work is "not without errors." Gwynne Kuhner Brown, "Whatever Happened to William Dawson's *Negro Folk Symphony*?" *Journal of the Society for American Music* 6, no. 4 (2012): 433–56.

35. NAACP, "Roy Wilkins," https://naacp.org/find-resources/history-explained/civil-rights-leaders/roy-wilkins, accessed February 16, 2021.

36. "Cornella Lampton Dawson, Pianist, Died Suddenly in Chicago Hospital," *New York Age*, August 25, 1928, 7.

37. *New York Times*, "A Tuskegee Symphony: Stokowski to Present Dawson's Pioneer Work on Negro Themes," *New York Times* (1923–); November 18, 1934; ProQuest Historical Newspapers: The *New York Times with Index*, p. X6.

38. Dawson continued to strive to speak German, taking a summer course at the University of Rochester in 1938, and auditing a course at the Central YMCA in Chicago in the summer of 1940. The instructor in Chicago indicated on the grade record that Dawson would have had an A had he registered for the course. William Levi Dawson papers, Stuart A. Rose Manuscript, Archives, and Rare Books Library, Emory University.

39. Gamble Music Company, "About Us," https://www.gamblemusic.com/about-us/, accessed January 4, 2022.

40. Biographical information about Doc Cook refers to the musician with a spelling discrepancy regarding his last name, as Cook and Cooke are both used. Richard Raichelson, "Doc Cook," personal correspondence, November 21, 2021.

41. "Doc Cook and His 14 Doctors of Syncopation," Syncopated Times, https://syncopatedtimes.com/doc-cook-and-his-14-doctors-of-syncopation/, accessed February 16, 2021.

42. Raichelson, "Doc Cook."

43. Jazz educators/performers Raoul Jerome and Lawrence Panella contributed to the assessment of the Doc Cook recordings.

44. George Hulme and Andy Simons, "The Brian Rust Discographies," *International Association of Jazz Record Collectors Journal* 43, no. 2 (2010): 8–18.

45. Willie Strong indicated that along with his work with Otterstrom, Dawson studied composition with another composer, Felix Borowski. Both Otterstrom and Borowski were at the Chicago Musical College approximately 1930–31. However, Dawson did not mention Borowski during personal interviews. Strong also reported that Dawson engaged in further graduate study at Eastman School of Music in Rochester, New York, as well as compositional tutelage at the Conservatory of Music in Hamburg, Germany, yet Dawson did not mention this in interviews, nor did he list that schooling in his unpublished "Highlights of the Career of William L. Dawson." As mentioned in an earlier endnote, Dawson did take a course in German at the University of Rochester (NY) in the summer of 1938, under whose aegis Eastman School of Music exists. However, documentation of further compositional study may still exist. Willie Strong, "Dawson, William Levi," *International Dictionary of Black Composers*, Vol. 1, ed. Samuel A. Floyd Jr., 354–57 (Chicago: Fitzroy Dearborn, 1999).

46. "Interview with William Levi Dawson, Philadephia, Pennsylvania, October 8, 1979," William Levi Dawson Papers, Stuart A. Rose Manuscript, Archives, and Rare Book Library, Emory University.

CHAPTER 2: THE DEVELOPMENT OF THE MUSIC SCHOOL AT TUSKEGEE INSTITUTE: 1930–55

1. Mark Hugh Malone, interviews with William L. Dawson, Tuskegee, AL, March 23, 1979, January 24, 1981, February 7, 1981, February 21, 1981; William L. Dawson and Bess Bolden Walcott, interview by author, Tuskegee, AL, October 10, 1981.

2. Robert Russa Moton, *Finding a Way Out: An Autobiography* (Garden City, NY: Doubleday, Page, 1921), 221.

3. Ruth Ann Stewart. *Portia: The Life of Portia Washington Pittman* (New York: Doubleday, 1977), 103.

4. William H. Hughes, and Frederick D. Patterson, *Robert Russa Moton of Hampton and Tuskegee* (Chapel Hill: University of North Carolina Press, 1956), 231.

5. Hughes and Patterson, *Robert Russa Moton of Hampton and Tuskegee*, 222.

6. *Tuskegee Normal and Industrial Institute Bulletin* 20, no. 1 (1925): 13.

7. Hughes and Patterson, *Robert Russa Moton of Hampton and Tuskegee*, 211.

8. David Lee Johnson. "The Contributions of William L. Dawson to the School of Music at Tuskegee Institute and to Choral Music (Alabama)." ProQuest Dissertations, 1987, 52.

9. Johnson, "Contributions of William L. Dawson," 52.

10. Mark Hugh Malone, interviews with William L. Dawson, Tuskegee, AL, March 23, 1979, January 24, 1981, February 7, 1981, February 21, 1981; William L. Dawson and Bess Bolden Walcott, interview by author, Tuskegee, AL, October 10, 1981.

11. Johnson, "Contributions of William L. Dawson," 52–53.

12. Johnson, "Contributions of William L. Dawson," 52; Mark Hugh Malone, interviews with William L. Dawson, Tuskegee, AL, March 23, 1979, January 24, 1981, February 7, 1981, February 21, 1981; William L. Dawson and Bess Bolden Walcott, interview by author, Tuskegee, AL, October 10, 1981.

13. Mark Hugh Malone, interviews with William L. Dawson, Tuskegee, AL, March 23, 1979, January 24, 1981, February 7, 1981, February 21, 1981. William L. Dawson and Bess Bolden Walcott, interview by author, Tuskegee, AL, October 10, 1981.

14. Mark Hugh Malone, interviews with William L. Dawson, Tuskegee, AL, March 23, 1979, January 24, 1981, February 7, 1981, February 21, 1981; William L. Dawson and Bess Bolden Walcott, interview by author, Tuskegee, AL, October 10, 1981. *Normal and Industrial Institute Bulletin* 9, no. 2 (1915): 38.

15. *Tuskegee Normal and Industrial Institute Bulletin* 8, no. 2 (1914): 41.

16. *Tuskegee Normal and Industrial Institute Bulletin* 24, no. 2 (1930–31): 6; *Tuskegee Normal and Industrial Institute Bulletin* 25, no. 2 (1931–32): 116.

17. Mark Hugh Malone, interviews with William L. Dawson, Tuskegee, AL, March 23, 1979, January 24, 1981, February 7, 1981, February 21, 1981; William L. Dawson and Bess Bolden Walcott, interview by author, Tuskegee, AL, October 10, 1981.

18. Mark Hugh Malone, interviews with William L. Dawson, Tuskegee, AL, March 23, 1979, January 24, 1981, February 7, 1981, February 21, 1981.

19. Ruth Ann Stewart, *Portia: The Life of Portia Washington Pittman* (New York: Doubleday, 1977), 103–4, 106.

20. Herb Boyd, "Extraordinary Pianist and Gifted Teacher Hazel Harrison," *Amsterdam News: Arts-Entertainment in the Classroom*, May 10, 2019, pp. 1–4, accessed December 12, 2021. Boyd delved into the relationship between Hazel Harrison and her Tuskegee student Ralph Ellison, who came to study music with Dawson and went on to literary fame after his education at the institute. Ellison remembered the advice Harrison always proclaimed: "You must always play your best even if it's in the Chehaw Station, because in this country there'll always be a little man hidden behind the stove . . . the little man whom you don't expect,

and he'll know the music, and the tradition, and the standards of musicianship required for whatever you set out to perform."

21. *Tuskegee Normal and Industrial Institute Bulletin* 25, no. 2 (1931–32): 116.

22. Jean Snyder, *Harry T. Burleigh: From Spiritual to the Harlem Renaissance* (Champaign: University of Illinois Press, 2016), 163–65. Heather Peterson, "Abbie Mitchell," *BlackPast*, July 2, 2008, https://www.blackpast.org/african-american-history/Mitchell-abbie-1884-1960/, accessed November 16, 2021. Mitchell's stage credits included performances of *In Dahomey, Abraham's Bosom, Mulatto, Coquette* (with Helen Hayes), and *The Little Foxes*, singing with Sissieretta Jones's ensemble, Black Patti Troubadours, and featured actress with Harlem's Lafayette Theatre. "Mitchell, Abbie (1884–1960)," in *Dictionary of Women Worldwide: 25,000 Women through the Ages*, ed. Anne Commire and Deborah Klezmer, vol. 2 (Farmington Hills, MI: Yorkin, 2007, p. 1335. Gale eBooks, link.gale.com/apps/doc/CX2588816742/GVRL?u=tall85761&sid=bookmark-GVRL&xid=144e9360, accessed November 16, 2021.

23. *Tuskegee Normal and Industrial Institute Bulletin* 25, no. 2 (1931–32): 116.

24. "Tuskegee Organizes School of Music," *Tuskegee Messenger*, July, 1932, 6.

25. *Tuskegee Normal and Industrial Institute Bulletin* 25, no. 2 (1931–32): 119–34.

26. *Tuskegee Normal and Industrial Institute Bulletin* 25, 119–34.

27. *Tuskegee Normal and Industrial Institute Bulletin* 25, 124–27.

28. *Tuskegee Normal and Industrial Institute Bulletin* 25, 21–23.

29. Mark Hugh Malone, interviews with William L. Dawson, Tuskegee, AL, March 23, 1979, January 24, 1981, February 7, 1981, February 21, 1981; William L. Dawson and Bess Bolden Walcott, interview by author, Tuskegee, AL, October 10, 1981.

30. Malone, interviews with William L. Dawson.

31. In 1989, following the celebration of William Dawson's ninetieth birthday in Tuskegee, Dan Williams, archivist in the Hollis Burke Frissell Library at Tuskegee University, sent me a package of documents from the events surrounding the observance of Dawson's birth. Contained in the parcel was a letter containing a tribute and birthday greeting from Dawson's former student Ralph Ellison, author of *Invisible Man, Shadow and Act*, and *Juneteenth*. The letter is reprinted in Appendix C.

32. *Tuskegee Normal and Industrial Institute Bulletin* 26, no. 2 (1932–33)" 131.

33. Tim Brooks and Richard L. Spottswood. *Lost Souls: Blacks and the Birth of the Recording Industry, 1890–1919*. Urbana-Champaign: University of Illinois Press, 2004, 499–500. Proquest Ebook Central, http://ebookcentral.proquest.com/lib/fsu/detail.action?docID=3413942. Created from fsu on 2021-11-15 00:52:00.

34. Tuskegee Normal and Industrial Institute Bulletin 30, no. 2 (1936–37): 165.

35. *Tuskegee Normal and Industrial Institute Bulletin* 30, no. 2 (1936–37): 165–82.

36. *Tuskegee Normal and Industrial Institute Bulletin* 31, no. 2 (1937–38): 121.

37. *Tuskegee Normal and Industrial Institute Bulletin* 31, 121.

38. *Tuskegee Normal and Industrial Institute Bulletin* 31, 121–27.

39. *Tuskegee Normal and Industrial Institute Bulletin* 34, no. 2 (1941–2), 14.

40. "Legacy: The Story," Tuskegee Airmen, https://tuskegeeairmen.org/legacy/the-story, accessed June 4, 2021.

41. *Tuskegee Normal and Industrial Institute Bulletin* 36, no. 2 (1943–4), 15, 148–50.

42. *Tuskegee Normal and Industrial Institute Bulletin* 36, no. 2, 143–44.

43. *Tuskegee Normal and Industrial Institute Bulletin* 37, no. 2 (1944–5), 150.
44. *Tuskegee Normal and Industrial Institute Bulletin* 37, 151.
45. *Tuskegee Normal and Industrial Institute Bulletin* 37, 151.
46. *Tuskegee Normal and Industrial Institute Bulletin* 38, no. 2 (1945–46): 162.
47. *Tuskegee Normal and Industrial Institute Bulletin* 44, no. 2 (1951–52): 245–46.

CHAPTER 3: THE RISE OF THE TUSKEGEE CHOIR TO NATIONAL PROMINENCE: 1933–55

1. Mark Hugh Malone, interviews with William L. Dawson, Tuskegee, AL, March 23, 1979, January 24, 1981, February 7, 1981, February 21, 1981; William L. Dawson and Bess Bolden Walcott, interview by author, Tuskegee, AL, October 10, 1981.

2. Mark Hugh Malone, interviews with William L. Dawson, Tuskegee, AL, March 23, 1979, January 24, 1981, February 7, 1981, February 21, 1981; William L. Dawson and Bess Bolden Walcott, interview by author, Tuskegee, AL, October 10, 1981; Booker T. Washington, *The Story of My Life and Work* (Chicago: J. L. Nichols, 1900), 320.

3. Washington, *Story of My Life and Work*, 391–92.

4. Dawson also referred to these as Negro religious folk songs.

5. Mark Hugh Malone, interviews with William L. Dawson, Tuskegee, AL, March 23, 1979, January 24, 1981, February 7, 1981, February 21, 1981; William L. Dawson and Bess Bolden Walcott, interview by author, Tuskegee, AL, October 10, 1981.

6. *Tuskegee Normal and Industrial Institute Bulletin* 25, no. 2 (1931–32): 116.

7. *Tuskegee Normal and Industrial Institute Bulletin* 25, 116–17.

8. Tuskegee University Archives, "Tuskegee Institute Choir Program," April 15, 1936, Tuskegee University Archives Repository, Tuskegee Institute.

9. Tuskegee University Archives, "Tuskegee Institute Choir Program," April 15, 1936.

10. Tuskegee University Archives, "Tuskegee Institute Concert Program," April 13, 1931, Tuskegee University Archives Repository, Tuskegee Institute.

11. Tuskegee University Archives, "Tuskegee Institute Concert Program."

12. Lawrence Jackson, "Session 4: William Dawson, Ralph Ellison and Discipline," March 3, 2005, DVCAM, 2hr36m, "In Celebration of William Levi Dawson" symposium records, William Levi Dawson papers, Stuart A. Rose Manuscript, Archives, and Rare Books Library, Emory University.

13. William Levi Dawson, "Highlights of the Career of William L. Dawson," unpublished manuscript, 1.

14. John Lovell Jr., *Black Song: The Forge and the Flame* (New York: Macmillan, 1972), 417.

15. Eileen Southern, *The Music of Black Americans: A History* (New York: W. W. Norton, 1971), 451; Hildred Roach, *Black American Music, Past and Present* (Boston: Crescendo, 1973), 236.

16. Maude Cuney-Hare, *Negro Musicians and Their Music* (Washington, DC: Associated Publishers, 1936), 251–52.

17. "Music Review," *New York Times*, December 25, 1932, 1.

18. Lawrence Jackson, "Session 4: William Dawson, Ralph Ellison and Discipline," March 3, 2005, DVCAM, 2hr36m, "In Celebration of William Levi Dawson" symposium records,

William Levi Dawson papers, Stuart A. Rose Manuscript, Archives, and Rare Books Library, Emory University.

19. National Public Radio, "Interview with William Levi Dawson—The Sunday Show, 1982," William Levi Dawson Papers, Stuart A. Rose Manuscript, Archives, and Rare Book Library, Emory University.

20. Mark Hugh Malone, interviews with William L. Dawson, Tuskegee, AL, March 23, 1979, January 24, 1981, February 7, 1981, February 21, 1981; William L. Dawson and Bess Bolden Walcott, interview by author, Tuskegee, AL, October 10, 1981.

21. Mark Hugh Malone, interviews with William L. Dawson, Tuskegee, AL, March 23, 1979, January 24, 1981, February 7, 1981, February 21, 1981.

22. John Lovell Jr., *Black Song: The Forge and the Flame* (New York: Macmillan, 1972), 418.

23. "Music Review," *New York Times*, December 28, 1932, 1.

24. Brooks Atkinson, "Music Hall's Opening," *New York Times*, December 28, 1932, 14.

25. Atkinson, "Music Hall's Opening," 14.

26. "Theatre Review," *Wall Street Journal*, December 31, 1932, 3.

27. "A Striking Contribution to Musical America," *American Business Survey*, April 1933, 24.

28. National Public Radio, "Interview with William Levi Dawson—The Sunday Show, 1982," William Levi Dawson Papers, Stuart A. Rose Manuscript, Archives, and Rare Book Library, Emory University. A contradiction as to the site of the birthday concert for FDR being at Hyde Park or in New York City is noted (see endnote 35). Despite FDR's enthusiastic invitation to Dawson to bring the Tuskegee Choir to the White House during his tenure as president of the United States, a concert in that venue for the Roosevelts did not happen.

29. "Music Review," *New York Times*, February 9, 1933, 15.

30. "Music Review," 15.

31. Stirling Bowen, "The Theatre," *Wall Street Journal*, February 10, 1033, 3.

32. Bowen, "The Theatre," 3.

33. Bowen, "The Theatre," 3.

34. Bowen, "The Theatre," 3.

35. Mitchell, Abbie Mitchell, "A Colleague's Appreciation—Excerpts from Papers of the Late Abbie Mitchell on Her Teaching Experience at Tuskegee," reprinted in *William Dawson: A Umum Tribute and a Marvelous Journey* (Philadelphia: Creative Artists' Workshop, 1981), 6. Mitchell indicated that the Tuskegee Choir sang at FDR's city residence in New York City, while Dawson and others indicate both Hyde Park and New York City. Given the size of the choir, it seems more plausible that the visit to celebrate FDR's birthday would have been in his New York City residence.

36. National Public Radio, "Interview with William Levi Dawson—The Sunday Show, 1982," William Levi Dawson Papers, Stuart A. Rose Manuscript, Archives, and Rare Book Library, Emory University.

37. National Public Radio, "Interview with William Levi Dawson—The Sunday Show, 1982," William Levi Dawson Papers, Stuart A. Rose Manuscript, Archives, and Rare Book Library, Emory University.

38. National Public Radio, "Interview with William Levi Dawson—The Sunday Show, 1982," William Levi Dawson Papers, Stuart A. Rose Manuscript, Archives, and Rare Book Library, Emory University.

39. Mark Hugh Malone, interviews with William L. Dawson, Tuskegee, AL, March 23, 1979, January 24, 1981, February 7, 1981, February 21, 1981; William L. Dawson and Bess Bolden Walcott, interview by author, Tuskegee, AL, October 10, 1981; William Levi Dawson, "Highlights of the Career of William L. Dawson," unpublished manuscript, 3–4.

40. Mark Hugh Malone, interviews with William L. Dawson, Tuskegee, AL, March 23, 1979, January 24, 1981, February 7, 1981, February 21, 1981; William L. Dawson and Bess Bolden Walcott, interview by author, Tuskegee, AL, October 10, 1981.

41. Mark Hugh Malone, interviews with William L. Dawson, Tuskegee, AL, March 23, 1979, January 24, 1981, February 7, 1981, February 21, 1981; William L. Dawson and Bess Bolden Walcott, interview by author, Tuskegee, AL, October 10, 1981; William Levi Dawson, "Highlights of the Career of William L. Dawson," unpublished manuscript, p. 2.

42. "Interview with William Levi Dawson—The Sunday Show (National Public Radio), 1982," William Levi Dawson Papers, Stuart A. Rose Manuscript, Archives, and Rare Book Library, Emory University.

43. Mark Hugh Malone, interviews with William L. Dawson, Tuskegee, AL, March 23, 1979, January 24, 1981, February 7, 1981, February 21, 1981; William L. Dawson and Bess Bolden Walcott, interview by author, Tuskegee, AL, October 10, 1981. Poem used by special permission of Mr. Dawson

44. Mark Hugh Malone, iInterviews with William L. Dawson, Tuskegee, AL, March 23, 1979, January 24, 1981, February 7, 1981, February 21, 1981.

45. Used by special permission of Mr. Dawson (view full letter in Appendix C).

46. Used by special permission of Mr. Dawson (view full letter in Appendix C).

47. Mark Hugh Malone, interviews with William L. Dawson, Tuskegee, AL, March 23, 1979, January 24, 1981, February 7, 1981, February 21, 1981; William L. Dawson and Bess Bolden Walcott, interview by author, Tuskegee, AL, October 10, 1981; William Levi Dawson, "Highlights of the Career of William L. Dawson," unpublished manuscript, 3.

48. Mark Hugh Malone, interviews with William L. Dawson, Tuskegee, AL, March 23, 1979, January 24, 1981, February 7, 1981, February 21, 1981; William L. Dawson and Bess Bolden Walcott, interview by author, Tuskegee, AL, October 10, 1981.

49. Lovell, *Black Song*, 442.

50. "The Pocket Diaries of William Levi Dawson," 1919–1921, William Levi Dawson Papers, Stuart A. Rose Manuscript, Archives, and Rare Book Library, Emory University. See photo.

51. Mark Hugh Malone, interviews with William L. Dawson, Tuskegee, AL, March 23, 1979, January 24, 1981, February 7, 1981, February 21, 1981; William L. Dawson and Bess Bolden Walcott, interview by author, Tuskegee, AL, October 10, 1981.

52. Malone, Mark Hugh Malone, iInterviews with William L. Dawson, Tuskegee, AL, March 23, 1979, January 24, 1981, February 7, 1981, February 21, 1981.

53. Samuel Coleridge-Taylor, *Twenty-Four Negro Melodies* (Boston: Oliver Ditson, 1905).

54. Mark Hugh Malone, interviews with William L. Dawson, Tuskegee, AL, March 23, 1979, January 24, 1981, February 7, 1981, February 21, 1981; William L. Dawson and Bess Bolden Walcott, interview by author, Tuskegee, AL, October 10, 1981; William Levi Dawson, "Highlights of the Career of William L. Dawson," unpublished manuscript, 3.

55. "Booker T. Washington Stamp Commemoration," April 7, 1940, William Levi Dawson Papers, Stuart A. Rose Manuscript, Archives, and Rare Book Library, Emory University.

56. Wayne Barr, DMA, Director of Choral Activities at Tuskegee University, confirmed that no copies of either piece exist in the choral library at the school; interview with Wayne Barr, November 15, 2021, archives at Tuskegee University.

57. Mark Hugh Malone, interviews with William L. Dawson, Tuskegee, AL, March 23, 1979, January 24, 1981, February 7, 1981, February 21, 1981; William L. Dawson and Bess Bolden Walcott, interview by author, Tuskegee, AL, October 10, 1981; William Levi Dawson, "Highlights of the Career of William L. Dawson," unpublished manuscript, 3.

58. Mark Hugh Malone, interviews with William L. Dawson, Tuskegee, AL, March 23, 1979, January 24, 1981, February 7, 1981, February 21, 1981; William L. Dawson and Bess Bolden Walcott, interview by author, Tuskegee, AL, October 10, 1981; William Levi Dawson, "Highlights of the Career of William L. Dawson," unpublished manuscript, 3–4.

59. "Booker T. Washington Honored as Bust Is Added to Hall of Fame," *New York Times*, May 24, 1946, 21.

60. "Booker T. Washington Honored as Bust Is Added to Hall of Fame."

61. Mark Hugh Malone, interviews with William L. Dawson, Tuskegee, AL, March 23, 1979, January 24, 1981, February 7, 1981, February 21, 1981; William L. Dawson and Bess Bolden Walcott, interview by author, Tuskegee, AL, October 10, 1981; William Levi Dawson, "Highlights of the Career of William L. Dawson," unpublished manuscript, 4.

62. Louis Biancolli, "Tuskegee Choir Shows Finesse in Memorial," *New York World Telegram*, May 28, 1946, 25.

63. Biancolli, "Tuskegee Choir Shows Finesse in Memorial," 25.

64. "Tuskegee Choir Pays Tribute to Founder," *New York Times*, May 28, 1946, 25.

65. Mark Hugh Malone, interviews with William L. Dawson, Tuskegee, AL, March 23, 1979, January 24, 1981, February 7, 1981, February 21, 1981; William L. Dawson and Bess Bolden Walcott, interview by author, Tuskegee, AL, October 10, 1981; William Levi Dawson, "Highlights of the Career of William L. Dawson," unpublished manuscript, p. 4.

66. Samuel L. Singer, "Tuskegee Unit Gives Concert," *Philadelphia Inquirer*, May 29, 1946, 19.

67. Singer, "Tuskegee Unit Gives Concert," 19.

68. Max de Schauensee, "Tuskegee Institute Choir Offers Fine Program of Spirituals," *Evening Bulletin* (Philadelphia, PA), May 29, 1946, 17.

69. de Schauensee, "Tuskegee Institute Choir Offers Fine Program of Spirituals," 17.

70. Mark Hugh Malone, interviews with William L. Dawson, Tuskegee, AL, March 23, 1979, January 24, 1981, February 7, 1981, February 21, 1981; William L. Dawson and Bess Bolden Walcott, interview by author, Tuskegee, AL, October 10, 1981; William Levi Dawson, "Highlights of the Career of William L. Dawson," unpublished manuscript, p. 4.

71. "Music Review," *Washington Post*, June 4, 1946, 1.

72. Mark Hugh Malone, interviews with William L. Dawson, Tuskegee, AL, March 23, 1979, January 24, 1981, February 7, 1981, February 21, 1981; William L. Dawson and Bess Bolden Walcott, interview by author, Tuskegee, AL, October 10, 1981.

73. Glenn Dillard Gunn, "Capacity Crowd Hears Concert By Tuskegee Choir," *Times-Herald* (Washington, DC), June 4, 1946, 13.

74. Gunn, "Capacity Crowd Hears Concert By Tuskegee Choir," 13.

75. Alice Eversman, "Sheer Beauty Marks Local Concert By Tuskegee Choir," *Evening Star* (Washington, D.C.), June 4, 1946, 14.

76. Eversman, "Sheer Beauty Marks Local Concert by Tuskegee Choir," 14.

77. Eversman, "Sheer Beauty Marks Local Concert by Tuskegee Choir," 14.

78. Helen deMotte, "Fine Program Given by Group from Tuskegee," *Richmond Daily Leader* (Richmond, VA), June 5, 1946, 20.

79. deMotte, "Fine Program Given by Group from Tuskegee," 20.

80. William Levi Dawson, "Highlights of the Career of William L. Dawson," unpublished manuscript, 4.

81. William Levi Dawson, "Highlights of the Career of William L. Dawson," unpublished manuscript, 5.

82. William Levi Dawson, "Highlights of the Career of William L. Dawson," unpublished manuscript, 5.

83. William Levi Dawson, "Highlights of the Career of William L. Dawson," unpublished manuscript, 5-6.

84. William Levi Dawson, "Highlights of the Career of William L. Dawson," unpublished manuscript, 6.

85. William Levi Dawson, "Highlights of the Career of William L. Dawson," unpublished manuscript, 6; Mark Hugh Malone, interviews with William L. Dawson, Tuskegee, AL, March 23, 1979, January 24, 1981, February 7, 1981, February 21, 1981; William L. Dawson and Bess Bolden Walcott, interview by author, Tuskegee, AL, October 10, 1981.

86. William Levi Dawson, "Highlights of the Career of William L. Dawson," unpublished manuscript, 6; Mark Hugh Malone, interviews with William L. Dawson, Tuskegee, AL, March 23, 1979, January 24, 1981, February 7, 1981, February 21, 1981;. William L. Dawson and Bess Bolden Walcott, interview by author, Tuskegee, AL, October 10, 1981.

87. Used by special permission of Mr. Dawson. See full letter in Appendix C.

88. Mark Hugh Malone, interviews with William L. Dawson, Tuskegee, AL, March 23, 1979, January 24, 1981, February 7, 1981, February 21, 1981; William L. Dawson and Bess Bolden Walcott, interview by author, Tuskegee, AL, October 10, 1981.

89. Mark Hugh Malone, interviews with William L. Dawson, Tuskegee, AL, March 23, 1979, January 24, 1981, February 7, 1981, February 21, 1981; William L. Dawson and Bess Bolden Walcott, interview by author, Tuskegee, AL, October 10, 1981; William Levi Dawson, "Highlights of the Career of William L. Dawson," unpublished manuscript, 6.

CHAPTER 4: DAWSON THE COMPOSER: 1921-90

1. Mark Hugh Malone, interviews with William L. Dawson, Tuskegee, AL, March 23, 1979, January 24, 1981, February 7, 1981, February 21, 1981; William L. Dawson and Bess Bolden Walcott, interview by author, Tuskegee, AL, October 10, 1981.

2. Milton Randolph Jr., "Session 2: William Dawson, Up Close," March 3, 2005, DVCAM, 2hr36m, "In Celebration of William Levi Dawson" symposium records, William Levi Dawson Papers, Stuart A. Rose Manuscript, Archives, and Rare Books Library, Emory University.

3. Milton Randolph Jr., "Session 2: William Dawson, Up Close," March 3, 2005, DVCAM, 2hr36m, "In Celebration of William Levi Dawson" symposium records, William Levi Dawson Papers, Stuart A. Rose Manuscript, Archives, and Rare Books Library, Emory University.

4. Robert O'Meally, "Session 4: William Dawson, Ralph Ellison and Discipline," March 3, 2005, DVCAM, 2hr36m, "In Celebration of William Levi Dawson" symposium records, William Levi Dawson Papers, Stuart A. Rose Manuscript, Archives, and Rare Books Library, Emory University.

5. Jean E. Snyder, *Harry T. Burleigh: From the Spiritual to the Harlem Renaissance* (Champaign: University of Illinois Press, 2016), 77.

6. Jay van Straaten, Jay, *Slavonic Rhapsody: The Life of Antonin Dvorak* (New York: Allen, Town, and Heath, 1948), 76. Jean Snyder questions whether the newspaper quote was verbatim. Snyder, *Harry T. Burleigh*, 84.

7. "An 'American Sound'—Identity of Simplification," *Music 345: Race, Identity, and Representation in American Music* (blog), October 24, 2019, https://pages.stolaf.edu/americanmusic/.

8. W. J. Batzell, *Critical and Historical Essays* (Boston: Arthur P. Schmidt, 1912), 258.

9. J. Rublowsky, *Black Music in America* (New York: Basic Books, 1971).

10. Gilbert Chase, *America's Music* (New York: McGraw Hill Book, 1966), 390.

11. "'American Sound'—Identity of Simplification."

12. Chase, *America's Music*, 390.

13. Snyder, *Harry T. Burleigh*, 79.

14. Henry E. Krehbiel, *Afro-American Folksongs* (New York: G. Schirmer, 1914), 2–3.

15. Krehbiel, *Afro-American Folksongs*, 2–3.

16. Krehbiel, *Afro-American Folksongs*, 14.

17. W. E. B. Du Bois, *The Souls of Black Folk* (New York: Blue Heron Press, 1953), 251.

18. Du Bois, *Souls of Black Folk*, 256.

19. James Weldon Johnson, ed., *The Book of American Negro Spirituals* (New York: Viking Press, 1925).

20. Alain Locke, *The Negro and His Music* (New York: Arno Press and the New York Times, 1969), 1.

21. Locke, *Negro and His Music*, 2.

22. Harry T. Burleigh, Letter to William Dawson, March 17, 1921, William Levi Dawson Papers, Stuart A. Rose Manuscript, Archives, and Rare Books Library, Emory University.

23. See photos.

24. Vernon Huff, "William Levi Dawson's Life in Speeches, Letters, and Writings," *Choral Journal* 55, no. 1 (2015): 66.

25. Snyder, *Harry T. Burleigh*, 186.

26. Nadia Nurhussein, "On Flowery Beds of Ease: Paul Lawrence Dunbar," *American Periodicals"* 20, no. 1 (2010): 46–67.

27. Nurhussein, "On Flowery Beds of Ease," 46–67.

28. Snyder, *Harry T. Burleigh*, 186.

29. Harry T. Burleigh to William Dawson, March 17, 1921, William Levi Dawson Papers, Stuart A. Rose Manuscript, Archives, and Rare Books Library, Emory University.

30. William Levi Dawson, "Jump Back, Honey, Jump Back" (Kansas City, MO: Wunderlichs Piano Company, 1923, William Levi Dawson Papers, Stuart A. Rose Manuscript, and Rare Book Library, Emory University.

31. No copy of the *Trio in A* exists in the Dawson Collection at Emory University, or in the archives at the University of Missouri-Kansas City, the repository for the Horner Institute of Fine Arts Archives.

32. "Music Supervisors of Nation Meet," *Musical Leader* (Chicago, IL), April 9, 1925, 1.

33. Eileen Southern, *The Music of Black Americans: A History* (New York: W. W. Norton, 1971), 452.

34. John Lovell Jr., *Black Song: The Forge and the Flame* (New York: Macmillan, 1972), 417.

35. William L. Dawson, "Interpretations of the Religious Folk Songs of the American Negro," *Etude* (Malvern, PA), March 1955, 11.

36. Dawson, "Interpretations of the Religious Folk Songs of the American Negro," 24.

37. Arthur C. Jones, *Wade in the Water—The Wisdom of Spirituals* (Maryknoll, NY: Orbis Books, 1993), 1.

38. Jones, *Wade in the Water*, 2.

39. Jones, *Wade in the Water*, 6.

40. James B. Kelley, "Song, Story, or History: Resisting Claims of a Coded Message in the African American *Spiritual*, 'Follow the Drinking Gourd,'" *Journal of Popular Culture* 41, no. 2 April (2008): 275.

41. Lydia Parrish, *Slave Songs of the Georgia Sea Islands* (New York: Creative Age Press, 1942), 54.

42. Lovell, *Black Song*, 111.

43. Lovell, *Black Song*, 111.

44. Lovell, *Black Song*, 58.

45. Eileen Guenther, *In Their Own Words: Slave Life and the Power of Spirituals* (St. Louis: Morningstar, 2016), 359; John Lovell Jr., "The Social Implications of the Negro Spiritual," *Journal of Negro Education* 8, no. 4 (October 1939): 642; Rebecca Lynn Raber, "Conducting the Coded Message Songs of Slavery: Context, Connotations, and Performance Preparation," doctoral diss., North Dakota State University, 2018, 19.

46. Miles Mark Fisher, *Negro Slave Songs in the United States* (Ithaca: Cornell University Press, 1953), viii–ix.

47. Guenther, *In Their Own Words*, 359.

48. Melva Costen, "Session 3: The Spirituals: Meaning and Mythology in African American Identity," March 3, 2005, DVCAM, 1hr43m, "In Celebration of William Levi Dawson" symposium records, William Levi Dawson Papers, Stuart A. Rose Manuscript, Archives, and Rare Books Library, Emory University.

49. Melva Costen, "Session 3: The Spirituals: Meaning and Mythology in African American Identity," March 3, 2005, DVCAM, 1hr43m, "In Celebration of William Levi Dawson" symposium records, William Levi Dawson Papers, Stuart A. Rose Manuscript, Archives, and Rare Books Library, Emory University.

50. Frederick Douglass, *My Bondage, My Freedom* (Project Gutenberg 2008), 214–15, https://www.gutenberg.org/files/202/202-h/202-h.htm, accessed February 8, 2021.

51. Douglass, *My Bondage, My Freedom*, 214–15.

52. Douglass, *My Bondage, My Freedom*, 214–15.

53. Booker T. Washington, *Up from Slavery: An Autobiography* (New York: Doubleday 1901), 20.

54. Lovell, *Black Song*, 223–24.

55. Guenther, *In Their Own Words*, 358.

56. Guenther, *In Their Own Words*, 359. Lovell, "Social Implications of the Negro Spiritual"; Raber, "Conducting the Coded Message Songs of Slavery, 19.

57. Jones, *Wade in the Water*, 51.

58. Scott Baretta and Mark Malone, *Mississippi Blues Trail: and Beyond—Teacher's Edition* (Jackson: Mississippi Arts Commission, 2013), Unit 5, Lesson 2.

59. Sarah Bradford, *Harriet Tubman: The Moses of Her People* (Mineola, NY: Dover, 2004), 33.

60. Bradford, *Harriet Tubman*, 37–38.

61. Kerry Walters, *The Underground Railroad: A Reference Guide* (Santa Barbara, CA: ABC-CLIO, 2012), 49.

62. The two phrases referring to "second class" and "difference in fare" may have been added in later years.

63. Walters, *Underground Railroad*, 45.

64. Walters, *Underground Railroad*, 31.

65. William L. Dawson, "Interpretations of the Religious Folk Songs of the American Negro," *Etude*, March 1955, 11.

66. Dawson, "Interpretations of the Religious Folk Songs of the American Negro," 58, 61.

67. Lawrence Jackson, "Session 4: William Dawson, Ralph Ellison and Discipline," March 3, 2005, DVCAM, 2hr36m, "In Celebration of William Levi Dawson" symposium records, William Levi Dawson Papers, Stuart A. Rose Manuscript, Archives, and Rare Books Library, Emory University.

68. Lawrence Jackson, "Session 4: William Dawson, Ralph Ellison and Discipline," March 3, 2005, DVCAM, 2hr36m, "In Celebration of William Levi Dawson" symposium records, William Levi Dawson Papers, Stuart A. Rose Manuscript, Archives, and Rare Books Library, Emory University.

69. William Levi Dawson, "King Jesus Is A-Listening" (Chicago: H. T. FitzSimons, 1925).

70. Dawson, "I Couldn't Hear Nobody Pray" (Chicago: H. T. FitzSimons, 1926).

71. William Levi Dawson, "Talk about a Child That Do Love Jesus" (Chicago: H. T. FitzSimons, 1927). FitzSimons published "Go to Sleep," a low-voice solo in 1926 that was also set for mixed, women's, and men's voices (SATB, SSA, TTBB); Willie Strong, "Dawson, William Levi," in *International Dictionary of Black Composers, Vol. 1*, ed. Samuel A. Floyd Jr., 354 (Chicago: Fitzroy Dearborn, 1999).

72. Alice Tischler, "William Levi Dawson." In *Fifteen Black American Composers: A Bibliography of Their Works*, Detroit Studies in Musical Bibliography, No. 45 (Detroit: Information Coordinators, 1981), 112; William Levi Dawson Papers, Stuart A. Rose Manuscript, Archives, and Rare Books Library, Emory University.

73. William Levi Dawson, "Jesus Walked This Lonesome Valley" (New York: Remick Music, 1927).

74. David Y. Yarbrough, "Critical Edition: Sonata for Violin and Piano by William Levi Dawson," doctoral diss., Peabody Conservatory of Music, 1999, 15–16.

75. Yarbrough, "Critical Edition: Sonata for Violin and Piano by William Levi Dawson," 15.

76. William Levi Dawson, "Highlights of the Career of William L. Dawson," unpublished manuscript, 6. However, the *Sonata* for Violin and Piano was recorded: Westminster W-9633; Strong, "Dawson, William Levi."

77. William Levi Dawson, "You Got to Reap Just What You Sow" (Chicago: Remick Music, 1928).

78. William Levi Dawson, "My Lord, What a Mourning" (Chicago: H. T. FitzSimons, 1927).

79. William Levi Dawson, "Out in the Fields" (Chicago: Gamble Hinged Music, 1929). Recorded: Desto DC-7107; Strong, "Dawson, William Levi." While the poem "Out in the Fields" was originally attributed to Louise Imogen Guiney, later consensus was that the words were written by Elizabeth Barrett Browning. Dawson acknowledged the finding and changed the citation in later publications of his musical settings.

80. William Levi Dawson, "The Mongrel Yank" (Chicago: Gamble Hinged Music, 1930).

81. William Levi Dawson, "The Rugged Yank" (Park Ridge, IL: Kjos Music, 1970).

82. Samantha Ege, "Composing a Symphonist: Florence Price and the Hand of Black Women's Fellowship," *Women and Music: A Journal of Gender and Culture* 4, no. 1 (2020): 7–27.

83. Ege, "Composing a Symphonist," 7–27.

84. Rodman Wanamaker, Letter to W. E. B. Du Bois, Rodman Wanamaker Contest in Music Compositions for Composers of the Negro Race to Crisis, December 23, 1929, W. E. B. Du Bois Papers (MS 312), Special Collections and University Archives, University of Massachusetts, Amherst Libraries.

85. William Levi Dawson, "Highlights of the Career of William L. Dawson," unpublished manuscript, 1; William Levi Dawson, "Jump Back, Honey, Jump Back" (Kansas City, MO: Wunderlichs Piano Company), 1923. Of these two compositions, only "Jump Back, Honey, Jump Back" is found listed as a composition in Dawson's papers at Emory University.

86. Marva Carter, "Session 6: 19th and 20th Century Notions of 'The Composer,'" March 4, 2005, DVCAM, 1hr58m, "In Celebration of William Levi Dawson" symposium records, William Levi Dawson Papers, Stuart A. Rose Manuscript, Archives, and Rare Books Library, Emory University.

87. Snyder, *Harry T. Burleigh*, 187.

88. William Levi Dawson, "Highlights of the Career of William L. Dawson," unpublished manuscript, 1.

89. Ege, "Composing a Symphonist," 7–27. A copy of Dawson's 1931 winning composition is not listed with compositions in the collection of his papers at Emory University.

90. Lawrence Jackson, "Session 4: William Dawson, Ralph Ellison and Discipline," March 3, 2005, DVCAM, 2hr36m, "In Celebration of William Levi Dawson" symposium records, William Levi Dawson Papers, Stuart A. Rose Manuscript, Archives, and Rare Books Library, Emory University; "Music Review," *New York Times*, February 9, 1933, 15.

91. Mark Hugh Malone, interviews with William L. Dawson, AL, March 23, 1979, January 24, 1981, February 7, 1981, February 21, 1981; William L. Dawson and Bess Bolden Walcott, interview by author, Tuskegee, AL, October 10, 1981.

92. Carter, Marva. "Session 6: 19th and 20th Century Notions of 'The Composer,'" March 4, 2005, DVCAM, 1hr58m, "In Celebration of William Levi Dawson" symposium records, William Levi Dawson Papers, Stuart A. Rose Manuscript, Archives, and Rare Books Library, Emory University; "Interview with William Levi Dawson, *The Sunday Show* (National Public

Radio), 1982, William Levi Dawson Papers, Stuart A. Rose Manuscript, Archives, and Rare Books Library, Emory University.

93. Mark Hugh Malone, interviews with William L. Dawson, Tuskegee, AL, March 23, 1979, January 24, 1981, February 7, 1981, February 21, 1981

94. Lawrence Jackson, "Session 4: William Dawson, Ralph Ellison and Discipline," March 3, 2005, DVCAM, 2hr36m, "In Celebration of William Levi Dawson" symposium records, William Levi Dawson Papers, Stuart A. Rose Manuscript, Archives, and Rare Books Library, Emory University.

95. "A Striking Contribution to Musical America," *American Business Survey*, April 1933, 24.

96. "Striking Contribution to Musical America," 24.

97. Catherine Reef, *William Grant Still: African American Composer* (Greensboro, NC: Morgan Reynolds, 2003), 59–60, 63, 69, 72, 94.

98. "Dawson: Negro Folk Symphony." Decca Records, DL 71077, 1962.

99. William L. Dawson, *Negro Folk Symphony Brochure*, published privately by William L. Dawson, n.d.

100. "TV Interview of Dawson at Houston, Texas, 1971-Side 1," William Levi Dawson Papers, Stuart A. Rose Manuscript, Archives, and Rare Book Library, Emory University.

101. Lawrence Jackson, "Session 4: William Dawson, Ralph Ellison and Discipline," March 3, 2005, DVCAM, 2hr36m, "In Celebration of William Levi Dawson" symposium records, William Levi Dawson Papers, Stuart A. Rose Manuscript, Archives, and Rare Books Library, Emory University.

102. Lawrence Jackson, "Session 4: William Dawson, Ralph Ellison and Discipline," March 3, 2005, DVCAM, 2hr36m, "In Celebration of William Levi Dawson" symposium records, William Levi Dawson Papers, Stuart A. Rose Manuscript, Archives, and Rare Books Library, Emory University.

103. Lawrence Jackson, "Session 4: William Dawson, Ralph Ellison and Discipline," March 3, 2005, DVCAM, 2hr36m, "In Celebration of William Levi Dawson" symposium records, William Levi Dawson Papers, Stuart A. Rose Manuscript, Archives, and Rare Books Library, Emory University.

104. Lawrence Jackson, "Session 4: William Dawson, Ralph Ellison and Discipline," March 3, 2005, DVCAM, 2hr36m, "In Celebration of William Levi Dawson" symposium records, William Levi Dawson Papers, Stuart A. Rose Manuscript, Archives, and Rare Books Library, Emory University; Mark Hugh Malone, interviews with William L. Dawson, Tuskegee, AL, March 23, 1979, January 24, 1981, February 7, 1981, February 21, 1981; William L. Dawson and Bess Bolden Walcott, interview by author, Tuskegee, AL, October 10, 1981.

105. Olin Downes, "Stokowski Gives American Works," *New York Times*, November 21, 1934, 22.

106. Downes, "Stokowski Gives American Works," 22.

107. Robert Simon, "Mr. Stokowski Chaperons an American Symphony—One Hand That Plays Two," *New Yorker*, December 1, 1934, 79.

108. Simon, "Mr. Stokowski Chaperons an American Symphony—One Hand That Plays Two," 79.

109. Lawrence Jackson, "Session 4: William Dawson, Ralph Ellison and Discipline," March 3, 2005, DVCAM, 2hr36m, "In Celebration of William Levi Dawson" symposium records,

William Levi Dawson Papers, Stuart A. Rose Manuscript, Archives, and Rare Books Library, Emory University.

110. Lawrence Jackson, "Session 4: William Dawson, Ralph Ellison and Discipline," March 3, 2005, DVCAM, 2hr36m, "In Celebration of William Levi Dawson" symposium records, William Levi Dawson Papers, Stuart A. Rose Manuscript, Archives, and Rare Books Library, Emory University.

111. Letters from the William Dawson Collection, William Levi Dawson Papers, Stuart A. Rose Manuscript, Archives, and Rare Book Library, Emory University; Marva Carter, "Session 6: 19th and 20th Century Notions of 'The Composer,'" March 4, 2005, DVCAM, 1hr58m, "In Celebration of William Levi Dawson" symposium records, William Levi Dawson Papers, Stuart A. Rose Manuscript, Archives, and Rare Books Library, Emory University.

112. Hildred Roach, *Black American Music: Past and Present* (Boston: Crescendo, 1973), 106.

113. Roach, *Black American Music: Past and Present*, 106.

114. Mark Hugh Malone, interviews with William L. Dawson, Tuskegee, AL, March 23, 1979, January 24, 1981, February 7, 1981, February 21, 1981; William L. Dawson and Bess Bolden Walcott, interview by author, Tuskegee, AL, October 10, 1981.

115. "Music Review," *Anniston Star*, November 18, 1934, 1.

116. Lawrence Jackson, "Session 4: William Dawson, Ralph Ellison and Discipline," March 3, 2005, DVCAM, 2hr36m, "In Celebration of William Levi Dawson" symposium records, William Levi Dawson Papers, Stuart A. Rose Manuscript, Archives, and Rare Books Library, Emory University.

117. Lawrence Jackson, "Session 4: William Dawson, Ralph Ellison and Discipline," March 3, 2005, DVCAM, 2hr36m, "In Celebration of William Levi Dawson" symposium records, William Levi Dawson Papers, Stuart A. Rose Manuscript, Archives, and Rare Books Library, Emory University.

118. Lawrence Jackson, "Session 4: William Dawson, Ralph Ellison and Discipline," March 3, 2005, DVCAM, 2hr36m, "In Celebration of William Levi Dawson" symposium records, William Levi Dawson Papers, Stuart A. Rose Manuscript, Archives, and Rare Books Library, Emory University.

119. Stephanie Li, *Zora Neale Hurston* (Santa Barbara, CA: ABC-CLIO, 2020), 1–2.

120. Lawrence Jackson, "Session 4: William Dawson, Ralph Ellison and Discipline," March 3, 2005, DVCAM, 2hr36m, "In Celebration of William Levi Dawson" symposium records, William Levi Dawson Papers, Stuart A. Rose Manuscript, Archives, and Rare Books Library, Emory University.

121. Lawrence Jackson, "Session 4: William Dawson, Ralph Ellison and Discipline," March 3, 2005, DVCAM, 2hr36m, "In Celebration of William Levi Dawson" symposium records, William Levi Dawson Papers, Stuart A. Rose Manuscript, Archives, and Rare Books Library, Emory University.

122. David Ewen, *American Composers Today: A Biographical and Critical Guide* (New York: H. N. Wilson, 1949), 78–79.

123. Lawrence Jackson, "Session 4: William Dawson, Ralph Ellison and Discipline," March 3, 2005, DVCAM, 2hr36m, "In Celebration of William Levi Dawson" symposium records, William Levi Dawson Papers, Stuart A. Rose Manuscript, Archives, and Rare Books Library, Emory University.

124. Lawrence Jackson, "Session 4: William Dawson, Ralph Ellison and Discipline," March 3, 2005, DVCAM, 2hr36m, "In Celebration of William Levi Dawson" symposium records, William Levi Dawson Papers, Stuart A. Rose Manuscript, Archives, and Rare Books Library, Emory University.

125. Lawrence Jackson, "Session 4: William Dawson, Ralph Ellison and Discipline," March 3, 2005, DVCAM, 2hr36m, "In Celebration of William Levi Dawson" symposium records, William Levi Dawson Papers, Stuart A. Rose Manuscript, Archives, and Rare Books Library, Emory University.

126. Lawrence Jackson, "Session 4: William Dawson, Ralph Ellison and Discipline," March 3, 2005, DVCAM, 2hr36m, "In Celebration of William Levi Dawson" symposium records, William Levi Dawson Papers, Stuart A. Rose Manuscript, Archives, and Rare Books Library, Emory University.

127. "Interview with William Levi Dawson, Philadelphia, Pennsylvania, October 8, 1979," William Levi Dawson Papers, Stuart A. Rose Manuscript, Archives, and Rare Book Library, Emory University.

128. "Interview with William Levi Dawson, Philadelphia, Pennsylvania, October 8, 1979."

129. William L. Dawson, "Africa Trip Travel Log," William Levi Dawson Papers, Stuart A. Rose Manuscript, Archives, and Rare Book Library, Emory University.

130. Dawson, "Africa Trip Travel Log."

131. Dawson, "Africa Trip Travel Log."

132. Design You Trust, "Inside a 1947 Boeing 377 Stratocruiser, The Largest And Fastest Aircraft in Commercial Service. https://designyoutrust.com/2020/02/inside-a-1947-boeing-377-stratocruiser-the-largest-and-fastest-aircraft-in-commercial-service/, accessed December 16, 2021.

133. Design You Trust, "Inside a 1947 Boeing 377 Stratocruiser."

William L. Dawson, "Africa Trip Travel Log," William Levi Dawson Papers, Stuart A. Rose Manuscript, Archives, and Rare Book Library, Emory University.

134. Dawson, "Africa Trip Travel Log."

135. Dawson, "Africa Trip Travel Log."

136. Dawson, "Africa Trip Travel Log"; Kimberly Francis. "Nadia Boulanger and Igor Stravinsky: Documents of the Bibliothèque Nationale de France," *Revue de musicology* 95, no. 1 (2009): 137–56.

137. John Inscoe, "Howard Swanson," The New Georgia Encyclopedia. https://www.georgiaencyclopedia.org/articles/arts-culture/howard-swanson-1907-1978/, accessed December 16, 2021.

138. William L. Dawson, "Africa Trip Travel Log," William Levi Dawson Papers, Stuart A. Rose Manuscript, Archives, and Rare Book Library, Emory University.

139. Dawson, "Africa Trip Travel Log."

140. Dawson, "Africa Trip Travel Log." Over 148 recordings of the African folk music made by William Dawson during his 1952–53 journey to Sierra Leone, Liberia, Ghana, Dahomey, and Nigeria were digitized by the staff at the Stuart A. Rose archives in the Woodruff Library at Emory University. "African Field Recordings," William Levi Dawson Papers, Stuart A. Rose Manuscript, Archives, and Rare Book Library, Emory University.

141. William L. Dawson, "Africa Trip Travel Log," William Levi Dawson Papers, Stuart A. Rose Manuscript, Archives, and Rare Book Library, Emory University.

142. William L. Dawson, "African Field Recordings," William Levi Dawson Papers, Stuart A. Rose Manuscript, Archives, and Rare Book Library, Emory University.

143. William L. Dawson, "Africa Trip Travel Log," William Levi Dawson Papers, Stuart A. Rose Manuscript, Archives, and Rare Book Library, Emory University.

144. Dawson, "Africa Trip Travel Log."

145. William L. Dawson, "African Field Recordings," William Levi Dawson Papers, Stuart A. Rose Manuscript, Archives, and Rare Book Library, Emory University.

146. Dawson, "African Field Recordings"; William L. Dawson, "Africa Trip Travel Log," William Levi Dawson Papers, Stuart A. Rose Manuscript, Archives, and Rare Book Library, Emory University.

147. Dawson, "Africa Trip Travel Log."

148. Dawson, "Africa Trip Travel Log"; William L. Dawson, "African Field Recordings," William Levi Dawson Papers, Stuart A. Rose Manuscript, Archives, and Rare Book Library, Emory University.

149. Dawson, "African Field Recordings."

150. William L. Dawson, "Africa Trip Travel Log," William Levi Dawson Papers, Stuart A. Rose Manuscript, Archives, and Rare Book Library, Emory University.

151. "TV Interview of Dawson at Houston, Texas, 1971-Side 1," William Levi Dawson Papers, Stuart A. Rose Manuscript, Archives, and Rare Book Library, Emory University.

152. Southern, *Music of Black American*, 427.

153. Gwynne Kuhner Brown, "What Ever Happened to William Dawson's *Negro Folk Symphony*?" *Journal for the Society for American Music* (2012) Volume 6, Number 4, 433–56.

154. Willie Strong, "William L. Dawson," In *International Dictionary of Black Composers, Vol. 1.*, ed. Samuel A. Floyd Jr., 354 (Chicago: Fitzroy Dearborn, 1999); Willie Strong, "Dawson, William Levi," *New Grove Dictionary of Music and Musicians* (Oxford: Oxford University Press, 2001).

155. *Negro Folk Symphony Brochure*, published privately by William Dawson.

156. Tom Huizenga, "Someone Finally Remembered William Dawson's 'Negro Folk Symphony,'" *NPR*, June 26, 2020, https://www.npr.org/sections/deceptivecadence/2020/06/26/883011513/someone-finally-remembered-william-dawsons-negro-folk-symphony, accessed July 25, 2020.

157. Marva Carter, "Session 6: 19th and 20th Century Notions of 'The Composer,'" March 4, 2005, DVCAM, 1hr58m, "In Celebration of William Levi Dawson" symposium records, William Levi Dawson Papers, Stuart A. Rose Manuscript, Archives, and Rare Books Library, Emory University.

158. Carter, "Session 6: 19th and 20th Century Notions of 'The Composer.'"

159. William Levi Dawson, "Highlights of the Career of William L. Dawson," unpublished manuscript, 3. Dawson's unpublished manuscript of important accomplishments during his life indicated February 20, 1940 as the first performance of *A Negro Work Song*, yet others report November 20, 1940 as the date of the recording of the broadcast.

160. William Levi Dawson, *A Negro Work Song*, William Levi Dawson Papers, Stuart A. Rose Manuscript, Archives, and Rare Books Library, Emory University.

161. Gwynne Kuhner Brown, "What Ever Happened to William Dawson's *Negro Folk Symphony*?" *Journal for the Society for American Music* 6, no. 4 (2012): 433–56.

162. William Levi Dawson, *A Negro Work Song*, William Levi Dawson Papers, Stuart A. Rose Manuscript, Archives, and Rare Books Library, Emory University.

163. William Levi Dawson, "Highlights of the Career of William L. Dawson," Unpublished Manuscript, 3, 5, 6.

164. Hildred Roach, *Black American Music: Past and Present* (Boston: Crescendo, 1973), 105–6.

165. John Haberlen, "Session 2: William Dawson, Up Close," March 3, 2005, DVCAM, 2hr36m, "In Celebration of William Levi Dawson" symposium records, William Levi Dawson Papers, Stuart A. Rose Manuscript, Archives, and Rare Books Library, Emory University.

166. William Levi Dawson, "Oh, What a Beautiful City," (Tuskegee, AL: Tuskegee Institute Steam Press, 1934).

167. William Levi Dawson, "Soon-Ah Will Be Done" (Tuskegee, AL: Tuskegee Institute Steam Press, 1934).

168. William Levi Dawson, "Ain-a That Good News" (Tuskegee, AL: Tuskegee Institute Steam Press, 1937).

169. William Levi Dawson, "There Is a Balm in Gilead," (Tuskegee, AL: Tuskegee Institute Steam Press, 1939).

170. Mark Hugh Malone, Interviews with William L. Dawson, Tuskegee, AL, March 23, 1979, January 24, 1981, February 7, 1981, February 21, 1981; William L. Dawson and Bess Bolden Walcott, interview by author, Tuskegee, AL, October 10, 1981.

171. William Levi Dawson, "Steal Away" (Tuskegee, AL: Tuskegee Institute Steam Press, 1942).

172. William Levi Dawson, "Ezekiel Saw de Wheel" (Tuskegee, AL: Tuskegee Institute Steam Press, 1942).

173. John Haberlen, "Session 2: William Dawson, Up Close," March 3, 2005, DVCAM, 2hr36m, "In Celebration of William Levi Dawson" symposium records, William Levi Dawson Papers, Stuart A. Rose Manuscript, Archives, and Rare Books Library, Emory University.

174. Lynn Abbott and Doug Seroff, Doug, *To Do This You Must Know How* (Jackson: University Press of Mississippi, 2013), 150.

175. Abbott and Seroff, *To Do This You Must Know How*, 149.

176. Abbott and Seroff, *To Do This You Must Know How*, 151.

177. William Levi Dawson, "Behold the Star" (Tuskegee, AL: Tuskegee Institute Steam Press, 1946).

178. William Levi Dawson, "Hail Mary" (Tuskegee, AL: Tuskegee Institute Steam Press, 1946).

179. William Levi Dawson, "Swing Low" (Tuskegee, AL: Tuskegee Institute Steam Press, 1946).

180. William Levi Dawson, "Ev'ry Time I Feel The Spirit" (Tuskegee, AL: Tuskegee Institute Steam Press, 1946).

181. It is also set for men.

182. William Levi Dawson, "Mary Had a Baby" (Tuskegee, AL: Tuskegee Institute Steam Press, 1947). There is some debate as to whether this composition was published in 1942 or 1947.

183. William Levi Dawson, "Lit'l' Boy Chile" (Tuskegee, AL: Tuskegee Institute Steam Press, 1947).

184. William Levi Dawson, "There's a Little Wheel A-Turnin' In My Heart" (Tuskegee, AL: Tuskegee Institute Steam Press, 1949).

185. William Levi Dawson, "Adawura B Me" (Chicago: Remick Music, 1955).

186. William Levi Dawson, "I Wan' to Be Ready" (Park Ridge, IL: Neil A. Kjos, 1967).

187. William Levi Dawson, "Zion's Walls" (Park Ridge, IL: Neil A. Kos, 1961).

188. William Levi Dawson, "The Rugged Yank" (Park Ridge, IL: Neil A. Kjos, 1974).

189. William Levi Dawson, "In His Care-O" (Park Ridge, IL: Neil A. Kjos, 1961); William Levi Dawson, "Feed-A My Sheep" (Park Ridge, IL: Neil A. Kjos, 1971); William Levi Dawson, "Slumber Song" (Park Ridge, Illinois: Neil A. Kjos, 1961).

190. William Levi Dawson, "Pilgrim's Chorus" (Park Ridge, IL: Neil A. Kjos, 1968).

191. William Levi Dawson, "Before the Sun Goes Down" (Park Ridge, IL: Neil A. Kjos, 1978). See composition for full text of the poem.

192. I found evidence of these compositions in Dawson's papers in both the Emory University archives and the Tuskegee University archives, as well as my own keepsakes from interviews, investigation notes for the original dissertation, and information received by mail.

193. Tuskegee University Archives, "Tuskegee Institute Concert Program," April 13, 1931, Tuskegee University Archives Repository, Tuskegee Institute.

194. "Hallelujah" in A Major, written in 3/4 meter, marked *Andante*. See composition for full text.

195. "Booker T. Washington Stamp Commemoration," NBC, April 7, 1940, William Levi Dawson Papers, Stuart A. Rose Manuscript, Archives, and Rare Book Library, Emory University.

196. Strong, Willie. "William Levi Dawson." In *International Dictionary of Black Composers, Vol. 1*. Samuel A. Floyd, Jr., ed., 354–59. Chicago: Fitzroy Dearborn, 1999, 358; William Levi Dawson, "Interlude," William Levi Dawson Papers, Stuart A. Rose Manuscript, Archives, and Rare Books Library, Emory University.

197. Dawson, "Interlude."

198. William L. Dawson, "Break, Break, Break," Unpublished manuscript from personal papers of the author.

199. Dawson, "Break, Break, Break"; William Levi Dawson Papers, Stuart A. Rose Manuscript, Archives, and Rare Book Library, Emory University. Viewing the manuscript, indulging myself by allowing my brain to give meaning to the music notation (to audiate, in Edwin Gordon's teaching), memories of William Dawson flooded back with a warm sense of who he was, what he accomplished, the many lives he touched, and the example he set.

200. William Levi Dawson, "Oppression," William Levi Dawson Papers, Stuart A. Rose Manuscript, Archives, and Rare Book Library, Emory University.

201. William Levi Dawson, "Dorabella" (Park Ridge, IL: Neil A. Kjos, 1981).

202. Samuel L. Singer, "A Gleeful Tribute for Conductor," *Philadelphia Inquirer*, November 23, 1980, A-22.

203. Robert K. Schwarz, "Composers Who Had to Triumph over Prejudice," *New York Times*, April 15, 1990, 22.

CHAPTER 5: DAWSON THE PEDAGOGUE: 1921–90

1. Mark Hugh Malone, interviews with William L. Dawson, Tuskegee, AL, March 23, 1979, January 24, 1981, February 7, 1981, February 21, 1981; William L. Dawson and Bess Bolden Walcott, interview by author, Tuskegee, AL, October 10, 1981.
2. Malone, interviews with William L. Dawson.
3. Malone, interviews with William L. Dawson.
4. Charles Ward, "The Will to Excel," *Houston Chronicle*, September 9, 1989, 1.
5. Ward, "The Will to Excel," 1.
6. Mark Hugh Malone, interviews with William L. Dawson, Tuskegee, AL, March 23, 1979, January 24, 1981, February 7, 1981, February 21, 1981; William L. Dawson and Bess Bolden Walcott, interview by author, Tuskegee, AL, October 10, 1981.
7. Robert O'Meally, "Session 4: William Dawson, Ralph Ellison and Discipline," March 3, 2005, DVCAM, 2hr36m, "In Celebration of William Levi Dawson" symposium records, William Levi Dawson Papers, Stuart A. Rose Manuscript, Archives, and Rare Books Library, Emory University.
8. O'Meally, "Session 4."
9. O'Meally, "Session 4."
10. "Session 4."
11. "Session 4."
12. "Session 4."
13. Milton Randolph Jr., "Session 2: William Dawson, Up Close," March 3, 2005, DVCAM, 2hr36m, "In Celebration of William Levi Dawson" symposium records, William Levi Dawson Papers, Stuart A. Rose Manuscript, Archives, and Rare Books Library, Emory University.
14. John Haberlen, "Session 2: William Dawson, Up Close," March 3, 2005, DVCAM, 2hr36m, "In Celebration of William Levi Dawson" symposium records, William Levi Dawson Papers, Stuart A. Rose Manuscript, Archives, and Rare Books Library, Emory University.
15. Haberlen, "Session 2: William Dawson, Up Close."
16. Haberlen, "Session 2: William Dawson, Up Close."
17. See later endnote about 1986 Mississippi ACDA Convention.
18. Robert O'Meally, "Session 4: William Dawson, Ralph Ellison and Discipline," March 3, 2005, DVCAM, 2hr36m, "In Celebration of William Levi Dawson" symposium records, William Levi Dawson Papers, Stuart A. Rose Manuscript, Archives, and Rare Books Library, Emory University.
19. Mark Hugh Malone, interviews with William L. Dawson, Tuskegee, AL, March 23, 1979, January 24, 1981, February 7, 1981, February 21, 1981; William L. Dawson and Bess Bolden Walcott, interview by author, Tuskegee, AL, October 10, 1981.
20. William Levi Dawson, "Highlights of the Career of William L. Dawson," unpublished manuscript, William Levi Dawson Papers, Stuart A. Rose Manuscript, Archives, and Rare Books Library, Emory University, 6.
21. American Embassy, "Unclassified Report," Antonio Gonzales de la Peña, Madrid, Spain, 1956, 1.
22. William Levi Dawson, "A Report to Mr. Robert D. Barton, Assistant Cultural Attaché, American Embassy, Madrid, Spain, on My Trip to Spain during the Summer," 1956, unpublished manuscript, 2.

23. American Embassy, "Unclassified Report," Antonio Gonzales de la Peña, Madrid, Spain, 1956, 1.

24. American Embassy, "Unclassified Report," 1–2.

25. American Embassy, "Unclassified Report," 2.

26. American Embassy, "Unclassified Report," 2.

27. American Embassy, "Unclassified Report," 3.

28. William Levi Dawson, "A Report to Mr. Robert D. Barton, Assistant Cultural Attaché, American Embassy, Madrid, Spain, on My Trip to Spain during the Summer," 1956, unpublished manuscript, 6–7.

29. William Levi Dawson, "Highlights of the Career of William L. Dawson," unpublished manuscript, William Levi Dawson Papers, Stuart A. Rose Manuscript, Archives, and Rare Books Library, Emory University, 7.

30. Amy Helene Kirshke, *Aaron Douglas: Art, Race, and the Harlem Renaissance* (Jackson: University Press of Mississippi, 1995), xiv; "Aaron Douglas Biography and Legacy." https://www.theartstory.org/artist/douglas-aaron/life-and-legacy, accessed November 10, 2021; "Aaron Douglas." https://unl.edu/one-of-ours/aaron-douglas, accessed November 10, 2021; "Aaron Douglas." https://kshs.org/kansapedia/aaron-douglas/12309, accessed November 10, 2021; Cheryl R. Ragan, "Plunging into the Very Depths of the Souls of Our People: The Life and Art of Aaron Douglas," doctoral dissertation, University of Kansas, 2008, accessed November 10, 2021; David C. Driskell, "The Significance of the Aaron Douglas Papers," speech given on the formal presentation of Douglas's papers to Fisk University, April 27, 1975. The speech was published as part of a special issue devoted to Douglas in *BANC!* a publication of Fisk University Library 4–5 (September 1974–June 1975), 3–4.

31. William Levi Dawson, "Highlights of the Career of William L. Dawson," unpublished manuscript, William Levi Dawson Papers, Stuart A. Rose Manuscript, Archives, and Rare Books Library, Emory University, 7.

32. Dawson, "Highlights of the Career of William L. Dawson," 8.

33. "The Conference All-State Organizations," *School Music News* 24, no. 5 (January 1961): 1.

34. William Levi Dawson, "Highlights of the Career of William L. Dawson," unpublished manuscript, William Levi Dawson Papers, Stuart A. Rose Manuscript, Archives, and Rare Books Library, Emory University, 8.

35. R. C. Hammerlich, "Musicians First, Students Prove in Concert Here," *Springfield (Massachusetts) Republican*, March 24, 1963, 1.

36. Hammerlich, "Musicians First, Students Prove in Concert Here," 1.

37. William Levi Dawson, "Highlights of the Career of William L. Dawson," unpublished manuscript, William Levi Dawson Papers, Stuart A. Rose Manuscript, Archives, and Rare Books Library, Emory University, 8.

38. Dawson, "Highlights of the Career of William L. Dawson," 8–9.

39. John Haskins, "A Concert of Modern Americana," *Kansas City Star* (Kansas City, MO), January 30, 1966, 15.

40. John Haskins, "The 65–66 Music Season—A Long Look Back," *Kansas City Star* (Kansas City, MO), June 5, 1966, 1.

41. William Levi Dawson, "Highlights of the Career of William L. Dawson," unpublished manuscript, William Levi Dawson Papers, Stuart A. Rose Manuscript, Archives, and Rare Books Library, Emory University, 9.

42. Dawson, "Highlights of the Career of William L. Dawson," 9.

43. Nicholas, Louis, "Fisk Music Fitting Centennial End," *Nashville Tennessean*, May 2, 1966, 16.

44. Werner Zepernick, "Fisk Festival Closes with Negro Symphonic Works," *Nashville Banner*, May 3, 1966, 3.

45. Zepernick, "Fisk Festival Closes with Negro Symphonic Works," 3.

46. William Levi Dawson, "Highlights of the Career of William L. Dawson," unpublished manuscript, William Levi Dawson Papers, Stuart A. Rose Manuscript, Archives, and Rare Books Library, Emory University, 9.

47. Dawson, "Highlights of the Career of William L. Dawson," 10–11.

48. Dawson, "Highlights of the Career of William L. Dawson," 11.

49. Dawson, "Highlights of the Career of William L. Dawson," 10–11.

50. Dawson, "Highlights of the Career of William L. Dawson," 10–11.

51. Dawson, "Highlights of the Career of William L. Dawson," 11.

52. Dawson, "Highlights of the Career of William L. Dawson," 13.

53. Dawson, "Highlights of the Career of William L. Dawson," 13.; Mark Hugh Malone, interviews with William L. Dawson, Tuskegee, AL, March 23, 1979, January 24, 1981, February 7, 1981, February 21, 1981; William L. Dawson and Bess Bolden Walcott, interview by author, Tuskegee, AL, October 10, 1981.

54. William Levi Dawson, "Highlights of the Career of William L. Dawson," unpublished manuscript, William Levi Dawson Papers, Stuart A. Rose Manuscript, Archives, and Rare Books Library, Emory University, 13–16, 19–21.

55. Dawson, "Highlights of the Career of William L. Dawson," 17–21.

56. Mark Hugh Malone, interviews with William L. Dawson, Tuskegee, AL, March 23, 1979, January 24, 1981, February 7, 1981, February 21, 1981; William L. Dawson and Bess Bolden Walcott, interview by author, Tuskegee, AL, October 10, 1981.

57. Having been a member of the American Choral Directors Association (ACDA) since 1979, I conducted a session at the 1980 Southern Division Convention in Knoxville, Tennessee, and sang in a choir selected for performance at the 1981 National Convention in New Orleans, Louisiana. I registered for the 1984 Southern Division Convention in Atlanta, Georgia, and attended Mr. Dawson's session. Afterward I reminisced with Mr. Dawson about the time we spent during interviews in his home in Tuskegee, Alabama. I later went on to serve ACDA as pianist for the Mississippi All-State Honor Showchoir, Southern Division Repertoire and Standards Chair for Jazz and Showchoir Music, Southern Division Repertoire and Standards Chair for Two-Year College Choirs, and National Repertoire and Standards Chair for Two-Year College Choirs.

58. As a newcomer to Mississippi in 1981, I quickly joined the Mississippi Chapter of ACDA. I founded the state newsletter and served as editor into the mid-1990s. When the idea was presented to start a state ACDA conference for the spring of 1986, I eagerly suggested that William Dawson be invited as the headliner for the event. Following my letter of invitation, Dawson responded affirmatively. During his time in Oxford, Mississippi, I served as chauffeur and caretaker for my friend. I remembered seeing the 1936 flyer from the Tuskegee Choir's upcoming concert at Mississippi State College in the archives at Tuskegee when researching information for my dissertation on Dawson's life and work. During his

conference introduction, I shared the significance of Mr. Dawson's appearance at the initial ACDA conference in the Magnolia State.

59. My article entitled, "William Dawson: The Tuskegee Choir," appeared in the March 1990 edition of the ACDA magazine, *Choral Journal*, to coincide with the salute being given to Mr. Dawson.

60. Used by special permission of William L. Dawson.

61. Lawrence Jackson, "Session 4: William Dawson, Ralph Ellison and Discipline," March 3, 2005, DVCAM, 2hr36m, "In Celebration of William Levi Dawson" symposium records, William Levi Dawson Papers, Stuart A. Rose Manuscript, Archives, and Rare Books Library, Emory University.

62. Robert O'Meally, "Session 4: William Dawson, Ralph Ellison and Discipline," March 3, 2005, DVCAM, 2hr36m, "In Celebration of William Levi Dawson" symposium records, William Levi Dawson Papers, Stuart A. Rose Manuscript, Archives, and Rare Books Library, Emory University.

63. Robert, O'Meally, "Session 4: William Dawson, Ralph Ellison and Discipline," March 3, 2005, DVCAM, 2hr36m, "In Celebration of William Levi Dawson" symposium records, William Levi Dawson Papers, Stuart A. Rose Manuscript, Archives, and Rare Books Library, Emory University.

APPENDIX B:
AWARDS AND HONORS RECEIVED BY WILLIAM LEVI DAWSON

1. Compiled with information gleaned from the following: William L. Dawson, interview by author, Tuskegee, AL, March 23, 1979, January 24, 1981, February 7, 1981, February 21, 1981; William L. Dawson and Bess Bolden Walcott, interview by author, Tuskegee, AL, October 10, 1981; William Levi Dawson, "Highlights of the Career of William L. Dawson," unpublished manuscript, 1; Willie Strong. "Dawson, William Levi." in *International Dictionary of Black Composers, Vol. 1*, ed. Samuel A. Floyd Jr., 354 (Chicago: Fitzroy Dearborn, 1999).

BIBLIOGRAPHY

Abbott, Lynn and Doug Seroff. *To Do This You Must Know How*. Jackson: University Press of Mississippi, 2013.
American Embassy. "Unclassified Report." Antonio Gonzales de la Peña. Madrid, Spain, 1956.
"An 'American Sound'—Identity of Simplification." *Music 345: Race, Identity, and Representation in American Music* (blog), October 24, 2019. https://pages.stolaf.edu/americanmusic/. Accessed October 14, 2021.
Atkinson, Brooks. "Music Hall's Opening." *New York Times*, December 28, 1932.
Baretta, Scott, and Mark Malone. *Mississippi Blues Trail: and Beyond*. Teacher's ed. Jackson: Mississippi Arts Commission, 2013.
Barr, Wayne. Personal interview, November 15, 2021.
Batzell, W. J. *Critical and Historical Essays*. Boston: Arthur P. Schmidt, 1912.
Biancolli, Louis. "Tuskegee Choir Shows Finesse in Memorial." *New York World Telegram* (New York, NY), May 28, 1946.
Book of American Negro Spirituals. Edited by James Weldon Johnson. New York: Viking Press, 1925.
"Booker T. Washington Honored as Bust Is Added to Hall of Fame." *New York Times*, May 24, 1946.
"Booker T. Washington Stamp Commemoration," April 7, 1940, William Levi Dawson Papers, Stuart A. Rose Manuscript, Archives, and Rare Book Library, Emory University.
Bowen, Stirling. "The Theatre." *Wall Street Journal*, February 10, 1933.
Boyd, Herb. "Extraordinary Pianist and Gifted Teacher Hazel Harrison." *Amsterdam News: Arts-Entertainment in the Classroom*, May 10, 2019, 1-4. Accessed December 12, 2021.
Bradford, Sarah. *Harriet Tubman: The Moses of Her People*. Mineola, NY: Dover, 2004.
Brooks, Tim, and Richard L. Spottswood. *Lost Souls: Blacks and the Birth of the Recording Industry, 1890-1919*. Urbana-Champaign: University of Illinois Press, 2004. Proquest Ebook Central, http://ebookcentral.proquest.com/lib/fsu/detail.action?docID=3413942. Created from FSU on 2021-11-15 00:52:00.
Brown, Rae Linda. "William Grant Still, Florence Price, and William Dawson: Echoes of the Harlem Renaissance" In *Black Music in the Harlem Renaissance: A Collection of Essays*, edited by Samuel A. Floyd, Jr., 71-86. Westport, CT: Greenwood Press, 1990.
Burleigh, Harry T. Letter to William Dawson, March 17, 1921. William Levi Dawson Papers, Stuart A. Rose Manuscript, Archives, and Rare Books Library, Emory University.

Burlington Free Press. "Redpath Chautauqua Opens Auspiciously." *Burlington Free Press*, August 17, 1921.

Carter, Marva. William Levi Dawson Papers. Stuart A. Rose Manuscript, Archives and Rare Book Library, Emory University.

Chase, Gilbert. *America's Music*. New York: McGraw Hill, 1966.

Coleman, Nancy. "Why We're Capitalizing Black." *New York Times Insider*, July 5, 2020. http://nytimes.com/2020/07/05/insider/capitalized-black.html. Accessed February 15, 2021.

Coleridge-Taylor, Samuel. *Twenty-Four Negro Melodies*. Boston: Oliver Ditson, 1905.

Commier, Anne, and Deborah Klezmer, eds. "Mitchell, Abbie ("1884–1960)," *Dictionary of Women Worldwide: 25,000 Women through the Ages*, vol. 2. Farmington Hills, MI: Yorkin, 2007, p. 1335. Gale eBooks, link.gale.com/apps/doc/CX2588816742/GVRL?u=tall85761&sid=bookmark-GVRL&xid=144e9360. Accessed November 16, 2021.

Cone, James H. *The Spirituals and the Blues: An Interpretation*. San Francisco: Harper and Row, 1972.

"The Conference All-State Organizations." *School Music News* 24, no. 5 (January 1961).

Conyers, James L. *Black Lives: Essays in African American Biography*. New York: Routledge, 1999. https://search-ebscohost-com.proxy.lib.fsu.edu/login.aspx?direct=true&db=nlebk&AN=24531&site=ehost-live. Accessed November 15, 2021.

Costen, Melva. "In Celebration of William Levi Dawson" symposium records, William Levi Dawson Papers, Stuart A. Rose Manuscript. Archives, and Rare Books Library, Emory University.

Creative Artists' Workshop. "Talking It Over with Roy Wilkins." *Kansas City Call*, December 13, 1934. In *William Dawson: A Umum Tribute and a Marvelous Journey*, Philadelphia: Creative Artists' Workshop, 1981.

Cuney-Hare, Maude. *Negro Musicians and Their Music*. Washington, DC: Associated Publishers, 1936.

Dawson, William L. "Adawura Bo ME." (Chicago: Remick Music, 1955).

Dawson, William L. "Africa Trip Travel Log." William Levi Dawson Papers, Stuart A. Rose Manuscript, Archives, and Rare Books Library, Emory University.

Dawson, William L. "African Field Recordings." William Levi Dawson Papers, Stuart A. Rose Manuscript, Archives, and Rare Book Library, Emory University.

Dawson, William L. "Ain-a That Good News." Tuskegee, AL: Tuskegee Institute Steam Press, 1937.

Dawson, William L. "Before the Sun Goes Down." Park Ridge, IL: Neil A. Kjos Co., 1978.

Dawson, William L. "Behold the Star." Tuskegee, Alabama: Tuskegee Institute Steam Press, 1946.

Dawson, William L. "Break, Break, Break." William Levi Dawson Papers, Stuart A. Rose Manuscript, Archives, and Rare Book Library, Emory University.

Dawson, William L. "Dorabella." Park Ridge, IL: Neil A. Kjos, 1981.

Dawson, William L. "Ev'ry Time I Feel the Spirit." Tuskegee, AL: Tuskegee Institute Steam Press, 1946.

Dawson, William L. "Ezekiel Saw de Wheel." Tuskegee, AL: Tuskegee Institute Steam Press, 1942.

Dawson, William L. "Feed-A My Sheep." Park Ridge, IL: Neil A. Kjos, 1971.

Dawson, William L. "Hail Mary." Tuskegee, AL: Tuskegee Institute Steam Press, 1946.

Dawson, William L. "Highlights of the Career of William L. Dawson." Unpublished manuscript.

Dawson, William L. "I Couldn't Hear Nobody Pray." Chicago: H. T. FitzSimons, 1926.
Dawson, William L. "In His Care-O." Park Ridge IL: Neil A. Kjos, 1961.
Dawson, William L. "I Wan' to Be Ready." Park Ridge, IL: Neil A. Kjos, 1967.
Dawson, William L. "Interpretations of the Religious Folk Songs of the American Negro." *Etude* (Malvern, PA), March 1955.
Dawson, William L. "Jesus Walked This Lonesome Valley." New York: Remick Music, 1927.
Dawson, William L. "Jump Back, Honey, Jump Back." Kansas City, MO: Wunderlichs Piano Company, 1923.
Dawson, William L. "King Jesus Is A-Listening." Chicago: H. T. FitzSimons, 1925.
Dawson, William L. "Lit'l' Boy Chile." Tuskegee, AL: Tuskegee Institute Steam Press, 1947.
Dawson, William L. "Mary Had a Baby." Tuskegee, AL: Tuskegee Institute Steam Press, 1947.
Dawson, William L. "The Mongrel Yank." Chicago: Gamble Hinged Music, 1930.
Dawson, William L. "My Lord, What a Mourning." Chicago: H. T. FitzSimons, 1927.
Dawson, William L. *Negro Folk Symphony* Brochure. Published privately by William L. Dawson, n.d.
Dawson, William L. "Negro Work Song." William Levi Dawson Papers, Stuart A. Rose Manuscript, Archives, and Rare Books Library, Emory University.
Dawson, William L. "Oh, What a Beautiful City." Tuskegee, AL: Tuskegee Institute Steam Press, 1934.
Dawson, William L. "Oppression." William Levi Dawson Papers, Stuart A. Rose Manuscript, Archives, and Rare Book Library, Emory University.
Dawson, William L. "Out in the Fields." Chicago: Gamble Hinged Music, 1929.
Dawson, William L. "Pilgrim's Chorus." Park Ridge, IL: Neil A. Kjos, 1968.
Dawson, William L. "A Report to Mr. Robert D. Barton, Assistant Cultural Attaché, American Embassy, Madrid, Spain, on My Trip to Spain during the Summer," 1956, unpublished manuscript.
Dawson, William L. "The Rugged Yank." Park Ridge, IL: Kjos Music, 1970.
Dawson, William L. "Slumber Song." Park Ridge, IL: Neil A. Kjos, 1961.
Dawson, William L. "Soon-Ah Will Be Done." Tuskegee, AL: Tuskegee Institute Steam Press, 1934.
Dawson, William L. "Steal Away." Tuskegee, AL: Tuskegee Institute Steam Press, 1942.
Dawson, William L. "Swing Low." Tuskegee, AL: Tuskegee Institute Steam Press, 1946.
Dawson, William L. "Talk about a Child That Do Love Jesus." Chicago: H. T. FitzSimons, 1927.
Dawson, William L. "There Is a Balm in Gilead." Tuskegee, AL: Tuskegee Institute Steam Press, 1939.
Dawson, William L. "There's a Little Wheel A-Turnin' in My Heart." Tuskegee, AL: Tuskegee Institute Steam Press, 1949.
Dawson, William L. "You Got to Reap Just What You Sow." Chicago: H.T. FitzSimons, 1928.
Dawson, William L. "Zion's Walls." Park Ridge, IL: Neil A. Kos, 1961.
deMotte, Helen. "Fine Program Given by Group from Tuskegee." Richmond (Virginia) Daily Leader, June 5, 1946.
de Schauensee, Max. "Tuskegee Institute Choir Offers Fine Program of Spirituals," *Evening Bulletin* (Philadelphia, PA), May 29, 1946.
Design You Trust. "Inside A 1947 Boeing 377 Stratocruiser, The Largest And Fastest Aircraft In Commercial Service. https://designyoutrust.com/2020/02/inside-a-1947-boeing-377

-stratocruiser-the-largest-and-fastest-aircraft-in-commercial-service/. Accessed December 16, 2021.

"Doc Cook and his 14 Doctors of Syncopation." *The Syncopated Times*. Accessed February 16, 2021. https://syncopatedtimes.com/doc-cook-and-his-14-doctors-of-syncopation/.

Douglass, Frederick. "Letter to Mrs. Stowe," Frederick Douglass' Papers. The University of Virginia. December 2, 1853. http://utc.iath.virginia.edu/africam/afar03agt.html. Accessed February 10, 2021.

Douglass, Frederick. *My Bondage, My Freedom*. Project Gutenberg, 2008. https://www.gutenberg.org/files/202/202-h/202-h.htm.

Downes, Olin. "Stokowski Gives American Works." *New York Times*, November 21, 1934.

Driskell, David C. "The Significance of the Aaron Douglas Papers," Speech given on the formal presentation of Douglas's papers to Fisk University, April 27, 1975. The speech was published as part of a special issue devoted to Douglas in *BANC!* a publication of Fisk University Library 4–5 (September 1974–June 1975). Accessed November 10, 2021.

Du Bois, W. E. B. (William Edward Burghardt). Letter from W. E. B. Du Bois to Encyclopaedia Britannica, May 12, 1926 (MS 312), W. E. B. Du Bois Papers, Special Collections and University Archives, University of Massachusetts Amherst Libraries.

Du Bois, W. E. B. *The Souls of Black Folk*. New York: Blue Heron Press, 1953.

Du Bois, W. E. B. W. E. B. Du Bois Papers. Special Collections and University Archives, University of Massachusetts Amherst Libraries.

Ege, Samantha. "Composing a Symphonist: Florence Price and the Hand of Black Women's Fellowship." *Women and Music: A Journal of Gender and Culture* 24, no. 1 (2020): 7–27.

Eversman, Alice. "Sheer Beauty Marks Local Concert by Tuskegee Choir." *Evening Star* (Washington, DC), June 4, 1946.

Ewen, David. *American Composers Today: A Biographical and Critical Guide*. New York: H. N. Wilson, 1949.

Farrah, Scott David. *Signifyin(g): A Semiotic Analysis of Symphonic Works by William Grant Still, William Levi Dawson, and Florence Price*. Doctoral diss., Florida State University, 2007.

Fisher, Miles Mark. *Negro Slave Songs in the United States*. Ithaca: Cornell University Press, 1953.

Francis, Kimberly. "Nadia Boulanger and Igor Stravinsky: Documents of the Bibliothèque Nationale de France." *Revue de musicology* 95, no. 1 (2009).

Gaillet, Lynée Lewis, Diana Eidson, and Don Gammill. *Landmark Essays on Archival Research*. New York: Routledge/Taylor & Francis, 2016.

Gamble Music Company. "About Us." https://www.gamblemusic.com/about-us/. Accessed January 4, 2022.

Grout, Donald J. *A History of Western Music*. New York: W. W. Norton, 1988.

Guenther, Eileen. *In Their Own Words: Slave Life and the Power of Spirituals*. St. Louis: Morningstar, 2016.

Gunn, Glenn Dillard. "Capacity Crowd Hears Concert by Tuskegee Choir." *Times-Herald* (Washington, DC), June 4, 1946.

Haberlen, John B. "William Dawson and the Copyright Act (A Victim of Arrangers)." *Choral Journal* 23, no. 7 (1983): 5–8.

Haberlen, John. William Levi Dawson Papers, Stuart A. Rose Manuscript. Archives, and Rare Books Library, Emory University.

Hammerlich, R. C. "Musicians First, Students Prove in Concert Here." *Springfield Republican* (Springfield, MA), March 24, 1963.

Harrington, T. C. *Official Record of the Proceedings of the Board of Park Commissioners*, Kansas City, MO, May 25, 1922.

Haskins, John. "A Concert of Modern Americana." *Kansas City Star* (Kansas City, MO), January 30, 1966.

Haskins, John. "The 65–66 Music Season—a Long Look Back." *Kansas City Star* (Kansas City, MO), June 5, 1966.

Hood, Marcia Mitchell. William Levi Dawson and His Music: A Teacher's Guide to Interpreting His Choral Spirituals. Doctoral diss., University of Alabama, 2004.

Horner, John. "Graduation Music in 1925." Unpublished manuscript, part 3.

Horowitz J. A Symphony to Link Africa and America; William Levi Dawson's 'Negro Folk Symphony' Is a Celebration of the Vernacular in a Traditional, European Form. *Wall Street Journal (Online)*. Feb 07, 2020. https://login.proxy.lib.fsu.edu/login?url=https://www.proquest.com/newspapers/symphony-link-africa-america-william-levi-dawsons/docview/2352112160/se-2?accountid=4840.

Huff, Vernon Edward. William Levi Dawson: An Examination of Selected Letters, Speeches and Writings. Doctoral diss., Arizona State University, 2013.

Huff, Vernon Edward. "William Levi Dawson's Life in Speeches, Letters, and Writings." *Choral Journal* 55, no. 1 (2015).

Hughes, William H., and Frederick D. Patterson. *Robert Russa Moton of Hampton and Tuskegee*. Chapel Hill: University of North Carolina Press, 1956.

Huizenga, Tom. "Someone Finally Remembered William Dawson's 'Negro Folk Symphony.'" NPR, June 26, 2020. https://www.npr.org/sections/deceptivecadence/2020/06/26/883011513/someone-finally-remembered-william-dawsons-negro-folk-symphony. Accessed July 25, 2020.

Hulme, George, and Andy Simons. "The Brian Rust Discographies." *International Association of Jazz Record Collectors Journal* 43, no. 2 (June 2010): 18.

Inscoe, John, ed. "Howard Swanson." In *The New Georgia Encyclopedia*. https://www.georgiaencyclopedia.org/articles/arts-culture/howard-swanson-1907-1978/. Accessed December 16, 2021.

"Interview with William Levi Dawson, Philadelphia, Pennsylvania, October 8, 1979," William Levi Dawson Papers, Stuart A. Rose Manuscript, Archives, and Rare Book Library, Emory University.

Jackson, Lawrence. William Levi Dawson Papers, Stuart A. Rose Manuscript, Archives, and Rare Books Library, Emory University.

Johnson, David Lee. The Contributions of William L. Dawson to the School of Music at Tuskegee Institute and to Choral Music. Ed.D. thesis, University of Illinois at Urbana-Champaign, 1987.

Johnson, James Weldon, ed. *The Book of American Negro Spirituals*. New York: Viking Press, 1925.

Johnson, John Andrew. "William Dawson, 'THE NEW NEGRO,' and His Folk Idiom." *Black Music Research Journal* 19, no. 1 (Spring 1999): 43. Gale Academic OneFile, link.gale.com

/apps/doc/A61574100/AONE?u=tall85761&sid=bookmark-AONE&xid=e382c3c9. Accessed November 15, 2021.

Jones, Arthur C. *Wade in the Water—The Wisdom of Spirituals*. Maryknoll, NY: Orbis Books, 1993.

Kelley, James B. "Song, Story, or History: Resisting Claims of a Coded Message in the African American Spiritual 'Follow the Drinking Gourd.'" *Journal of Popular Culture* 41, no. 2 (2008): 262–80.

Kirschke, Amy Helene. *Aaron Douglas: Art, Race, and the Harlem Renaissance*. Jackson: University Press of Mississippi, 1995.

Kohos, Jacqueline. Sounds and Symbols: The Relationship between Auditory Processing and Reading. Master's thesis, Bank Street College of Education, New York, New York, 2015.

Krehbiel, Henry E. *Afro-American Folksongs*. New York: G. Schirmer, 1914.

"LeBron James: LA Lakers Star Says the Unrest in Washington Shows 'We Live in Two Americas.'" *Sky Sports*, February 8, 2021. https://www.skysports.com/nba/news/36226/12182098/lebron-james-la-lakers-star-says-the-unrest-in-washington-shows-we-live-in-two-americas. Accessed February 8, 2021.

"Legacy: The Story." Tuskegee Airmen. https://tuskegeeairmen.org/legacy/the-story. Accessed June 4, 2021.

Li, Stephanie. *Zora Neale Hurston*. Santa Barbara, CA: ABC-CLIO, 2020.

Locke, Alain. *The Negro and His Music*. New York: Arno Press and the New York Times, 1969.

Lovell, John Jr. *Black Song: The Forge and the Flame*. New York: Macmillan, 1972.

Lovell, John Jr. "The Social Implications of the Negro Spiritual." *Journal of Negro Education* 8, no. 4 (October 1939): 634–43.

MacMillan, William Robert. *The Choral Music of William Dawson*. D.A. thesis, University of Northern Colorado, 1991.

Malone, Mark Hugh. Interview with William L. Dawson, Tuskegee, AL, March 23, 1979, January 24, 1981, February 7, 1981, February 21, 1981. William L. Dawson and Bess Bolden Walcott, interview by author, Tuskegee, AL, October 10, 1981.

Middleton, Lanice P. *Tuskegee University Cemetery Stories: The Lives That Built a Great American Educational Institution*. Montgomery: NewSouth Books, 2021.

Mitchell, Abbie. "A Colleague's Appreciation—Excerpts from Papers of the Late Abbie Mitchell on Her Teaching Experience at Tuskegee." Rpt. in *William Dawson: A Umum Tribute and a Marvelous Journey*. Philadelphia: Creative Artists' Workshop, 1981.

"Mitchell, Abbie (1884–1960)." *Dictionary of Women Worldwide: 25,000 Women through the Ages*, edited by Anne Commire and Deborah Klezmer, 2:1335. Farmington Hills, MI: Yorkin, 2007. Gale eBooks, link.gale.com/apps/doc/CX2588816742/GVRL?u=tall85761&sid=bookmark-GVRL&xid=144e9360. Accessed 16 Nov. 2021.

Moton, Robert Russa. *Finding a Way Out: An Autobiography*. Garden City, NY: Doubleday, Page, 1921.

"Music Review." *Anniston Star*, November 18, 1934.

"Music Review." *New York Times*, December 28, 1932.

"Music Review." *Washington Post*, June 4, 1946.

"Music Supervisors of Nation Meet." *Musical Leader* (Chicago, IL), April 9, 1925

NAACP. "Roy Wilkins." https://naacp.org/find-resources/history-explained/civil-rights-leaders/roy-wilkins. Accessed February 16, 2021.

National Public Radio. "Interview with William Levi Dawson—The Sunday Show, 1982," William Levi Dawson Papers, Stuart A. Rose Manuscript, Archives, and Rare Book Library, Emory University.

Nicholas, Louis. "Fisk Music Fitting Centennial End." *Nashville Tennessean*, May 2, 1966.

Nurhussein, Nadia. "On Flowery Beds of Ease: Paul Lawrence Dunbar." *American Periodicals* 20, no. 1 (2010): 46–67.

O'Meally, Robert. William Levi Dawson Papers, Stuart A. Rose Manuscript, Archives, and Rare Books Library, Emory University.

Orchard, Hugh A. *Fifty Years of Chautauqua: Its Beginnings, Its Development, Its Message, and Its Life*. Cedar Rapids, IA: Torch Press, 1923.

Parrish, Lydia. *Slave Songs of the Georgia Sea Islands*. New York: Creative Age Press, 1942.

Perry, Frank Jr. "William Levi Dawson." *Afro-American Vocal Music: A Select Guide to Fifteen Composers*, Edited by Frank Perry, 34–38. Berrien Springs, MI: Vande-Vere, 1991.

Peterson, Heather. "Abbie Mitchell." *BlackPast*, July 2, 2008. https://www.blackpast.org/african-american-history/Mitchell-abbie-1884-1960/. Accessed November 16, 2021.

Phillips, Ulrich. *Life and Labor in the Old South*. Boston: Little, Brown, 1929.

Raber, Rebecca Lynn. "Conducting the Coded Message Songs of Slavery: Context, Connotations, and Performance Preparation." Doctoral diss., North Dakota State University, 2018.

Ragan, Cheryl R. "Plunging into the Very Depths of the Souls of Our People: The Life and Art of Aaron Douglas." Doctoral diss., University of Kansas, 2008.

Raichelson, Richard. "Doc Cook." Personal correspondence, November 21, 2021.

Randolph, Milton Jr. William Levi Dawson Papers. Stuart A. Rose Manuscript, Archives, and Rare Book Library, Emory University.

Reef, Catherine. *William Grant Still: African American Composer*. Greensboro, NC: Morgan Reynolds, 2003.

Roach, Hildred. *Black American Music, Past and Present*. Boston: Crescendo, 1973.

Rublowsky, J. *Black Music in America*. New York: Basic Books, 1971.

Schwarz, K. Robert. "Composers Who Had to Triumph over Prejudice." *New York Times*, April 15, 1990.

Shingles, Samuel D. *William Levi Dawson: The Man and His Music*. Master's thesis, Bowling Green State University, 1994.

Simon, Robert. "Mr. Stokowski Chaperons an American Symphony—One Hand That Plays Two." *New Yorker*, December 1, 1934.

Singer, Samuel L. "A Gleeful Tribute for Conductor." *Philadelphia Inquirer*, November 23, 1980.

Singer, Samuel L. "Tuskegee Unit Gives Concert." *Philadelphia Inquirer*, May 29, 1946.

Smith, Jessie Carney, ed. "William Levi Dawson," *Notable Black American Men, Book II*. Gale, 1998. Gale in Context: Biography, link.gale.com/apps/doc/K1622000107/BIC?u=tall85761&sid=bookmark-BIC&xid=5239426c. Accessed 18 Nov. 2021. Gale Document Number: GALE|K162200010

Snyder, Jean. *Harry T. Burleigh: From Spiritual to the Harlem Renaissance*. Champaign: University of Illinois Press, 2016.

Southern, Eileen. *The Music of Black Americans: A History*. New York: W. W. Norton, 1971.
Stewart, Ruth Ann. *Portia: The Life of Portia Washington Pittman*. New York: Doubleday, 1977.
Stone, Jeffrey Carroll II. "A Legacy of Hope in the Concert Spirituals of Robert Nathaniel Dett (1882–1943) and William Levi Dawson (1899–1990)." North Dakota State University, doctoral diss., 2017.
"A Striking Contribution to Musical America." *American Business Survey*, April 1933.
Strong, Willie. "Dawson, William Levi." New Grove Dictionary of Music and Musicians Oxford: Oxford University Press, 2001.
Strong, Willie. "William Levi Dawson." In *International Dictionary of Black Composers, Vol. 1*, edited by Samuel A. Floyd Jr., 354–59. Chicago: Fitzroy Dearborn, 1999.
Thompson, Jacqueline Kay. William Levi Dawson (b. 1898 and an Analysis of His Negro Folk Symphony (1932, rev. 1952). Master's thesis, Conservatory of Music, University of Missouri, Kansas City, 1979.
Tischler, Alice. "William Levi Dawson." In *Fifteen Black American Composers: A Bibliography of Their Works*. Detroit Studies in Musical Bibliography, No. 45. Detroit: Information Coordinators, 1981.
"Tuskegee Choir Pays Tribute to Founder." *New York Times*, May 28, 1946.
Tuskegee Normal and Industrial Institute Bulletin 8, no. 2 (1914).
Tuskegee Normal and Industrial Institute Bulletin 9, no. 2 (1915).
Tuskegee Normal and Industrial Institute Bulletin 20, no. 1 (1925).
Tuskegee Normal and Industrial Institute Bulletin 24, no. 2 (1930–31).
Tuskegee Normal and Industrial Institute Bulletin 25, no. 2 (1931–32).
Tuskegee Normal and Industrial Institute Bulletin 26, no. 2 (1932–33).
Tuskegee Normal and Industrial Institute Bulletin 30, no. 2 (1936–37).
Tuskegee Normal and Industrial Institute Bulletin 34, no. 2 (1941–42).
Tuskegee Normal and Industrial Institute Bulletin 36, no. 2 (1943–44).
Tuskegee Normal and Industrial Institute Bulletin 37, no. 2 (1944–45).
Tuskegee Normal and Industrial Institute Bulletin 38, no. 2 (1945–46).
Tuskegee Normal and Industrial Institute Bulletin 44, no. 2 (1951–52).
"Tuskegee Organizes School of Music." *Tuskegee Messenger*, July 1932.
"A Tuskegee Symphony: Stokowski to Present Dawson's Pioneer Work on Negro Themes." *New York Times* (1923–); November 18, 1934; ProQuest Historical Newspapers: The *New York Times* with Index.
Tuskegee University Archives. "Tuskegee Institute Concert Program," April 13, 1931. Tuskegee University Archives Repository, Tuskegee Institute.
Tutor, Phillip. "Neglected for Decades, the 'Negro Folk Symphony' by Anniston Composer William Levi Dawson Is Reaching a New Generation." *Anniston Star*, April 24, 2021. https://www.annistonstar.com/features/neglected-for-decades-the-negro-folk-symphony-by-anniston-composer-william-levi-dawson-is-reaching/article_d2dcc54a-a445-11eb-a9b8-537615e1a963.html
"TV Interview of Dawson at Houston, Texas, 1971-Side 1." William Levi Dawson Papers, Stuart A. Rose Manuscript, Archives, and Rare Book Library, Emory University.
"Theatre Review." *Wall Street Journal*, December 31, 1932.

van Straaten, Jay. *Slavonic Rhapsody: The Life of Antonin Dvorak.* New York: Allen, Town, and Heath, 1948.

Walters, Kerry. *The Underground Railroad: A Reference Guide.* Santa Barbara, CA: ABC-CLIO, 2012.

Wanamaker, Rodman. Letter to W. E. B. Du Bois. "Rodman Wanamaker Contest in Music Compositions for Composers of the Negro Race to Crisis, December 23, 1929." W. E. B. Du Bois Papers (MS 312), Special Collections and University Archives, University of Massachusetts, Amherst Libraries.

Ward, Charles. "The Will to Excel." *Houston Chronicle*, September 9, 1989.

Washington, Booker T. "Atlanta Exposition Address, 1895." *Black History Bulletin* 68, no. 1 (2005).

Washington, Booker T. "Atlanta Exposition Speech-September 18, 1895." Booker T. Washington Papers, Manuscript Division, Library of Congress, Washington, DC. https:memory.loc.gov/cgi-bin/query/r?ammem/aaodyssey:@field(NUMBER)+@band(mssmisc+ady0605), accessed December 28, 2021.

Washington, Booker T. *The Story of My Life and Work* (Chicago: J. L. Nichols, 1900).

Washington, Booker T. *Up from Slavery: An Autobiography.* New York: Doubleday, 1901.

Weaver, David E. Black Diva of the Thirties: The Life of Ruby Elzy. Jackson: University Press of Mississippi, 2004.

Wilkins, Roy. "Talking It Over with Roy Wilkins." *William Dawson: A Umum Tribute and a Marvelous Journey* Philadelphia: Creative Artists' Workshop, 1981.

"William Levi Dawson." *The Black Perspective in Music* 18, no. 1/2 (1990): 218. http://www.jstor.org/stable/1214874.

"William Levi Dawson (1899–1990)." In L. Bracks, *African American Almanac: 400 Years of Triumph, Courage and Excellence.* Canton, MI: Visible Ink Press, 2012. Credo Reference: https://login.proxy.lib.fsu.edu/login?url=https://search.credoreference.com/content/entry/vipaaalm/william_levi_dawson_1899_1990/0?institutionId=2057.

William Levi Dawson Papers. Stuart A. Rose Manuscript, Archives, and Rare Book Library, Emory University.

Wilson, Charles Reagan. *The New Encyclopedia of Southern Culture: Volume 12: Music*, edited by Bill C. Malone, Chapel Hill: University of North Carolina Press, 2009. ProQuest Ebook Central, https://ebookcentral-proquest-com.proxy.lib.fsu.edu/lib/fsu/detail.action?docID=1663486. Accessed November 10, 2021.

Yarbrough, David Y. "Critical Edition: Sonata for Violin and Piano by William Levi Dawson." Doctoral diss. Peabody Conservatory of Music, 1999.

Zepernick, Werner. "Fisk Festival Closes with Negro Symphonic Works." *Nashville Banner*, May 3, 1966.

INDEX

ABC radio network, 66, 72, 131
Academy of Music, 59, 96
Accra, Gold Coast (now Ghana), 105
"Adawura B Me," 111–12
Afro-American Symphony, 95, 97, 108
"Ain-a That Good News," 71, 110, 130
Alabama Arts Hall of Fame, 141
Alabama State University, 47, 61
Alexander, Will, 38
American Business Survey, 57–58, 94–96
American Conservatory of Music, 32–33
American Symphony Orchestra, 107
Anderson, Marian, 64, 69
Anniston Star, 100
Atkinson, Brooks, 57
Atlanta Compromise, 11
Atlanta University, 38

Baretta, Scott, 85–86
Beethoven, Ludwig van, 19
"Before the Sun Goes Down," 112
"Behold the Star," 71, 111
Berlioz, Hector, 124
Biancolli, Louis, 67
Bibb, Henry, 88
Billington, Ray Allen, 83
Birmingham (Alabama) Symphony Orchestra, 99
Blackburn's Negro Concert Band, 26–27
Black Lives Matter Movement, 22–23
blues music origins, 85
Boatner, Edward, 100
Boeing 377 Stratocruiser, 102
Boulanger, Nadia, 103

Bowen, Stirling, 59
Bradford, Sarah, 86–87
"Break, Break, Break," 113–14, 184n199
Brown, Gwynne Kuhner, 5, 106–8, 166n34
Bullock, Ernest R., 44, 47
Burleigh, Harry T., 45, 54, 64, 67, 70, 75, 78–79, 91, 100
Busch, Carl, 30

Carnegie, Andrew, 17, 50
Carnegie Hall, 52, 58–59, 93, 97, 101, 109
Carter, Marva, 23–24, 92–94, 99, 108
CBS radio network, 66, 97, 108, 131
CBS television network, 131
Chase, Gilbert, 76
Chautauqua Movement, 20, 30
Chicago Bee, 36
Chicago Civic Orchestra, 33, 40
Chicago Daily News, 35
Chicago Defender, 36
Chicago Tribune, 91
Chicago World's Fair, 1933, Century of Progress, 35
civil rights movement, 23, 32
Clorindy, or the Origin of the Cakewalk, 44, 79, 92–93
Coleridge-Taylor, Samuel, 45, 54, 65, 124
Cole-Talbert, Florence, 47–48
Conway, Pat, 26–27
Cook, Charles (Charlie) "Doc," 34, 35, 167n40
Cook, H. O., 27, 32
Cook, Will Marion, 44–45, 79, 92–93, 95
Constitution Hall, 52, 69–70

Costen, Melva, 84
Cotonou, Dahomey (Benin), 106
Cotton States and International Exposition, 11
Crisis, The, 28, 32, 80, 92
Cuney-Hare, Maude, 55

Dakar, Senegal, 103–4
Dawson, Cecile De Mae Nicholson, 4, 61, 73, 112, 128
Dawson, Cornella Lampton, 33, 61
Dawson, Eliza Starkey, 8–9, 15
Dawson, George, 8–10, 14–15, 32
Dawson, William Levi, **works:** "Adawura B Me," 111; "Ain-A That Good News," 71, 110, 130; "Before the Sun Goes Down," 112; "Behold the Star," 71, 111; "Break, Break, Break," 113–14, 184n199; "Dorabella," 114–15; "Ev'ry Time I Feel the Spirit," 111, 124, 130; "Ezekiel Saw De Wheel," 110, 119; "Feed-A My Sheep," 112; "Forever Thine," 26, 31, 61, 79; "Go to Sleep," 90; "Hail Mary," 71, 111, 130; "Hallelujah," 54, 65, 113, 173n56; "I Couldn't Hear Nobody Pray," 90; "In His Care-O," 112; "I Wan' to Be Ready," 112; "Jesus Walked This Lonesome Valley," 53, 90–91; "Jump Back Honey, Jump Back," 79, 92, 178n85; "King Jesus Is A-Listening," 28, 80, 89–90; "Lit'l Boy Chile," 111; "Lovers Plighted," 93; "Mary Had a Baby," 111; "The Mongrel Yank," 91–92, 112; "My Lord a Mourning," 28, 64, 80, 91; *Negro Folk Symphony*, 61, 94–97, 99–101, 106–8, 115, 120, 125–27; *A Negro Work Song*, 108, 109, 182n159; "Oh, What a Beautiful City," 56, 109; "Oppression," 114; "Out in the Fields," 91, 146, 178n79; "Pilgrim's Chorus from *Tannhäuser*," 112; "The Rugged Yank," 92, 112; "Scherzo," 92; "Seeking for the City," 65, 113, 173n56; "Slumber Song," 112; *Sonata* for Violin and Piano, 90; "Soon Ah Will Be Done," 71, 109, 130; "Steal Away," 110; "Swing Low, Sweet Chariot," 111; "Talk about a Child That Do Love Jesus," 90; "There Is a Balm in Gilead," 71, 110, 130; "There's a Little Wheel A-Turnin' in My Heart," 111, 130; *Trio in A* for violin, cello, and piano, 30, 80, 176n31; "You Got To Reap Just What You Sow," 91; "Zion's Walls," 112
Dawson, William Levi, Sr., 163n1
"Deep River," 64, 88, 144
DeLamarter, Eric, 33, 167n38
deMotte, Helen, 71
Dennard, Brezeal, 130
Department of Music (Tuskegee), 48–50, 93, 148
Dett, Robert Nathaniel, 54, 64, 67, 70, 80, 110, 115, 127–28
Dillworth, Rollo, 93
"Dorabella," 114–15
Douglas, Aaron, 28–29, 80, 124, 161
Douglass, Frederick, 12, 84–85, 88
Downes, Olin, 97
Drye, Captain Frank L., 18–19, 42–44, 48–49
Du Bois, W. E. B., 11, 22–23, 32, 78, 92
Dulles, John Foster, 73
Dunbar, Paul Laurence, 44, 79, 92, 95
Dvořák, Antonin, 28, 72, 75, 77–81, 93–95, 100–101, 175n6

Ebenezer A.M.E. Church (Kansas City, Missouri), 29
Edgar Bergen and Charlie McCarthy Show, 72
elements of music, 46
Ellington, Duke, 67
Ellison, Ralph, 47, 118–20, 131–32, 140, 150–51, 157–60, 168n20, 169n31
Emory University Archives, 66, 90, 112–15, 129
Evening Bulletin (Philadelphia), 68
Eversman, Alice, 70–71
"Ev'ry Time I Feel the Spirit," 111, 124, 130
"Ezekiel Saw De Wheel," 110, 119

"Feed-A My Sheep," 112
Finding a Way Out, 37–38

INDEX

Fisher, William Arms, 28
Fisk Jubilee Singers, 9, 17, 47, 75, 81, 124, 161
Fisk University, 9, 54, 65, 81, 100, 124, 126–27
"Follow the Drinking Gourd," 87
"Forever Thine," 26, 31, 61, 79
Foster, Stephen, 60, 77–78
Freetown, Sierra Leone, 104

Gamble Hinged Music Company, 33–34, 89–91
Garrison, William Lloyd, 88
Geer, Will, 67
Girl's Glee Club (Women's Glee Club), 13, 52–53
"Go Down, Moses," 87
"Go to Sleep," 90
Gottschalk, Louis Moreau, 75
Grainger, Percy, 33
Great Depression, 35, 47–49, 56, 61
Gresham, S. W., 9–10, 42, 74
griots, 164n2
Guenther, Eileen, 83, 85
Gunn, Glenn Dillard, 69–71

Haberlen, John, 109–10, 119
"Hail Mary," 71, 111, 130
Hall, Regina G., 30, 120
"Hallelujah," 54, 65, 112, 173n56
Hammerich, R. C., 125
Hampton, Keith, 93
Hampton Institute, 11, 25, 37–38, 54, 64, 66–67, 126, 144
Hanson, Howard, 95
Harlem Renaissance, 28, 38, 40, 78, 124
Harrison, Hazel, 44, 47, 168n20
Haskins, John, 126
HBCUs (Historically Black Colleges and Universities), 22, 38, 72, 125–26
Hennagin, Herbert, 99
Hogan, Moses, 93
Hoover, Herbert, 60, 109–10
Hope, John, 38
Horner, Charles, 30
Horner, John, 30, 166n32
Horner Institute of Fine Arts, 29–32, 80, 128

Howse, O. Lexine, 44
H. T. FitzSimons Company, 28, 33–34, 89–91
Huff, Vernon Edward, 4
Huizinga, Tom, 107–8
Huneker, James Gibbons, 77
Hurst, Fannie, 67
Hurston, Zora Neale, 100

"I Couldn't Hear Nobody Pray," 90
Imes, G. Lake, 40, 54, 110, 113
"In His Care-O," 112
"Interlude," 113
Invisible Man, 119, 131–32
Ithaca Conservatory of Music, 26
"I Wan' to Be Ready," 112

Jackson, Clyde Owen, 117–18
Jackson, Lawrence, 54, 56, 89, 93–94, 97, 99–101
James, LeBron, 23
Jerome, Raoul, 167n43
"Jesus Walked This Lonesome Valley," 53, 90–91
Jim Crow Era, 11, 23, 69, 85
Johnson, Hall, 100
Johnson, James Weldon, 78
Jones, Arthur, 82, 85
"Jump Back Honey, Jump Back," 79, 92, 178n85

Kalish, Edna, 99
Kansas City, Missouri, 26, 29–31, 61, 80, 90, 124, 126, 128–29, 130, 150–51, 161
Kansas City Herald, 99
Kansas City Star, 126
Kansas Vocational College, 25–27, 79
Kelley, James B., 82
Kenny, Nick, 63, 143
"King Jesus Is A-Listening," 28, 80, 89–90
Kjos Company. *See* Neil A. Kjos Company
Krehbiel, Henry E., 77–78, 100
Kumasi, Gold Coast (Ghana), 105, 111

Lagos, Nigeria, 106
Langston, E. L., 10, 14

Lee, Jennie Cheatham, 17–18, 41, 65, 90, 124, 148, 161–62
Lincoln High School (Kansas City, Missouri), 27–28, 32, 80
List, Kurt, 73, 145
"Lit'l Boy Chile," 111
Locke, Alain, 11, 28, 78, 80
Lome, French Togoland (now Togo), 106
London, England, 103
Lovell, John, 55–56, 64, 81, 83, 85
"Lovers Plighted," 93

MacDowell, Edward, 76
"Mary Had a Baby," 111
McHose, Allen Irvine, 111
Men's Glee Club (Tuskegee), 13, 42, 52–53, 67
Milhaud, Darius, 99
Mills Brothers, 67
Mitchell, Abbie, 44, 169n22, 175n35
"Mongrel Yank, The," 91–92, 112
Monrovia, Liberia, 104
Montgomery, Bruce, 114–15
Moore, Emily C. *See* Neely, Emily C.
Morehouse College, 38
Morehouse College Glee Club, 129
Moton, Catherine, 44, 47
Moton, Robert Russa, 25, 37–41, 43, 46, 97, 99, 110
Musical Leader, 80
"My Lord, What a Mourning," 28, 64, 80, 91

Nashville Banner, 127
National Association for the Advancement of Colored People (NAACP), 28, 32, 80, 92
National Association of Negro Musicians, 92, 128
NBC radio network, 61–63, 65–66, 113, 131
NBC television network, 73
Neely, Captain Alvin J., 21, 22, 26, 165n18
Neely, Emily C., 41, 44, 148
Negro folk songs, 28, 35, 42, 46, 52, 64, 80–81, 83, 88–90, 93, 95–96, 110, 112, 122, 160, 170n4
Negro Folk Symphony, 41, 61, 94–97, 99–100, 106–8, 115, 120, 125–27, 140–41, 145–46

Negro Work Song, A, 108, 109, 181n159
Neil A. Kjos Company, 112, 114, 128
"New Negro," 38, 41
New Yorker, 98
New York Philharmonic Orchestra, 107
New York State School Music Association, 121, 124–25
New York Times, 22, 55–58, 66–67, 93, 97
Nicholas, Louis, 126–27

"Oh, What a Beautiful City," 56, 109
Oliver Ditson Company, 28, 89
O'Meally, Robert, 74, 118–20, 132
"Oppression," 114
ORF Vienna Radio Symphony Orchestra, 107
Otterstrom, Thorvald, 34–35, 93, 167n45
"Out in the Fields," 91, 146, 178n79

Panella, Lawrence, 167n43
Paris, France, 103
Parrish, Lydia, 83
Patterson, Frederick D., 39, 69
Patterson, Mrs. F. D., 47, 61
Peabody, George Foster, 54
Peña, Antonio Gonzales de la, 121–23
Philadelphia Forum, 60
Philadelphia Inquirer, 68, 114–15
Philadelphia Symphony Orchestra, 94, 97, 120
"Pilgrim's Chorus" from *Tannhäuser*, 112
Pittman, Portia Washington, 38, 43–44, 47–48
Pittsburgh Courier, 100
plantation melodies, 13, 42, 46, 81, 160
Porgy and Bess, 44
Price, Florence, 93, 115
Primus, Pearl, 67

Quade, Allen, 91

Raber, Rebecca, 85
racial discrimination, 5, 14, 20, 22–24, 25–26, 28–29, 31, 33, 35–36, 42, 56, 59, 62–63, 69, 77, 80, 85, 89, 93, 103, 115, 122, 130–31, 187n58

racial equality, 11, 27, 56, 99
Radio City Music Hall, 55–57, 66, 94, 109, 115
Randolph, Milton, Jr., 24, 74, 119
Rankin, George, 47–48
Ravel, Maurice, 99
Redpath Chautauqua Circuit, 20–24, 110
Remick Music Corporation, 34, 90–91, 112
Ritter, Kelly, 5
Roach, Hildred, 55, 99, 109
Robert Curtis Ogden Association, 92
Robeson, Paul, 91
Robinson, Bill, 67
Roosevelt, Eleanor, 171n35
Roosevelt, Franklin Delano, 56, 58, 65, 73, 171n28, 171n35
Rosemond, Andrew F., 44, 48, 61
Rothafel, Samuel Lionel (Roxy), 55–56, 59, 109
Rublowsky, John, 76
"Rugged Yank, The," 92, 112

Schauensee, Max de, 68
"Scherzo," 92, 178n85
Schoenberg, Arnold, 94
School Music News (New York), 124
School of Music at Tuskegee, 39–42, 44, 48, 53, 73, 109, 130
Schwarz, K. Robert, 115
"Seeking for the City," 65, 113, 173n56
segregation, 11, 20, 23–24, 28–31, 69, 115, 131
Shannon, Ireland, 102
Shaw, Robert, 111
Simmons, Alice Carter, 17, 41
Simon, Robert A., 98
Sims, Alberta, 44, 48–49
Singer, Samuel L., 68, 114–15
"Slumber Song," 112
Sowing and Reaping, 18
Small, Alonzo, 19–21
Smith, Al, 56
Smith, N. Clark, 27, 42
Sonata for Violin and Piano, 90, 178n76
"Soon Ah Will Be Done," 71, 109, 130
Southern, Eileen, 55, 81, 106

Spohn, George Weida, 62–63
"Steal Away," 110
Stearns, Henry V., 26, 32
Still, William Grant, 95, 97, 100, 108, 115
Stock, Frederick, 33, 167n38
Stokowski, Leopold, 95–98, 106–7, 120, 146
Straaten, Jay van, 75–76
Stravinsky, Igor, 103
Strong, Willie, 113, 117, 167n45
Sulton, Dorothy, 48
Suthern, Orrin, 48–49, 149
Swanson, Howard, 103
"Swing Low, Sweet Chariot," 111
Sympony No. 9 in E minor, "From the New World," 94–95, 101

"Talk about a Child That Do Love Jesus," 90
Tennesseean, 126–27
Tennyson, Alfred Lord, 113–14
Terry, Elizabeth, 44, 48
"There Is a Balm in Gilead," 68, 71, 110, 130
"There's a Lit'l Wheel A-Turnin' in My Heart," 111, 130
Tilghman, H. G., 63–64, 144
Times Herald (Washington, DC), 70
Towson, Adelaide, 41, 148–49
Trio in A for violin, cello, and piano, 30, 80, 176n31
Tubman, Harriet, 86–87
Tuskegee Airmen, 49, 66
Tuskegee Band, 10, 13, 18, 24, 36, 116
Tuskegee Choir, 13, 51, 73, 81, 90, 110–11, 120, 130–31, 150
Tuskegee Choir Series, 109, 112
Tuskegee Institute (Tuskegee Normal and Industrial Institute), 4, 6, 9–11, 14–17, 19–20, 23–25, 27, 36–43, 47, 50, 61, 65–66, 72, 78, 81, 87, 109–10, 112–13, 120, 130–31, 140, 144, 148
Tuskegee Male Quartette/Tuskegee Quintette, 19–23, 25, 27, 40, 52, 54, 78, 110, 117
Tuskegee Messenger, 45
Tuskegee Press, 109
Tuskegee University, 66

Underground Railroad, 87–88
United Negro College Fund (UNCF), 61, 67, 69–73
University of Missouri–Kansas City Conservatory of Music, 140

Victoria, Tomás Luis de, 121–22

"Wade in the Water," 88
Walcott, Bess Bolden, 4, 163n1
Wall Street Journal, 57, 59
Wanamaker Contest, 92–93
Warner Brothers Publications, 90–91
Washburn College, 25–26, 29, 32, 79
Washington, Booker T., 4, 11–13, 14, 17–19, 21, 23–24, 25, 27, 37–40, 42–43, 46, 50, 52–54, 65–67, 81, 84–85, 113, 164n8, 166n27
Washington Evening Star, 70–71
Washington Post, 69

Weidig, Adolph, 26, 32–33
Whalum, Wendell, 129
White House, 52, 60, 65, 109
Whitted, Van S., 47–48
Wilkins, Roy, 31–32
Williams, Daniel, 4, 113
Williamson, John Finley, 110
Woods, Charles Winter, 19
Work, Frederick, 65
Work, John Wesley, II, 64–65
Work, John Wesley, III, 65
World War II, 49, 61, 65–66, 102
Wyatt, Lucius, 24

Yarbrough, David, 90–91
"You Got to Reap Just What You Sow," 91

Zepernick, Werner, 127
"Zion's Walls," 112

ABOUT THE AUTHOR

With a career in education that spans forty-six years, **Mark Hugh Malone** has worked with students of all ages. Though a native of Miami, Florida, the majority of Malone's teaching has been in Mississippi at Pearl River Community College, William Carey University, and the University of Southern Mississippi. Choirs under Malone's direction made three European concert tours, sang for ACDA Southern Division and State Conventions, performed in New York, Washington, DC, Atlanta, Nashville, New Orleans, Anaheim, Seattle, aboard Carnival Cruise Lines, at Walt Disney World, and Six Flags Over Georgia. As curriculum designer for the Mississippi Arts Commission, Malone created arts-integrated and STEAM curricula that include: *The Mississippi Blues Trail and Beyond*, *Mississippi History through the Arts—A Bicentennial Journey*, *Footprints in the Dust—The Natchez Trace*, and three STEAM curricula to be published in the near future. Malone holds the BS in Social Studies Education from the Florida State University, the BA in Humanities from Rollins College, the Master of Music Education and the PhD in Music Education from the Florida State University, and completed postdoctoral study at Westminster Choir College.

www.ingramcontent.com/pod-product-compliance
Lightning Source LLC
Chambersburg PA
CBHW022015220426
43663CB00007B/1095